Post-Petroleum Design

Despite the growing demand for design strategies to reduce our petroleum use, no one has yet brought together the lessons of the world's leading post-petroleum designers into a single resource. *Post-Petroleum Design* brings them together for the first time.

Readers will be introduced to the most current, innovative, plastic- and petroleum-free products and projects in industrial design, architecture, transportation, electronics, apparel and more. *Post-Petroleum Design* explores firsthand the client and consumer motivations behind the demand, and shares the case studies, principles, best practices, risks, and opportunities of the world's leading post-petroleum design experts who are already meeting that demand. It introduces 40 inspiring individuals from across the globe; people like Eben Bayer, the American innovator whose company, Ecovative, is growing houses from mushrooms; Mohammed Bah Abba, whose Zeer Pot is helping families keep produce fresh in the sweltering Nigerian summer without electricity; and the engineers at Mercedes-Benz Advanced Design Studios whose Biome car evolves from genetically engineered DNA.

Post-Petroleum Design gives design professionals the information they need to research, evaluate, and select materials, technologies, and design strategies that meet the growing demand for sustainable design, plastic-free materials, and process energy conservation. Designer profiles, studies, statistics, and many color illustrations all highlight the work—some of the best design work to be found anywhere, and showcased here for the first time.

George Elvin is the founder of Gone Studio, the company pioneering post-petroleum design through zero-plastic, zero-waste, zero-electricity manufacturing. His designs have been featured by the Discovery Channel, Macworld, Treehugger, and over 50 other green design venues. The author of over 40 books and articles, his work on green design and technology has been published by Routledge, Wiley and Princeton Architectural Press, among others. Previous positions have included Assistant Professor of Architecture at the University of Illinois and Visiting Fellow at the University of Edinburgh. He is currently an Associate Professor of Architecture at Ball State University in Indiana.

Post-Petroleum Design

George Elvin

Routledge
Taylor & Francis Group

LONDON AND NEW YORK

First published 2015
by Routledge
2 Park Square, Milton Park, Abingdon, Oxon OX14 4RN

and by Routledge
711 Third Avenue, New York, NY 10017

Routledge is an imprint of the Taylor & Francis Group, an informa business

© 2015 George Elvin

British Library Cataloguing-in-Publication Data
A catalogue record for this book is available from the British Library

Library of Congress Cataloging-in-Publication Data
Elvin, George.
Post-petroleum design / George Elvin.
pages cm
Includes bibliographical references and index.
1. Product design. 2. Materials. 3. Green products. 4. Sustainable engineering.
5. Environmental protection. I. Title.
TS171.4.E48 2015
658.5'752--dc23
2015000651

ISBN: 978-1-138-85389-8 (hbk)
ISBN: 978-1-138-85390-4 (pbk)
ISBN: 978-1-315-72249-8 (ebk)

Typeset in Minion Pro 9.5/13.5 pt
by Fakenham Prepress Solutions, Fakenham, Norfolk NR21 8NN

Printed by Bell & Bain Ltd, Glasgow

Cover image: Phoenix car. Designers Kenneth Cobonpue and Albrecht Birkner teamed to create this concept car, which features the innovative use of rattan and other post-petroleum materials. Image courtesy of Kenneth Cobonpue.

To
Meg
———

– CONTENTS –

"It's just take-your-breath-away type explosions," one survivor was saying. Witnesses were telling how they could see the fireball from 35 miles away. As I watched the news reports about the BP Deepwater Horizon oil rig explosion in the Gulf of Mexico, my heart went out to the people and other living things affected. But, to be honest, I had other, more personal and positive things to deal with. Having spent most of my life designing buildings, I was embarking on a new adventure—one that would lead me into the uncharted world of post-petroleum design.

It began with a single piece of folded paper. Inspired by my then 10-year-old son's origami, I was working on a unique design for an iPad case. This particular summer morning, I was in the dining room pondering a prototype I'd made out of plastic. In the kitchen, the TV continued to blare reports of the millions of gallons of oil pouring from the Deepwater Horizon into the gulf, and the environmental havoc it was wreaking. Then it hit me. How could I put more petroleum-based plastic into this world? I felt like an accomplice to a terrible crime. I knew I couldn't live without plastic, but I made up my mind right then and there that if I was going to bring a new product into the world, I was going to make it plastic-free.

In that moment, Gone Studio was born—a company committed to designing and making products that people can feel good about. Now, more than five years later, we're not only plastic-free, we're also zero-waste and even zero-energy in all our manufacturing. We're dedicated to post-petroleum design, and to a cleaner, healthier world than the one we've made through our dependence on petroleum.

After my post-petroleum revelation as a result of the Gulf oil spill, I took all my plastic prototypes for the iPad case and dumped them in the recycling bin. I briefly considered making the case from recycled plastic, but I soon discovered that the recycling process can use a lot of energy, be toxic to workers, and create enormous carbon dioxide emissions. I also learned that very few of the products labeled as made from recycled material are 100 percent recycled. I even found that some iPad cases marketed as "made from recycled materials" had as little as 10 percent recycled content.

Armed with my new awareness of the plastic recycling process, I set out in search of the perfect plastic-free material to make my iPad case from. Few natural materials offer the padding necessary to protect a computer, but after investigating cotton, bamboo fiber, and even hemp, I settled on wool felt. You can't get any more natural than wool. Sheep grow it to keep warm, you shear it off, and they regrow it. I pictured those sheep and compared that image to the plastic-making process that sucks non-renewable fossil fuels from our Earth and creates side effects like the Gulf oil spill. I knew I had made the right choice.

As I developed my creation, my commitment to post-petroleum design grew. I also began to realize there was an entire global community of designers who shared my commitment. Robin Behrstock, co-owner of iZen Bamboo, invited me to design and make plastic-free wool cases for her company's bamboo keyboards; Eben Bayer, co-creator of Ecovative packaging made from mushroom mycelium, contacted me from the Davos conference about this book, and Mike LaVecchia and Brad Anderson, co-founders of Grain Surfboards, who use the same technology Boeing uses to make airplane wings in their wooden surfboards, spent over an hour on the phone with me from their shop in Maine.

But the more my connections to the post-petroleum design community grew, the more surprised I was that these designers weren't always aware of each other or of the plastic-free, post-petroleum theme running through their work. So as I continued to develop my own design, this book also began to take shape. It tells the story of the world's post-petroleum designers—designers who are working today to create a world less reliant on oil and plastic.

Around the world, more and more people are growing concerned about oil and its consequences and are moving toward new alternatives. This movement is happening at all scales, from major auto manufacturers developing biodegradable vehicles to individuals saying no to plastic bags at the supermarket. Governments are taking action too. What these governmental, corporate, and individual actions have in common is a commitment to reduce our dependence on oil through post-petroleum design and technologies. Governments recognize post-petroleum design as the way to energy independence and security; corporations are adopting it to build consumer loyalty by doing the right thing for the environment; and consumers are demanding it for the health of the planet and future generations.

The pages that follow are filled with the ideas that unite these diverse people and projects into a movement that is changing the way we make our world. Designers will see how their fellow creatives are using petroleum-free materials to shape bold new designs in everything from electronics to architecture. Businesspeople will learn how to manufacture products with less plastic, energy, and waste. Even those outside of design and business will enjoy its eye-opening revelation of innovations from leading designers in apparel, packaging, automobiles, and more.

Post-Petroleum Design celebrates their successes and, for the first time, weaves them together in a compelling story. Through its pages, you will travel the globe, visiting design studios, cutting-edge labs, and remote villages where post-petroleum designers are using everything from bamboo to bioplastics to shape a better future. Vernacular craft traditions, industrial-scale production, even the latest advances in nanotechnology, all hold secrets with the potential to lead us beyond our dependence on non-renewable resources, secrets that are now being unlocked by post-petroleum design.

Here you will share in my own journey into post-petroleum design and, I hope, share in the excitement I felt as I identified some of the common principles shared by its pioneers. These principles represent a new culture in design and commerce, and yet they are the same principles evolved over eons by nature herself. Many books on green design and sustainable business espouse principles based on nature, but this book, like my journey itself, is different. In this case, I discovered a community of like-minded designers working with shared interests, and then began to recognize their principles. The realization that they are the very principles that nature works by was profound. It gave me hope that we can go beyond our current petroleum-based paradigm and reduce the threat of climate change, toxic waste, and pollution. It is a grand task but, as we will see, it is one that is already being taken up by leading designers the world over. With the power to change the world and how we live in it, post-petroleum design is the new oil.

– ACKNOWLEDGMENTS –

Tʜɪs book wouldn't exist without the designers featured in it. It's their work and their dedication that inspired me to write it. I hope it helps them see how many like-minded creatives are working in similar ways to shape the world ahead. I'd also like to thank two designers who have influenced me for over 30 years—Scott Constable and Mike High. The book's excellent line art is the work of Maria Meza. And, finally, Fran Ford, Senior Architecture Editor, and Editorial Assistant Grace Harrison at Routledge. I couldn't have asked for a better publisher than Routledge, and Fran championed the project right from the start. Grace guided it (and me) through the manuscript preparation. Copy-editor Liz Dawn honed the text, and production editor Alanna Donaldson oversaw the weaving of word and image into the form you see here.

Meg, Jack, Annie, thank you, you are my inspiration in everything I do.

I also want to acknowledge all the good people working in oil, plastic, and related fields. This book is not a condemnation of them or their work; it is an exploration of opportunities to design and make things that bring us all the benefits that oil and plastic have brought us without all the environmental and health concerns that have accompanied them. Sooner than we think, we will all be post-petroleum designers. Most people working in oil, plastic, and related fields know this and are working to find cleaner, healthier alternatives before the petroleum that drives their businesses runs out.

And, finally, I want to acknowledge you. Whatever your attitude is toward oil and plastic and their uses, I'm glad you've taken the time to explore the issues further. Whether you're a designer or in another field, I wish you great success and hope you find inspiration in the pages that follow.

O F all the materials found on Earth, none has had the impact of oil. With it we have trans-formed life on the planet and the atmosphere that life depends on. Every barrel of oil we burn releases nearly a thousand pounds of carbon dioxide into the air, and as carbon dioxide increases, so does global warming. Oil, which gave us the power to change the Earth, now threatens the health of every living thing on it. But in a world that runs on oil, cutting back is not easy.[1]

A single barrel of oil contains more energy than a human being produces laboring by hand for ten years, and some fear living without it would mean a return to our pre-petroleum days of toil. Yet it doesn't have to be that way. We can create a post-petroleum world rich in the good things that oil has brought us but without its negative side effects. Before we can create it, however, we have to design it. And we can't wait for the wells to run dry or the atmosphere to overheat to begin. By then, we could find ourselves passengers on a dying planet, doing too little too late to reverse the effects of a climate out of control.

Designing a post-petroleum world, however, is no easy task. It requires us to rethink how we make things, what we make them from, how we move them—how we power our entire economy. Clean energy alternatives like solar and wind will help, as will alternative fuels like ethanol, but they are not enough. The production of plastics alone consumes two-and-a-half billion barrels of oil per year. It also generates two billion tons of carbon dioxide, enough to perpetuate global climate change even if we were to switch to clean energy and biofuels today. We need to change the way we make everything—our cars, our houses, the products we use every day, all the petroleum-based conveniences we enjoy—and we need a clear plan to do it.[2]

That plan is post-petroleum design, a new way of designing and making things that uses much less oil. It is already taking shape in design studios, factories, and laboratories around the world. There, post-petroleum designers are forging an alternative to a future fouled by oil. Working with new materials and old, the most advanced technologies and the most ancient wisdoms, these pioneers are working to shape our post-petroleum future. But before we can make sense of the post-petroleum era, we need to understand how we became so dependent on oil.

Notes

1   U.S. Environmental Protection Agency, "Carbon Dioxide Emissions Coefficients," February 14, 2013, www.eia.gov/environment/emissions/co2_vol_mass.cfm

2   U.S. Environmental Protection Agency, "Inventory of U.S. Greenhouse Gas Emissions and Sinks: 1990–2012," April 2014, www.epa.gov/climatechange/ghgemissions/usinventoryreport.html

PART ONE

Oil and Its Impacts

The Golden Age of Oil

Crazy Drake's Folly

Today, the hills of northwestern Pennsylvania are scarred by strip mining and mountain topping. But 150 years ago they were wilderness. Black bears and wolves roamed the woods, pausing to drink from mountain creeks that ran cold and clear. It was along one of these creeks that Colonel Edwin Drake and his band of explorers clambered in search of oil. The year was 1858, and a youthful United States of America was growing fast, taking the reins of the industrial revolution from Great Britain with the help of a seemingly endless supply of natural resources. Coal from the hills of northwestern Pennsylvania powered the locomotives and ships carrying the U.S. to global preeminence, but coal wasn't easy to get at. In those days before strip mining and mountain topping, deep mining was the only way, and that was dangerous and expensive.

Drake and his men weren't looking for coal, though. They had their eye on the next big thing, a fuel with 66 percent more energy per pound than coal. They were after oil, so plentiful in northwestern Pennsylvania that in some places it covered the ground with a swampy slick. Some creeks sparkled with the rainbow-colored sheen of perpetual oil slicks as oil bubbling up from below ground was carried downstream. It's no wonder that Drake chose to search along one of these, the one called Oil Creek.

As they trudged along its wooded banks, his men carried a kind of rigging never before used in the search for oil. Before Drake, oil had only been harvested from surface slicks, called seeps, like the ones that dotted northwestern Pennsylvania. But Drake was after bigger game than that. He and his men were hauling timbers, pipes, and augers to make the kind of rigging that until then had only been used by salt miners to extract subterranean salt brine. No one had ever thought to go to the trouble of drilling for oil. But with the new nation's thirst for fuel skyrocketing, the Seneca Oil Company had hired Drake to try his brash new scheme.

Things went poorly at first, earning the rig the nickname "Drake's Folly" and the Colonel the nickname "Crazy Drake." But Drake would have the last laugh. In 1859, he and his crew struck oil at a depth of 69 feet. A new "oil rush" was underway, and soon oil rigs were sprouting up all over northwestern Pennsylvania. Suddenly, America had a bold new source to power its expansion westward, and the supply appeared to be as endless as the demand. Only one obstacle

Figure 1.1: Drake's Folly
The first oil well in the U.S. was 69 feet deep. Today's wells can reach
deeper than seven miles in search of oil. Image courtesy of Drake
Well Museum, Pennsylvania Historical and Museum Commission.

stood in the way. The crude oil discovered by Drake and others was of little use in its natural state, and oil refineries barely existed in the 1860s.

One enterprising young man, however, saw oil's potential to power the nation's westward expansion. This son of a snake oil salesman saw coal prices rise by 50 percent over the course of the Civil War, and he saw oil as an attractive alternative. He also saw the missing link between the oil wells of Pennsylvania and the rising demand for power to the west: refineries. In 1862, at just 21 years of age, he began amassing the resources to buy a small Cleveland refinery located along the new Atlantic & Great Western Railroad that would link the Pennsylvania oil fields to the American West. By 1865 the refinery was his, and within six years he and his partners owned every refinery in Cleveland. Eight years later, his company was refining nine out of every ten barrels of oil produced in the United States. By 1890, the Standard Oil Company would be one of the world's wealthiest companies, and the young man, John D. Rockefeller, would be the nation's first billionaire—a wealth built on oil.

Fueling the American Dream

How did oil grow from Drake's Folly to become the world's most profitable commodity in just 30 years? The answer can be found in a bicycle shop in Germany. In 1885, just as John D. Rockefeller was becoming the world's richest man, Karl Benz was putting the finishing touches on his new invention, an "automobile fueled by gas." Sales were slow at first, since no one but

Benz had ever considered gasoline as a fuel. In fact, his first customers had to buy gasoline from pharmacies that sold it as a cleaning product. By the end of the nineteenth century, however, Benz was producing over 500 cars per year. Within four years, sales would top 3,500.

But gas was by no means the only power source for this new mode of transportation. In 1906, American Fred Marriott set a land speed record of 127 mph in a Stanley Steam Racer, and Stanleys were some of the most popular vehicles in the fledgling U.S. auto industry. Only the Columbia Automobile Company, with its line of electric cars, outsold Stanley. But the Steamer didn't require an electrical outlet (scarce in 1906) or a stop at the gas station. Instead, drivers simply pulled up to a horse watering trough and siphoned out what they needed. The Steamer, however, became a victim of its own success. More cars on the street meant fewer horses, and that meant fewer watering troughs. Soon finding one to refuel from became harder than finding an electric car refueling station is today.

But it wasn't just the nation's vanishing horse troughs that brought about the decline in steam- and electric-powered vehicles. While the Stanley and Columbia factories in Connecticut and Massachusetts made the Northeast the center of the U.S. auto industry, a former sawmill operator from Michigan was hard at work on another power source. In 1908, he and his partners ponied up $28,000 to start a new company making gas-powered cars they hoped would rival Stanley and Columbia. By 1916, nearly half a million cars per year would be rolling off the assembly lines of their Ford Motor Company. Their Model T cars sold for under $400, while the Stanley Steamer cost almost ten times as much, putting to rest any doubts about which fuel would power the world's cars.

And while resistance would prove futile in the long run, other, often more efficient fuels continued to shape the American transportation landscape for years to come. Even Henry Ford designed his early cars to run on ethanol, calling it "the fuel of the future." Electricity was another alternative, not for automobiles but for mass transit. As late as 1920, public mass transit was still the nation's first choice for travel, and if you looked up from the city streets filling with cars, you would see the overhead lines of electric trolleys. To the oil and auto companies, however, those trolley cars were full of lost customers. Starting in 1936, two major bus lines working with investments from General Motors, Standard Oil, Philips Petroleum, and others, began buying up trolley systems across America. They tore down the overhead electric lines, tore up the tracks, and junked the cars. Eventually, GM and other companies would be convicted of conspiring to monopolize the sale of the buses that replaced the trolleys, but the damage was done—petroleum-powered buses and cars had won out over mass transit, electric and steam power.[1]

Figure 1.2: Stanley Steam Racer
In 1906, Fred Marriott set a land speed record of 127 mph in a Stanley Steam Racer at a time when steam-, electric-, and gasoline-powered cars vied for dominance of the world's roads. Image courtesy of Scientific American.

Figure 1.3: Trolley Car and "Trackless Trolley"
World War II-era Baltimore commuters hustle to catch an electrically powered trolley (left) and a gas-powered "trackless trolley" (better known today as a bus). Image courtesy of Library of Congress; photo by Marjory Collins.

By 1960, Americans were driving 13 miles for every 1 they traveled by mass transit. One hundred years after Drake first struck black gold in the hills of northwestern Pennsylvania, over 70 million gas-powered vehicles would be rolling across the United States. Outnumbering single-family homes by more than ten to one, the car had supplanted the home as the new American Dream. For the auto and oil industries, it was a dream come true. General Motors was the nation's largest company, Ford Motor Company was second, and Esso, now called Exxon Mobil and a direct descendant of the U.S. Supreme Court's 1911 antitrust breakup of Standard Oil, was third. The four-wheeled American Dream ran on gas, and together these mega-corporations virtually ran the country. But a single event in the early 1970s would lead us to wonder what happens when the pipeline that fuels the American Dream starts to run dry?[2]

Notes

1   Wood, John Cunningham and Wood, Michael C., eds., *Alfred P. Sloan: Critical Evaluations in Business and Management*, London: Routledge, 2003.

2   U.S. Census Bureau, "Statistical Abstract of the United States: 2012," www.census.gov/history/pdf/12s1101.pdf

The End of Oil

Peak Oil

"A nation that runs on oil can't afford to run short," was the 1972 mantra of the American Petroleum Institute. The API had good reason to be concerned: two years earlier, in 1970, U.S. oil production, which had led the world since the days of Drake's Folly, had begun to decline. To make matters worse, America's thirst for oil was on the rise, doubling between 1950 and 1970. With consumption going up and domestic supplies going down, oil imports skyrocketed. Relying on foreign oil to fuel the American Dream, however, proved to be risky business.

The last place I wanted to be as a teenager in the summer of 1973 was stuck in the back of my parents' station wagon, waiting in line to buy gas. It could take hours, and with purchases sometimes limited to ten gallons, it wasn't long before we were back in line. By the end of the year, the shortages and high prices resulting from the boycott by the Organization of Arab Petroleum Exporting Countries were so severe that President Nixon declared a nationwide maximum speed limit of 50 mph. "Fifty is Thrifty" public service announcements soon flowed from the radios of cars stuck in the gas lines. Within a year, one in five gas stations was without gas, and the price of what was left had nearly doubled.

Figure 2.1: Oil Embargo Gas Lines
Long lines to buy gas during the 1973 oil embargo by Arab members of the Organization of Petroleum Exporting Countries gave U.S. citizens their first taste of life with less oil. Image courtesy of Library of Congress; photo by Warren K. Leffler.

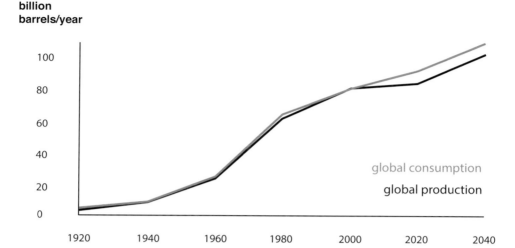

billion barrels/year

Figure 2.2: World Oil Production and Consumption
We now consume more oil than we produce, with the gap
expected to widen in coming years. Illustration by Maria Meza.

Since then, the cost of gas has doubled again. But do we still need to be concerned about oil shortages? Can't we always find more, thanks to technological advances and undiscovered sources? Thanks to increasing production from offshore wells and unconventional oil deposits like shale oil, the U.S. Energy Information Administration (EIA) predicts that global crude oil production will rise over the next few years. Oil advocates are quick to take that as a sign that we no longer have to worry about the end of oil. The same prediction, however, shows global crude production falling increasingly short of global demand after 2020. One study published in *Energy Policy* puts the peak for both conventional and unconventional oil at 2016, but another study in the same journal places peak production for unconventional oil at around 2080. The difference between the two shows the difficulty of predicting just how soon we will run out of oil.[1]

Learning from Peak Gas

Not far from my home in Muncie, Indiana, there was once a coalmine. Back in 1876, miners working 600 feet below ground bored into something that caused a loud explosion. Some of the miners thought they'd broken through the ceiling of hell, and they plugged the hole and abandoned the mineshaft. Eight years later, a company, hearing of natural gas discoveries in Ohio, opened the shaft and drilled deeper. At about 1,000 feet down, they tapped into what came to be called the Trenton Gas Field. It proved to be the largest natural gas field in the country, covering 2,500 square miles. Fumes rose up the shaft, and when they were lit, flames shot into the air and could be seen 15 miles away in Muncie.

The gas was so plentiful that local settlements burned it for lighting and heating, and whole new towns sprung up to support the resulting industrial boom—towns with names like Gas City and Gaston. Muncie was able to lure the Ball Brothers Glass Manufacturing Company, makers of the famous Ball mason jars, from Buffalo, New York, with the promise of unlimited free gas. Towns and companies were so sure the gas would last that they lit "flambeaus," continuously burning gas pipes tapping the fields below. As a result of these and other wasteful practices, nine out of every ten cubic feet of gas tapped went to waste.

Gas was being used up so fast that pressure within the subterranean field dropped quickly, and by 1902 the gas boom was over. Less than 20 years after extraction began, central Indiana had used up its seemingly unlimited supply of easily accessed natural gas. The industries that consumed it moved on or shut down, and its economy has yet to recover.

The Trenton Gas Field reached peak production in 1900, and by 1915 production had fallen by 95 percent. Indiana was "out of gas." Like the natural gas deposits of central Indiana one hundred years ago, today's oil supplies are finite. The difference is that at the global scale, there will be nowhere else to move to, no other deposits to use up.

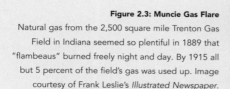

Figure 2.3: Muncie Gas Flare
Natural gas from the 2,500 square mile Trenton Gas Field in Indiana seemed so plentiful in 1889 that "flambeaus" burned freely night and day. By 1915 all but 5 percent of the field's gas was used up. Image courtesy of Frank Leslie's *Illustrated Newspaper*.

Exactly when we will run out of oil is hard to say. Currently, we're in the midst of an intensified global effort to find new sources of oil and squeeze more from existing deposits. Both global and domestic oil production are on the rise. But the current oil rush only means we're using a finite resource faster than ever, and we will run out that much sooner. Still, even as we burn through nearly 90 million barrels of oil per day, there are those who argue we can stave off peak oil if we improve on current methods of oil exploration and extraction, conserve what's left, or substitute alternative fuels. Can any of these options help us postpone the inevitable end of oil? Conservation is one option. If we could curb our 90 million barrel per day habit, we could certainly make the world's oil supply last longer. Three primary conservation strategies could be used: regulation, taxation, and higher prices. Let's look first at higher gas prices because in the immediate future it's not the end of oil we have to worry about, it's the $10 per gallon gas.

$10 Gas

> It's blackmail for people like me who don't live in a big city and can't take public transport.
>
> (Italian commuter Costanza Cappelli, on paying $9.50 per gallon for gas)

Like other Italians in the summer of 2012, Costanza Cappelli was complaining about gasoline prices, which had reached $9.50 per gallon. At that price, the average Italian family was spending more on fuel than food. Not surprisingly, auto sales dropped 20 percent that summer. But despite the hardship, Italians cut back on fuel consumption by less than 10 percent. Nearly one-third of commuters in Milan, Rome, and Naples said the price increase didn't change their driving habits at all.[2]

In the U.S., drivers began cutting back on driving in 2008, after a steady increase dating back to World War II. But experts ranging from the U.S. Department of Transportation to the U.S. Energy Information Administration predict that driving will renew its upward trend in the next few years and maintain it for the foreseeable future. And like their Italian counterparts, American drivers seem relatively unfazed by rising gas prices. Even in 2011, when gas prices reached almost $4 per gallon, one-quarter of Americans still said the increase didn't affect their travel plans, and public transit ridership increased less than 5 percent. Lack of access to public transportation is, in fact, the main reason we keep driving when gas costs go up, as it was for Costanza Cappelli in his Tuscan village.[3,4]

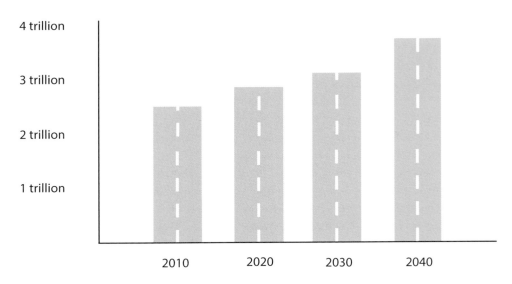

Figure 2.4: Light-Duty Vehicle Miles Traveled
Despite hindrances like a recession and high gas prices, Americans continue to drive more. Illustration by Maria Meza.

The other reason we keep driving despite rising gas prices is that our infrastructure demands it. The Interstate Highway System of the 1950s and 1960s created impenetrable barriers for bikes and pedestrians, leaving millions of Americans too isolated to walk or bike, and without adequate mass transit. No wonder mass transit accounts for less than 2 percent of all passenger miles traveled on U.S. roads.[5]

When faced with traveling any distance, we drive, not necessarily because we want to but because we feel we have to. As energy expert Robert Hirsch explained,

> The idea of moving towards a world that is less dependent on liquid fuel is a good one, and eventually, that's going to have to happen simply because we are depleting the liquid fuels that are available or are going to be available from coal or shale or other sources. The problem is that we have an enormous infrastructure that's dependent on liquid fuels now. We all have our cars and we get our food from trucks, and trains, and we fly around in airplanes, and so forth. And to change that infrastructure in a dramatic way is going to take a great deal of time because that equipment has long lifetimes, and it's going to cost a lot of money.

Our lack of transportation alternatives and an "asphalt nation" built for cars mean that many who may not want to drive feel they have to, no matter how high gas prices go. All of these factors make voluntary conservation an unlikely means to reduce oil consumption significantly.[6]

One Nation under Regulation

EVEN if paying more at the pump won't make us cut back on driving, can't the government simply force conservation by imposing stricter regulations for fuel efficiency? It wouldn't be the first time, as we saw when the federal government imposed a nationwide 55 mph speed limit and Corporate Average Fuel Economy (CAFE) standards in the wake of the 1973 oil embargo. But since those conservation measures took effect, U.S. oil consumption has more than doubled, suggesting that governmental regulation doesn't automatically cut oil consumption.

Automakers don't appear too eager to adopt CAFE standards either. The National Automobile Dealers Association has argued that stricter fuel economy rules would add $5,000 to the price of a new vehicle. The leaders of General Motors, Ford, and Chrysler warned Congress in 2007 that stricter standards "would destroy the domestic auto industry." But while stricter fuel economy standards don't appear to be forcing conservation, they haven't killed off the auto or oil industries either. Three of 2011's four largest U.S. companies were oil companies, their $60 billion in profits exceeding the gross domestic product of some countries. These companies will likely continue to resist higher fuel efficiency laws in years to come.[7,8]

The Death of Taxes

> It's a hot afternoon in July. Your air conditioner is keeping the house cooled to 79 degrees; you're watching the ballgame on a 50-inch flat screen TV; and you're doing a load of laundry. A blip on a computer screen alerts an unseen bureaucrat that your home is consuming far too much energy, given demands. Automatically, your thermostat will shift to 84 degrees, the TV will be turned off until evening, and the washer/dryer won't work again until after dark.
>
> (Brian Sussman, "Big Brother's Next Car: Your Car")[9]

This is the kind of scenario that comes to some people's minds when they think of governmental regulation and taxation. But if stricter federal regulations won't reduce oil consumption, could higher taxes do the trick? California pushed to the forefront of that debate in 2011 when the state doubled its gasoline tax from 17.3 cents per gallon to 35.3 cents. But did Californians cut back on their driving after the gas tax was imposed? They did, but there's a catch. They had already cut their driving in the six months prior to the tax hike by 1.7 percent over the previous year, a reduction most experts attribute to the recession. "This would really be something to celebrate if we were in a period of economic growth," said Tom Kloza, chief oil analyst for the Oil Price Information Service. "We could cite government leadership. We could celebrate people deciding to buy a lot more fuel-efficient vehicles. But I think a great deal of it is a manifestation of the misery out there of people living paycheck to paycheck."[10]

Rauli Partanen, co-author of *The World After Cheap Oil*, sees the same trend in oil consumption across European industries. "Some reduction," he said, "is due to better mileage and alternative ways to heat homes and other efficiency-gains. But given that many of the countries hit by the euro-crisis have lost almost a third of their oil demand in just a few years, I would have to argue that most of the lost demand is due to economic problems."[11]

Despite the thinning paychecks suffered by many as a result of the recession, the average American household still pays over $4,000 per year to fill their gas tanks. In fact, we spend more on transportation, including fuel, than on any other living expense except housing. Perhaps the old adage that all we really need is food, clothing, and shelter should be updated to shelter, car, and food, the true order of our spending.[12]

Would a federal gas tax hike that kicked prices even higher be more effective? Probably not. The Congressional Budget Office estimated that achieving a 10 percent reduction in gasoline consumption would require raising gas taxes by 46 cents per gallon. Considering that the federal gas tax hasn't been raised since 1993, a significant rise in gasoline taxes seems highly unlikely.

Rising Giants, Shrinking Oil

There's one more reason why we can't reduce our oil consumption fast enough to compensate for rising prices and declining production: rising demand from industrializing nations. "In the past," writes *Wall Street Journal* correspondent Russell Gold,

> when U.S. drivers cut back, that has dented global demand for oil and depressed prices. After a lag, the lower prices would help the economy regain its footing—or at least remove a substantial headwind. But many oil experts believe that scenario won't play out this time, because U.S. drivers are no longer calling the shots. The rapidly industrializing economies of China, India, Brazil and even Saudi Arabia are.

China alone consumes over four million more barrels of oil per day than they did ten years ago.[13] Global demand for oil led by countries outside the Organization for Economic Cooperation and Development (OECD) isn't a future scenario either; it's today's reality. In 2014, liquid fuel use by non-OECD nations eclipsed that of OECD nations for the first time. The pace of oil consumption in Asia alone is nothing less than astonishing, more than doubling in the last 20 years.[14]

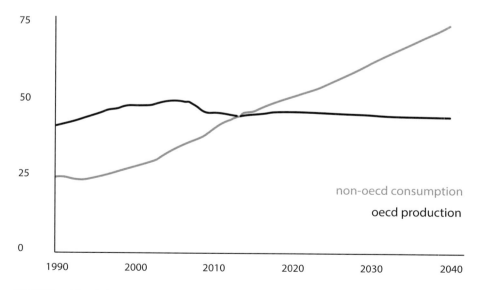

billion barrels/year

non-oecd consumption

oecd production

Figure 2.5: OECD and Non-OECD Liquid Fuel Use Forecast
As oil use plateaus in the Organization for Economic Co-operation and Development countries (U.S., U.K., Germany, Japan, and 30 others), skyrocketing use by rapidly developing non-OECD nations like China, Brazil, and India drives global consumption upward. Illustration by Maria Meza.

World oil consumption is rising, with no sign of letting up. Noting that his company expects global energy demand to increase 40 percent by 2030, BP CEO Bob Dudley said, "That's like adding one more China and one more U.S. to the world's energy demand by 2030. Nearly all that growth—96% in fact—is expected to come from the emerging economies with more than half coming from China and India alone." Can we produce enough oil to keep up with a 40 percent increase in demand? World oil production is increasing, but our thirst for oil is rising faster. The EIA estimates that, thanks in large part to rapidly increasing oil use by non-OECD nations, global consumption will exceed production by more than 5 billion barrels per year by 2040.[15,16]

Despite taxation, regulation, and rising prices, global liquid fuel use continues to climb. When we factor in the skyrocketing consumption in industrializing nations, conservation has an even smaller impact. But even if conservation isn't working, can't we simply find more oil, digging deeper or developing new technologies to extract the billions of barrels held in untapped deposits? If we can, we won't have to worry about finding alternative energy sources or post-petroleum solutions like reduced plastic use—we can simply carry on as "a nation that runs on oil."

Notes

1   U.S. Energy Information Administration, "International Energy Outlook 2014," Report, Washington, DC, 2014, www.eia.gov/forecasts/ieo/more_overview.cfm; Guseo, Renato, "Worldwide Cheap and Heavy Oil Productions: A Long-term Energy Model," *Energy Policy*, Volume 39, Issue 9 (2011): 5572–5577; Moore, S.H. and Evans, G.M., "Long Term Prediction of Unconventional Oil Production," *Energy Policy*, Volume 38, Issue 1 (2010): 265–276.

2   Vasarri, Chiara, and Ebhardt, Tommaso, "Italians Squeezed by $9.50-a-Gallon Gas Face Costly Drive," *Bloomberg News*, August 31, 2012, www.bloomberg.com/news/2012-08-30/italians-squeezed-by-9-50-a-gallon-gas-face-costly-drive-home.html; Bowman, Zach, "You Think Gas Prices are Bad Here, Italians are Paying $9.50/gal," Autoblog, September 6, 2012, www.autoblog.com/2012/09/06/you-think-gas-prices-are-bad-here-italians-are-paying-9-50-gal/

3   U.S. Public Interest Research Group, "A New Direction: Our Changing Relationship with Driving and the Implications for America's Future," Report, Washington, DC, 2013, 2.

4   Martin, Hugo, "Despite High Gas Prices, Southern Californians Plan to Hit the Road Over Memorial Day Weekend," *Los Angeles Times*, May 24, 2011, http://articles.latimes.com/2011/may/24/business/la-fi-memorial-day-20110525; Helman, Christopher, "America's Most Gas-Guzzling Cities," Forbes.com, June 10, 2011, www.forbes.com/sites/christopherhelman/2011/05/10/americas-biggest-and-least-gas-guzzling-cities/

5   U.S. Bureau of Transportation Statistics, "National Transportation Statistics," Table 1-40: U.S. Passenger-Miles, 2012, www.rita.dot.gov/bts/sites/rita.dot.gov.bts/files/publications/national_transportation_statistics/html/table_01_40.html www.fhwa.dot.gov/pressroom/fhwa1103.cfm

6   U.S. Energy Information Administration, "International Energy Outlook 2014."

7   Ramsey, Mike, "Car Dealers Oppose New Fuel Economy Standards," Wall Street Journal Blog, January 17, 2012, http://blogs.wsj.com/drivers-seat/2012/01/17/car-dealers-oppose-new-fuel-economy-standards/

8   Thomas, Ken, "Auto Execs Discuss Mileage With Congress," *Washington Post* Online, June 6, 2007, www.washingtonpost.com/wp-dyn/content/article/2007/06/06/AR2007060600306_pf.html

9   Sussman, Brian, "Big Brother's Next Car: Your Car," americanthinker.com, April 24, 2012, www.american-thinker.com/2012/04/big_brothers_next_target_your_car.html

10   White, Ronald, "California Motorists Leading the Way on Using Less Gasoline," *Los Angeles Times*, http://articles.latimes.com/2011/oct/01/business/la-fi-california-gas-20111002

11   Partanen, Rauli, "Peak Oil Demand or Peak Oil Supply?" kaikenhuippu.com, September 9, 2014, http://kaiken-huippu.com/2014/09/09/peak-oil-demand-or-peak-oil-supply/

12   "Missing $4,155? It Went Into Your Gas Tank This Year," cnbc.com, December 19, 2011, www.cnbc.com/id/45727242; U.S. Bureau of Labor Statistics, "Consumer Expenditure Survey," 2014, www.bls.gov/cex/

13   Gold, Russell, "Drivers Cut Back on $4 Gas," *Wall Street Journal* Online, April 28, 2011, http://online.wsj.com/articles/SB10001424052748703367004576289292254881456

14   U.S. Energy Information Administration, "International Energy Outlook 2014."

15   Dudley, Bob, "Energy Outlook 2030," Speech at release of report, London, January 18, 2012, www.bp.com/en/global/corporate/press/speeches/energy-outlook-20300.html

16   U.S. Energy Information Administration, "International Energy Outlook 2014."

3

Grasping for More

"Drill, Baby, Drill"

> Don't come crying when we are facing a shortage. We're going to face huge challenges
> to bring additional capacity on stream.
>
> (Christophe de Margerie, CEO of Total, Europe's third-largest oil company)[1]

"Drill, baby, drill," is a familiar refrain from those who believe that more exploration and extraction
will boost supplies and delay the advent of peak oil. New technologies, they argue, will help us
reach deposits hidden in oil shales, tar sands, and offshore areas. As conventional sources of oil
run low, these sources of unconventional or tight oil look increasingly inviting. North America's
reserves alone may exceed all the conventional oil left in the Middle East. By 2040, a Carnegie
Endowment report predicts, nearly half of our oil will be from unconventional sources.[2,3]

Tight oil recovery technologies are indeed advancing, but we don't know yet how well they
will work in the long run or what their impact on the environment will be. We do know it costs a
lot more to access unconventional oil—$30 to $80 per barrel more than conventional oil. Costs in

million $ us

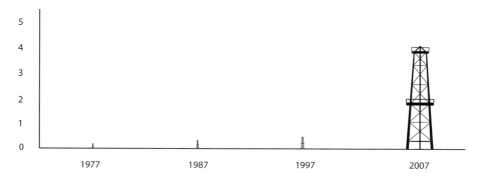

Figure 3.1: Cost of Oil Extraction
The cost per rig to drill for oil more than quadrupled in the
first decade of this century. Illustration by Maria Meza.

the billions per field are now commonplace as the industry struggles to find oil in deeper, rockier, and harder-to-access locations. For example, Europe's third-largest oil company, Total, recently spent $4.6 billion to develop just one new field, the Dalia field 83 miles off the coast of West Africa. And over the last six years, the top 50 oil and gas companies have doubled their domestic drilling costs compared to the previous six years.[4,5,6]

"We are approaching the end of easily accessible, relatively homogeneous oil," concluded the authors of the Carnegie report, *Understanding Unconventional Oil*, "and many experts claim that the era of cheap oil may also be ending." The cost to the environment may be higher too. "As output ramps up to meet increasing global demand for high-value petroleum products," they continued, "unconventional oils will likely deliver a higher volume of heavier hydrocarbons, require more intensive processing and additives, and yield more byproducts that contain large amounts of carbon." A survey by the Congressional Research Service put numbers to those concerns, suggesting that carbon dioxide emissions from Canadian oil sands crude are roughly twice those for conventional crude. Burning all the Alberta tar sand oil, according to John Abraham of the University of Saint Thomas in Minnesota, would raise global temperatures by 0.72 degrees Fahrenheit. Oil sand extraction also uses more water and more energy. Currently, it takes two barrels of oil worth of energy to produce three barrels of oil from oil sands. In 2007, oil sand extraction in Alberta used about one billion cubic feet of natural gas per day—roughly 40 percent of Alberta's total usage. Water consumption is even worse, as extraction and processing use between 2.5 and 4 barrels of water for each barrel of bitumen produced.[7,8,9,10,11]

In addition to releasing more carbon and requiring more energy and water to access, much of our unconventional oil is found in environmentally sensitive areas like the Alaska National Wildlife Refuge and the outer continental shelf. The EIA estimates that opening up waters currently closed to drilling off the East Coast, West Coast, and the west coast of Florida would yield an extra 500,000 barrels of oil per day—about 3 percent of today's consumption—by 2030. The environmental price for that 3 percent would likely be unacceptable, and it would have little impact on gas prices, according to the EIA study. Despite these concerns, unconventional oil will make up more of our future supply simply because we've already used all the easy oil; but it will do so at a higher economic and environmental cost.[12]

Black Gold, Gray Wolves

If you flew low over the plains of Alberta, Canada a few years ago, you would have seen deer, caribou and, if you were lucky, a few of the gray wolves that prey on them. Today, this landscape is known as the "oil fields" of Alberta, and you may be more likely to see fracking equipment than caribou. "The woodland caribou, which is a dominant species in the area, is at risk of extinction," said Samuel Wasser, director of the Center for Conservation Biology at the University of Washington. "To stabilize these caribou populations," he said, "the Alberta government has proposed, and even conducted already, intensive wolf reduction programs in the ecosystem." Wolf reduction programs use bait tainted with strychnine and hunting from airplanes to thin the population.

Wasser has measured the wolf population's declining numbers by using specially trained scat-sniffing dogs. With their help, he found that wolves are not to blame for declining caribou populations in the region. "The problem," he explained, "is that the primary prey of wolves in the system are currently the invading deer population, not the caribou." His study showed that rising deer populations were in fact driving wolves away from the caribou. And he sees a possible connection between the declining caribou population and human development like fracking. "Modifying landscape-level human-use patterns," he concluded, "may be more effective at managing this ecosystem than intentional removal of wolves."

"If we're going to do anything here," he concluded, "we really need to start by first managing ourselves in the system and quit crying wolf, to use a cliché. The human use levels are really quite considerable in system, and this is largely driven by global demand for oil."[13]

"Frack 'em and Forget 'em"

Hydraulic fracturing, or fracking, is a common method for extracting unconventional oil from sand and rock. Squeezing oil from rock gives us access to considerable reserves we haven't been able to tap before. But some communities exposed to fracking for natural gas have encountered serious environmental consequences. As one Pennsylvania resident put it, "The more you learn about hydraulic fracturing in the states ahead of us in these fast moving gas ventures, the more concern you have for our local environment."

Smells like Death

"It smells like a cross between something dead and diesel fuel," said Deb Thomas of the Powder River Basin Resources Council in Pavillion, Wyoming. "It's a very chemical bad smell." Pavillion is one community with firsthand experience in the effects of fracking. During the 1990s, the number of production wells in Pavillion doubled. And with the increase in drilling, residents began to notice an objectionable taste and odor in their well water.

For over ten years, the residents complained to the state government about the problem. Finally, in 2008, the U.S. Environmental Protection Agency (EPA) stepped in and began an investigation. When their initial tests found methane and dissolved hydrocarbons in wells, they decided to dig deeper. The monitoring wells they drilled in 2010 turned up high concentrations of benzene and xylenes (both known carcinogens), along with other substances used in fracking and not normally found in the local groundwater. One monitoring well measured benzene levels above the maximum permitted level. With that, the EPA recommended that several Pavillion-area residents with private water wells find alternate sources of water for drinking and cooking. The EPA's draft report, released in 2011, concluded that, "the data indicates likely impact to ground water that can be explained by hydraulic fracturing." In other words, fracking was contaminating local drinking water with high levels of known carcinogens.[14,15,16]

Concerns about fracking are especially strong in the American West, where property laws can divide ownership of land and the minerals beneath it. "It's just this land-grab, rape-and-pillage mentality," said Colorado cattle rancher Landon Deane, whose fields cover mineral deposits up for bid by fracking companies. She is just one of thousands of landowners in the West facing the prospect of fracking on their own property without their consent. Their voices join others around the world speaking out against fracking. At a town hall meeting in England, where community members gathered to discuss leasing their land to gas company executives, one local put British decorum aside, yelling, "Frack 'em and forget 'em, isn't it? It's all about the money!"[17,18]

Because of concerns over fracking, several European countries, as well as some U.S. states, have placed moratoria on the practice. Given the current level of resistance and environmental concern, it's questionable that fracking will be used to extract oil at a large scale.

Imitation Oil

I LIVE in a college town in Indiana, surrounded by cornfields. When I first moved here from California, I pictured all that corn going to feed people. But as it turns out, only one out of every ten ears goes to feed people. Four times as much is taken to ethanol plants for conversion to fuel. Nearly all of that ethanol goes to power motor vehicles. And ethanol offers environmental

Figure 3.2: Fracking Rig
Fracking rigs are becoming more commonplace in North America, but are also raising environmental and health concerns. iStock.com image; photo by Bob Ingelhart.

advantages over gasoline. A 2007 study by Argonne National Laboratory found that using corn-based ethanol instead of gasoline reduces life cycle greenhouse gas emissions by anywhere from 19 to 52 percent.[19]

Already, 95 percent of all gas sold in the U.S. is 10 percent ethanol, due in part to a federal mandate requiring an increase in U.S. biofuel consumption from 4.7 billion gallons in 2007 to 36 billion gallons in 2022. Millions of flex-fuel vehicles capable of burning blends up to E85 (85 percent ethanol) already roam the streets. But are we on track to increase that percentage? Unfortunately, obstacles abound.[20]

Open the gas cap on some new cars and you'll be confronted with a warning label: "E15–E85" with a circle and slash through it. Almost all automakers warn their customers to avoid fuel blends with more than the standard 10 percent ethanol. They claim that using higher ethanol content blends can damage engines, and even warn that using them will void the vehicle's warranty. There are obstacles on the other side of the pump as well. The cost of modifying a gas station to sell even E15 (just 5 percent more ethanol than conventional gas) is one. Pump conversion can cost tens of thousands of dollars, with no guarantee that customers will accept the new fuel.[21]

"Don't Put It in the Car "

"Don't put it in the car," Debbie Konrade's husband told her. He was referring to the E15 gas sold at a local east Kansas filling station. While the fuel's 15 percent ethanol content is just slightly more than ordinary gas, he had heard the warnings from automakers to stay away from it or risk engine damage. And although the Environmental Protection Agency has approved the fuel for cars with a model year of 2001 and later, the stigma has hindered ethanol sales nationwide.

"We should have seen it coming," lamented Doug Sommer, plant manager for ethanol producer East Kansas Agri-Energy. He'd seen production slip from 45,000 bushels of corn per day to 36,000 in the past year. And his plight is echoed through refineries across the country. In 2012, the industry posted its first production drop in 17 years and it was a big one—14 percent—forcing nearly 10 percent of the nation's plants to close.

"It's been hard on every business up and down Main Street," said Christopher Jackson, Mayor of Walhalla, North Dakota after the 2012 closing of a local plant. "I don't know that people realized how big of an impact that plant closing had on the community. Now we're a year into it; everybody's feeling the pinch."

Those hard times left the industry as a whole 500 million gallons shy of the amount they're required to produce under the 2007 Renewable Fuel Standard, a federal law designed to amp up biofuel sales and help "wean the U.S. off oil." The 2012 losses led the governors of eight states and almost 200 members of Congress to petition the EPA to suspend the law. Their efforts failed though, and the industry continues to struggle, posting losses of 36 cents per gallon in 2012 after earning 24 cents per gallon the year before.[22,23]

Figure 3.3: "No E15" Gas Tank Lid
Many automakers warn that using gas with as little as 15 percent ethanol content can void engine warranties. Image courtesy of Wikimedia Commons; photo by Mario Roberto Durán Ortiz.

Other objections to ethanol come from some environmental advocates. Corn farming at the large scale necessary to feed our cars can result in nitrogen runoff from fertilizer, soil erosion, and excessive water consumption. Just growing enough corn to produce one gallon of ethanol requires about 1,800 gallons of water. But even if the environmental and economic obstacles to ethanol are overcome, its contribution to total fuel consumption may be marginal. "The growth opportunity that existed some years ago is still out there in theory," said Todd Sneller, the administrator of the Nebraska Ethanol Board, "but the reality is that it's going to take an awful lot of time, money and political battles to realize that opportunity." According to the EIA, it may never fully materialize. By their estimate, the practical limit for domestic ethanol production is about 700,000 barrels per day, about one-third of 1 percent of current U.S. oil consumption. And they don't even consider that tiny amount a realistic figure until 2030.[24,25]

Charge It!

Like the age of ethanol, the age of electric cars has been slow to arrive. One reason is limited range. No one wants to be stranded with a dead battery, and electric charging stations in the U.S. are still few and far between. "You really have to calculate where you're going," said Steven Siegelaub, an early adopter and owner of a Tesla Roadster. Another issue is service. Chevrolet, for example, put the electric hybrid Volt on the market with no certified technicians to service it. In smaller markets, mechanics may still be scratching their heads when they look under the hood of an electric vehicle.[26]

Despite these hurdles, electric drive vehicle sales continue to grow, and there are now over a million on the roads of America. A new breed of electrics like the Tesla S, which received the highest auto rating ever given by Consumer Reports, 99.5 out of 100, could bring new customers. But for now, sales of electrics are less than 4 percent of total auto sales, not much relief for our gas-guzzling transportation system. A report by Lux Research paints a dim future for them as well, predicting that even if the price of oil reaches $140 per barrel by 2020, a 40 percent increase over the 2013 price, over 95 percent of our vehicles will still be gas-powered.[27,28]

The Rise of Renewables

WHILE you can't run your car on wind or solar power (yet), could these renewable sources take over enough of our non-transportation energy needs to leave plenty of oil for auto fuels and even plastic? Renewable energy has made great progress in recent years, and is expected to account for about one-third of the new electricity generation added in the U.S. from 2013 to 2016. But the EIA predicts that renewables will account for less than 20 percent of our electricity in 2040.[29,30]

In an interview with *The Times*, former Shell CEO Jeroen van der Veer called for a "reality check" on renewables and warned that the world's energy crisis cannot be solved by them alone.

> Contrary to public perceptions, renewable energy is not the silver bullet that will soon solve all our problems. Just when energy demand is surging, many of the world's conventional oilfields are going into decline. The world is blinding itself to the reality of its energy problems, ignoring the scale of growth in demand from developing countries and placing too much faith in renewable sources of power.[31]

Renewable energy is the world's future power source; it has to be if we want to survive. But like other alternatives, it is proving slow to arrive and may have limits to growth we have yet to acknowledge. And as we've seen, whether through drilling more wells or employing new technologies to drain what's left from rock, shale, and sand, it appears unlikely we can extract enough oil from unconventional sources to keep up with growing global energy demand. Despite the growing use of renewable energy like wind and solar, oil use is expected to grow in coming years, reaching nearly 120 million barrels per day by 2040.[32,33]

How Will It End?

How, exactly, the end of oil will play out on the global stage depends on a number of factors. Will it be sudden or gradual? Will it be a peaceful transition or a violent calamity? Even when gas prices hit $9.50 per gallon in Italy in 2012, there was concern about severe economic and social impacts. "If fuel prices remain so high," warned Emiliano Brancaccio, a professor of political economy at the University of Sannio, "we could face an inflationary depression." Robert Hirsch, in a 2005 report for the U.S. Department of Energy, concluded that, "Without mitigation, the peaking of world oil production will almost certainly cause major economic upheaval." And former Secretary of Energy James Schlesinger told the U.S. Senate in the same year, "Unless we take serious steps to prepare for the day that we can no longer increase production of conventional oil, we are faced with the possibility of a major economic shock—and the political unrest that would ensue."[34,35]

A 2012 working paper from the International Monetary Fund entitled, "Oil and the World Economy: Some Possible Futures", was more precise about what the end of oil could look like. If oil fields continue at their current rate of depletion, the author concluded, "Annual growth rates in the industrial countries would decline by one full percentage point." That's in contrast to growth rates over 3 percent for the U.S. since World War II, and over 9 percent for China since 1989.[36]

"Our economic model is based on growth," added energy specialist Dr. Tom Murphy. "When it becomes clear that growth cannot continue, the ramifications can be sudden and severe." Those ramifications could be even more severe than climate change, according to Murphy. "I see climate change as a serious threat to natural services and species survival, perhaps ultimately having a very negative impact on humanity. But resource depletion trumps climate change for me, because I think this has the potential to effect far more people on a far shorter timescale with far greater certainty." Economies built on oil face a catch-22. The end of cheap oil could slow them significantly, but, as *The World After Cheap Oil* co-author Rauli Partanen observed, "if their economy starts to grow, so will their demand for oil." That would cause oil to run out faster, leading to further shocks. Lower prices in the long run appear unlikely though. "In the IEO2014 Reference case," said the EIA referring to their most recent forecast, "world oil prices fall from $113 per barrel (2012 dollars) in 2011 to $92 per barrel in 2017, then rise steadily to $141 per barrel in 2040."[37,38,39,40]

The passing of peak oil, whenever it comes, will be a critical threshold for nations that run on oil. Every day it is drawing nearer. And we need to remember that while oil companies like to talk about oil "production," humankind has never produced one single drop of crude oil. We simply take it out of the ground and use it up. Currently, oil companies take over 80 million barrels of oil per day from the planet. And we're consuming it at an even faster rate—nearly 90 million barrels per day. New technologies for oil exploration and extraction will help and improved fuel efficiency will help; and while alternative fuels like biofuels, electricity and, perhaps, hydrogen will help too, we are still using irreplaceable oil at a phenomenal pace. What matters is not exactly when we will squeeze the last drop of oil from the ground, but when it will become too expensive to extract economically, forcing us to find alternatives or do without the fuel, plastics, cars, and other basic commodities we've become accustomed to. As supplies run out, prices will rise, squeezing first the poor, then middle-income people and, finally, the most wealthy.

Oil is running out. And despite our best efforts to conserve it and find alternatives in transportation, heating, cooling, manufacturing, and electrical power generation, these options aren't putting much of a dent in our oil consumption. As it runs out, we will need to use less of it in everything we do, and everything we make. Manufacturing will be key, as industry and transportation are expected to account for 92 percent of global liquid fuel use by 2040. And when we look for ways to cut back, one area, previously overlooked, stands out. Plastic uses over 1.3 billion barrels of oil per year. As cars become more fuel-efficient, as more of them go electric, and as we learn to use less oil in heating, cooling, manufacturing, and electrical power generation, the percentage of our petroleum that ends up as plastic will only increase. In fact, the percentage of our petroleum that goes to plastic production has increased more than fivefold since 1976. Reducing petroleum-based plastic now means more oil for other uses, a cleaner environment, and reduced health risks. Aside from the health and environmental concerns associated with plastic, the fact is we're running out of the non-renewable fossil fuels we use to make it. Ultimately, we have no choice but to find alternatives to plastic. [41,42,43]

Notes

1   Voss, Stephen, "Total, Shell Chief Executives Say 'Easy Oil' Is Gone," bloomberg.com, April 5, 2007, www.bloomberg.com/apps/news?pid=newsarchive&sid=aH57.uZe.sAI

2   Steele, Michael, 2008 Republican National Convention, St. Paul, Minnesota, September 1, 2008.

3   Gordon, Deborah, "Understanding Unconventional Oil," Report, Carnegie Endowment, Washington, DC, 2012, http://carnegieendowment.org/files/unconventional_oil.pdf

4   Seljom, Pernille, "Unconventional Oil & Gas Production," Report, Energy Technology Systems Analysis Programme, May 10, 2010, www.iea-etsap.org/web/E-TechDS/PDF/P02-Uncon%20oil&gas-GS-gct.pdf

5   Voss, "Total, Shell Chief Executives Say 'Easy Oil' Is Gone."

6   Krauss, Clifton and Lipton, Eric, "After the Boom in Natural Gas," *New York Times*, October 20, 2012, www.nytimes.com/2012/10/21/business/energy-environment/in-a-natural-gas-glut-big-winners-and-losers.html?pagewanted=all&_r=0

7   Gordon, "Understanding Unconventional Oil."

8   Seljom, "Unconventional Oil & Gas Production."

9   Biello, David, "How Much Will Tar Sands Oil Add to Global Warming?" *Scientific American*, January 23, 2013, www.scientificamerican.com/article.cfm?id=tar-sands-and-keystone-xl-pipeline-impact-on-global-warming

10 McColl, David and Slagorsky, Martin, "Canadian Oil Sands Supply Costs and Development Projects," Report, Canadian Energy Research Institute, November 2008.

11 U.S. Securities and Exchange Commission, Exhibit 99.1, "OriginOil's Second Licensing Agreement Targets Canadian Oil Sands Market," Washington, DC, www.sec.gov/Archives/edgar/data/1419793/000101376212002227/ex991.htm

12 Hargreaves, Steve, "Drill baby drill won't lower gas prices," April 25, 2011, CNN Money, http://money.cnn.com/2011/04/25/news/economy/oil_drilling_gas_prices/index.htm; Reed, Stanley, "Planning for a Post-Oil World at a Time of Crisis," *New York Times*, nytimesonline.com, May 30, 2012, www.nytimes.com/2012/05/31/world/middleeast/31iht-m31-abudhabi-taqa.html?_r=2&

13 Wasser, Samuel, Keim, Johah, Taper, Mark, and Lele, Subhash, "The Influences of Wolf Predation, Habitat Loss, and Human Activity on Caribou and Moose in the Alberta Oil Sands," *Frontiers in Ecology and the Environment*, Volume 9, Issue 10, 546–551, www.esajournals.org/doi/abs/10.1890/100071

14 Banerjee, Neela, "EPA Says 'Fracking' Probably Contaminated Well Water in Wyoming," *Los Angeles Times*, December 8, 2011, http://articles.latimes.com/2011/dec/08/nation/la-na-fracking-20111209

15 Lachelt, Gwen, "Groups Denounce Attack on EPA Investigation of Fracking Contamination," January 17, 2012, Earthworks, www.earthworksaction.org/earthblog/detail/groups_denounce_attack_on_epa_investigation_of_fracking_contamination

16 Bleizeffer, Dustin, "Pavillion, Wyoming-Area Residents Told Not to Drink Water," *Casper Star Tribune*, September 1, 2010, http://trib.com/news/state-and-regional/article_a7529206-b5ef-11df-8439-001cc4c002e0.html

17 Healy, Jack, "Colorado Communities Take On Fight Against Energy Land Leases," *New York Times*, February 2, 2013, www.nytimes.com/2013/02/03/us/colorado-communities-take-on-fight-against-energy-land-leases.html?_r=0

18 Booth, Robert, "No Fracking in Home Counties, Village Residents Tell Oil Company," *The Guardian*, January 12, 2012, www.guardian.co.uk/environment/2012/jan/12/fracking-oil-west-sussex-caudrilla

19 U.S. Department of Energy, "Ethanol Vehicle Emissions," www.afdc.energy.gov/vehicles/flexible_fuel_emissions.html

20 U.S. Department of Energy, "Ethanol Fuel Basics," www.afdc.energy.gov/fuels/ethanol_fuel_basics.html

21 Wald, Matthew L., "In Kansas, Stronger Mix of Ethanol," *New York Times*, www.nytimes.com/2012/07/12/business/energy-environment/at-kansas-station-e15-fuel-reaches-the-masses.html?pagewanted=all&_r=0

22 Parker, Mario, "U.S. Ethanol Production Headed for Decline," *Minneapolis Star Tribune*, November 7, 2012, www.startribune.com/business/177788401.html?refer=y

23 Wald, Matthew L., "In Kansas, Stronger Mix of Ethanol."

24 Eligon, John and Wald, Matthew L., "Days of Promise Fade for Ethanol," *New York Times*, www.nytimes.com/2013/03/17/us/17ethanol.html?pagewanted=all

25 U.S. Energy Information Administration, Report, "Ethanol Production Capacity Little Changed in Past Year," May 20, 2013, www.eia.gov/todayinenergy/detail.cfm?id=11331

26 Koretzky, Michael, "5 Reasons NOT to Buy an Electric Car," *Money Talks News*, February 8, 2011, www.moneytalksnews.com/2011/02/28/5-reasons-not-to-buy-an-electric-car/

27 Electric Drive Transportation Association, "Cumulative U.S. Plug-in Vehicle Sales," www.electricdrive.org/index.php?ht=d/sp/i/20952/pid/20952

28 Lux Research, Report, "Global Automotive Sales in 2020 by Vehicle Type: Three Scenarios," www.luxresearchinc.com/blog/2009/11/global-automotive-sales-in-2020-by-vehicle-type-three-scenarios/

29 U.S. Energy Information Administration, Report, "Annual Energy Outlook 2010," www.eia.gov/oiaf/aeo/electricity.html

30 Kumhof, Michael and Muir, Dirk, "Oil and the World Economy: Some Possible Futures," *Philosophical Transactions of the Royal Society*, December 2, 2013, http://web.stanford.edu/~kumhof/oilroyalsoc.pdf; U.S. Energy Information Administration, "Annual Energy Outlook 2014," Report, www.eia.gov/forecasts/aeo/pdf/0383(2013).pdf

31 Mortished, Carl, "Energy Crisis Cannot Be Solved by Renewables, Oil Chiefs Say," *The Times of London*, June 25, 2007, www.thetimes.co.uk/tto/business/industries/naturalresources/article2180851.ece

32 BP, "Outlook to 2035," 2014, www.bp.com/en/global/corporate/about-bp/energy-economics/energy-outlook/outlook-to-2035.html

33 U.S. Energy Information Administration, Report, "Annual Energy Outlook 2014."

34   Vasarri, Chiara and Ebhardt, Tommaso, "Italians Squeezed by $9.50-a-Gallon Gas Face Costly Drive," *Bloomberg News*, August 31, 2012, www.bloomberg.com/news/2012-08-30/italians-squeezed-by-9-50-a-gallon-gas-face-costly-drive-home.html

35   Hirsch, Robert, Bezdek, Roger, and Wendling, Robert, "Peaking of World Oil Production: Impacts, Mitigation & Risk Management," Report, February 2005, www.netl.doe.gov/publications/others/pdf/oil_peaking_netl.pdf

36   Whipple, Tom, "The Peak Oil Crisis: Alternative Futures," Falls Church News-Press, November 14, 2012, http://fcnp.com/2012/11/14/the-peak-oil-crisis-alternative-futures/

37   Stafford, James, "Tom Murphy Interview: Resource Depletion is a Bigger Threat than Climate Change," oilprice.com, March 22, 2012, http://oilprice.com/Interviews/Tom-Murphy-Interview-Resource-Depletion-is-a-Bigger-Threat-than-Climate-Change.html

38   Partanen, Rauli, "Peak Oil Demand or Peak Oil Supply?" kaikenhuippu.com, September 9, 2014, http://kaiken-huippu.com/2014/09/09/peak-oil-demand-or-peak-oil-supply/

39   U.S. Energy Information Administration, Report, "Annual Energy Outlook 2014."

40   Ibid.

41   Ibid.

42   "What Happens to Plastics When the Oil Runs Out and When Will It Run Out?" British Plastics Federation, August 19, 2008, www.bpf.co.uk/Press/Oil_Consumption.aspx; U.S. Energy Information Administration, "International Energy Statistics," 2014, www.eia.gov/cfapps/ipdbproject/IEDIndex3.cfm?tid=5&pid=53&aid=1

43   PlasticsEurope, "Plastics—the Facts 2012: An Analysis of European Plastics Production, Demand and Waste Data for 2011," Report, www.plasticseurope.org/documents/document/20121120170458-final_plastic-sthefacts_nov2012_en_web_resolution.pdf; U.S. Energy Information Administration, "International Energy Statistics."

PART TWO

Oil and Plastic

4

Just One Word—Plastic

A World Wrapped in Plastic

Cheap oil and low plastic prices are a thing of the past.

(Mike Kmetz, President of IDES plastics consultancy)

"The true question," says Kmetz, "is when will the global demand for oil exceed the ability to produce it? Many believe that this will happen sooner rather than later and when it occurs, our lives will get much more interesting. The impact on many industries, including plastics, is likely to be profound." As we've seen, global demand already exceeds production. We can minimize the impacts of that shortfall by reducing our dependence on petroleum-based plastics now, but this may be no easy task. Plastic has been around not much more than a hundred years, yet we've produced enough to wrap the entire planet six times. We love it, and we've loved it since we first set eyes on it in the late nineteenth century.[1]

Elephants and Billiard Balls

I esteem celluloid of such inestimable value to the profession, that I should regard it as criminal not to give my unqualified testimony in its favor, which, after using it for more than three years, it affords me pleasure to do.

(D. Burrill, February 8, 1878)

The celluloid Mr Burrill esteemed was one of the first plastics invented. Its origins are a story in itself. It was, in fact, elephants and billiard balls that started us down the path to today's trillion-dollar-a-year plastics industry. In the mid-nineteenth century, the game of billiards was evolving from a pastime for English gentlemen into the mainstream American phenomenon we now call pool. But growth was stalling because billiard balls were made from ivory, and more ivory meant fewer elephants. Those that were left were not about to give up their tusks without a fight, and it was not uncommon for them to turn their hunters into prey. By 1863, the industry was so concerned about the shortage of ivory that one manufacturer, Phelan and Collender, offered a prize of $10,000 (nearly $175,000 in today's dollars) to anyone who could come up with a viable alternative. The prize was never claimed, but it may have served as inspiration for one man.

Ten years prior to Phelan and Collender's challenge, John Wesley Hyatt had dropped out of the seminary to take up work as a printer. One day, he accidentally knocked over a bottle of collodion, a mix of ether and ethanol, in his print shop in Albany, New York. Later, when he tried to clean up the spill, he found it had dried to a hard but flexible film. After much trial and error, he found that adding camphor created a material strong enough to make billiard balls. He even started a successful billiard ball company. But his new material is best remembered for its application in the rapidly growing film industry. He called his camphor and collodion concoction celluloid.

While the movies were just catching on in America, billiards was booming, and with it the sales of Hyatt's billiard balls. Celluloid, however, had one problem—one that would later plague the movie industry in a grand way. Around 1900, Hyatt began receiving complaints from alarmed billiard parlor owners that the balls would occasionally explode when they struck each other. Some were said to catch fire if left in contact with a cigar. They were discovering what we now know—celluloid is extremely flammable—and it would fuel many a future theater fire.[2]

Plastic Is Petroleum

CELLULOID, the first commercial plastic, had many advantages. It was strong, light, flexible, and could be molded into almost any shape. Leo Hendrick Baekeland made the material yet to be known as plastic even more popular with a substance he cooked up in his garage in Yonkers. In 1909, he unveiled the first synthetic thermoset plastic (meaning it could be synthesized from inorganic chemicals and shaped by heating). Bakelite, as he called it, quickly caught on across a wide range of industries. Originally used as wire insulation, we now remember it best for its use in jewelry.

One of the ingredients in Baekeland's new wonder material was phenol, a chemical derived from coal tar in his day. Today we make phenol from oil—lots of oil. Other building blocks of today's plastics can be made from either oil or natural gas. The ethylene used to make polyethylene (the most common plastic) can be made from both. In Australia, for instance, plastic grocery bags are made from natural gas, but two-thirds of the country's bags are imported from Southeast Asia, where they are made from oil.

It didn't take long for the plastic pioneered by Baekeland, Hyatt, and others to catch on. It was strong, lightweight, cheap, durable, and relatively easy to make; and its primary raw material, petroleum, was cheap and plentiful. By 1960 the plastics industry was producing 7 million tons of plastic per year. By 2000, annual production had reached 160 million tons, and by 2020, it is expected to reach nearly 540 million.[3]

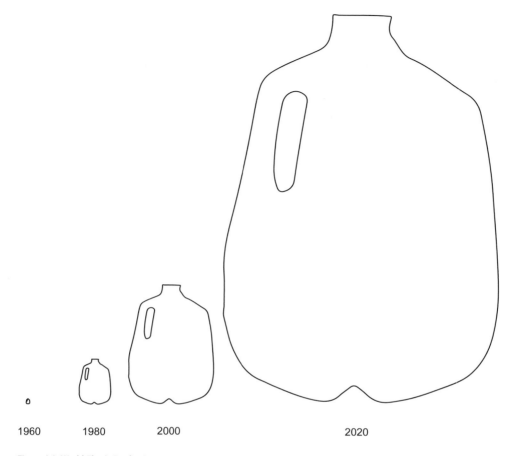

| 1960 | 1980 | 2000 | 2020 |

Figure 4.1: World Plastic Production
Global plastic production is expected to triple during the
first 20 years of this century. Illustration by Maria Meza.

Toys, utensils, storage bins—it seems that nearly everything today is made of plastic. Our purchases come wrapped in plastic, and we carry them home in plastic bags. If all the world's plastic production went only to make plastic shopping bags, we would have produced enough to stretch from here to the moon. And back. Thirty times. All that plastic takes over a billion barrels of oil per year to produce. Plastic proponents argue that, "The enormous convenience and the energy savings offered by plastics in a bewildering range of applications easily justify this minimal expenditure of fossil fuel." But is 1.3 billion barrels per year a "minimal expenditure of fossil fuel"? It's more than half of current U.S. oil production. And while global fossil fuel consumption by the plastics industry is expected to hover around 1.3 billion barrels per year through 2040, the shortfall of oil production compared to demand is expected to increase.[4,5,6]

Oil and Water

The average American uses 167 disposable plastic water bottles per year. How much oil does it take to make one of them? You can see the answer by filling a bottle one-quarter full with oil.

Figure 4.2: Oil Required to Make a Plastic Bottle
It takes approximately a quarter liter of oil to make a plastic liter bottle. Illustration by Maria Meza.

If oil supplies decline and we continue to dedicate over a billion barrels per year to plastic, there will be less oil left for transportation and other uses. Gasoline and heating oil prices will rise along with the cost of plastic. But we are paying other costs besides the price of oil when we buy plastic—environmental costs.

Notes

1   Kmetz, Mike, "What's Really Going On with Plastic Prices?" Report, UL, www.ides.com/articles/oil.asp

2   "The History of Celluloid," Plastics.com, www.plastics.com/content/articles/1/4/The-History-of-Celluloid/Page4.html

3   Pardos Marketing, "World Plastics Consumption Long Term, 1960–2020," www.pardos-marketing.com/hot04.htm

4   PlasticsEurope, "The Compelling Facts about Plastics 2009: An Analysis of European Plastics Production, Demand and Recovery for 2008," Report, September 26, 2009, www.plasticseurope.org/Documents/Document/20100225141556-Brochure_UK_FactsFigures_2009_22sept_6_Final-20090930-001-EN-v1.pdf

5   U.S. Energy Information Administration, "International Energy Outlook 2014" (Report, Washington, DC, 2014), www.eia.gov/forecasts/ieo/more_overview.cfm

6   Ibid.

5

Plastic Pollution

Producing Plastic

> Except for a small amount that's been incinerated, every bit of plastic manufactured in the world for the last fifty years or so still remains. It's somewhere in the environment.
>
> (Anthony Andrady, author, *Plastics and the Environment*)[1]

The world produces over a million disposable plastic grocery bags per minute, enough to make them the most common human-made object in the world. Like plastic water bottles, they're made from fossil fuel deposits that took hundreds of thousands of years to form. Only about one in ten will be recycled. Millions every year end up polluting our land and seas. The vast majority will end up in the landfill alongside the plastic water bottles and five billion tons of other plastic garbage. Estimates of how long they will remain there range from hundreds to hundreds of thousands of years, depending on the type of plastic and its local environment. Even when they seem to have disappeared, most plastics have simply broken down into smaller particles because the polymer chains that make them up can be extremely difficult to break.[2]

The cost of plastic pollution is immeasurable. We pay to clean up oil spills, air pollution, waterways, and stray plastic bags. In California, the city of San Jose spends roughly $1 million per year to repair recycling equipment jammed with plastic bags. San Francisco spends $8.5 million per year to clean up, recycle, and landfill its plastic bags. The state as a whole devotes about $25 million to landfilling plastic bags each year, and another $8.5 million to removing them from its streets.[3]

The Bag and the Bomb Scare

A New York representative once joked that the state flower should be a plastic bag stuck in a tree. But one particular New York City bag seemed so out of place as it perched among the branches of a locust tree at the corner of Bedford Avenue and North 5th Street that passersby began calling the police. Soon, the bomb squad was on the scene. The street was closed and, as a police helicopter circled above, firefighters scaled the tree. It proved to be just another New York City grocery bag, one of millions adrift in The City That Never Sleeps.[4]

Oceans of Plastic

> Our plastic footprint is taking a greater toll on marine life than our carbon footprint is.
>
> (Capt. Charles Moore, co-author, *Plastic Ocean*)[5]

A day at the beach sounds nice, but not to Patrick Chandler, Special Programs Coordinator for the Center for Alaskan Coastal Studies. On this day, he's leading a group of volunteers in a cleanup of Gore Point on Alaska's Kenai Peninsula. "After spending a long day pulling debris from logs, digging it out of sand and hauling it into piles for pickup," says Chandler, "the most disheartening thing to see is a section of beach so covered with small bits of foamed plastic that you know it's hopeless to try to pick it all up."

It's no wonder Chandler and his volunteers were overwhelmed—on one beach they found 93 times as much foamed plastic as in years past. But why the sudden increase in plastic pollution on a remote Alaskan beach? While Chandler and his volunteers were asking that question, scientists at the International Pacific Research Center were discovering the answer. Most of it originated thousands of miles away, in Japan. When the great tsunami of March 2011 hit Eastern Japan, it washed an estimated five million tons of debris into the ocean. Over the ensuing months, wind currents carried it east to Hawaii and, eventually, Alaska. But as vast as the quantity of plastic released into our oceans by the Japan tsunami was, it is insignificant compared to the amount from other sources. According to a report by the United Nations, 10 percent of the plastic produced every year winds up in the ocean, making plastic the single largest source of ocean pollution.[6]

Seven Seas, 5 Gyres, and 26 Million Tons of Plastic

What if you could see the Great Pacific Garbage Patch and the impact it's having on marine birds and fish firsthand? Anna Cummins took that challenge and it changed her life. In 2002, Cummins got a call from a friend inviting her to a talk by Captain Charles Moore, founder of the Algalita Marine Research Foundation and co-author of *Plastic Ocean*. Moore's vivid description of ocean plastic pollution and its effects haunted her for weeks. Finally, she picked up the phone and called him. It took about 20 calls, but Moore finally agreed to take her on his next trip, a 2004 research expedition to the small Pacific island of Guadalupe. There, Cummins had the unenviable job of collecting the boluses, or regurgitated stomach contents, of the albatross, the giant marine bird known to travel over 2,000 miles without stopping. "Every single bolus I collected had plastic fragments in it," she recalled.

The shock of what she saw on Guadalupe inspired her to join Moore on a second voyage. Together with Moore and Algalita's Research Director, Dr Marcus Eriksen, Cummins and three other volunteers set out on an expedition across the Pacific from Hawaii to Los Angeles. The journey gave Cummins a break from collecting albatross boluses only to find her gathering almost 700 lantern fish for dissection by a lab back on land. When the lab finished its work, their results were staggering: over one-third of these fish, found hundreds of miles from civilization, contained plastic in their guts.

"I came away from that trip with an overwhelming sense of just how enormous the problem truly is, and a frustration that so few people really seemed to know about it," she said. But her frustration inspired her to take on a new project to educate others about ocean plastic pollution. Her partner would be her new husband, Dr Marcus Eriksen, who had proposed halfway through the Pacific expedition, offering her an engagement ring woven from derelict plastic fishing nets he found floating in mid-ocean. Together with Joel Paschal, also of the Pacific expedition, the two dreamed up JUNKraft, a boat made from 15,000 empty plastic bottles that would sail from Los Angeles to Hawaii to raise awareness about the plastic fouling our seas.

Because the Pacific expedition was just Cummins's first ocean crossing, it was agreed that she would stay on land and orchestrate logistics rather than join Eriksen and Paschal aboard JUNKraft. As the main link between the vessel and the rest of the world, Cummins helped the two-man crew through some dire straits. Almost immediately after setting sail from Los Angeles, JUNKraft began taking on water as the ocean waves began to unscrew the caps from the plastic bottles keeping her afloat. After some strategizing, it was agreed the crew would dive in and glue the caps back on one by one. "Tedious, tiring work," Eriksen reported as he and Paschal labored to glue over a thousand caps. But once the task was complete, JUNKraft was able to complete its journey, with the crew still counting bottlecaps in their sleep.

With JUNKraft, Cummins and Eriksen began to shift their focus from identifying the problem of ocean plastic pollution to solving it. Since cleanup of the innumerable plastic particles that clog our oceans is logistically impossible (one of Moore's studies found plastic more plentiful than plankton in certain parts of the Pacific), the aim of JUNKraft and the projects that followed was to raise public awareness and keep plastic from reaching the world's waterways in the first place.

On Eriksen's return from Hawaii in 2009, the pair teamed again for JUNKride, a land-based excursion from Vancouver to Tijuana. Along the way, the husband-and-wife team gave over 40 talks and delivered 100 samples of the plastic-tainted ocean water they'd found to educators and government officials. And just as their JUNKraft covered the 2,600 miles from Los Angeles to Hawaii using only the wind for power, JUNKride was also a zero-energy endeavor; the pair covered the 2,000 miles from Vancouver to Tijuana on bikes.

Following JUNKride, Cummins and Eriksen consolidated their research efforts into 5 Gyres, an organization dedicated to bringing global attention to the issue of marine plastic pollution and promoting solutions. The name refers to the ocean gyres, large systems of rotating currents. Today's gyres are so polluted that Cummins refers to them, with a note of both sobriety and humor, as "massive toilet bowls that never flush."

While Cummins often uses her buoyant sense of humor to entertain as well as educate audiences, she recognizes that ocean-bound plastic waste is no laughing matter. It's estimated that every year as much as 26 million tons of plastic—10 percent of what we use—ends up in the oceans. "We've had a chance to research plastic pollution in all 5 oceanic gyres," she said, "and proven that this is indeed an international problem." It's a problem Cummins is all too familiar with, having logged over 25,000 miles at sea since that first voyage in 2004. In 2010 she was elected a National Fellow of the Explorers Club. And perhaps, if asked why she has dedicated her life to stopping plastic pollution, she would answer like a true explorer, "Because it's there."[7]

Figure 5.1: Anna Cummins
Together with husband and 5 Gyres
co-founder Dr Marcus Eriksen, Anna Cummins
has fostered exploration, education,
and action on ocean plastic pollution.
Image courtesy of Anna Cummins.

While plastic debris increasingly clogs the shores of even the world's most remote areas, most of it remains at sea. There, it can ensnare seals, birds, turtles, and other animals. These animals also mistake plastic bags and debris for food (to a sea turtle, plastic bags can look a lot like jellyfish). One study of Alaskan sea birds found that nearly two-thirds had ingested plastic. A similar study of fulmars, gull-like sea birds common to the Arctic, reported an even higher number. One Australian crocodile was found to have 25 plastic bags in its stomach.[8,9]

But plastic grocery bags posing as jellyfish aren't the only problem plastic creates for marine wildlife. Plastic floating near the ocean surface photodegrades, breaking down into smaller bits of plastic. These pieces keep breaking down until parts of our oceans become "plastic soup"—water so thick with plastic that the pieces can't even be counted using a microscope. A recent survey of Lake Erie found between 1,500 and 1,700,000 plastic particles per square mile. Over four-fifths of them measured less than two-tenths of an inch.[10]

These minute particles can accumulate in the animals that eat them and work their way up the food chain, ultimately affecting humans. Human intake is of particular concern because ocean plastic can accumulate polychlorinated biphenyl (PCBs) and other toxins from water. Concentrations of these toxins can increase as they move up the food chain. According to the EPA, "Some marine debris, especially some plastics, contains toxic substances that can cause death or reproductive failure in fish, shellfish, or any marine life. In fact, some plastic particles have even been determined to contain certain chemicals up to one million times the amount found in the water alone."[11,12]

The cost to coastal communities is high as well. One EPA study found that West coast cities and counties in the U.S. spend over half a billion dollars per year to fight litter and marine debris. Industries that rely on our oceans are also adversely affected. It's estimated, for example, that the Scottish fishing industry spends about $16 million per year dealing with the effects of marine debris. These numbers suggest that the annual global cost of marine plastic pollution is in the billions of dollars. And who can put a number on the cost to marine wildlife?[13,14]

Recycling Reality

I LIKE to think I'm doing my part to keep plastic out of the waste stream by recycling it. The Midwestern town I live in accepts most plastics, so I'm able to toss most of my used plastic in the bin for curbside pickup. But how much of that plastic actually gets recycled? "Depending on the bin, and on the city's recycling system," says author Roseann Cima, "between 60 and 80 percent of recycling is actually recycled." Exact percentages, however, can vary dramatically. A 2004 study of New York City recycling, for instance, found that nearly 90 percent of the plastic that residents placed in recycling bins actually ended up in landfills.[15,16]

According to the EPA, of the 31 million tons of plastic waste generated in the U.S. in 2010, 8 percent was recovered. That leaves 28.5 million tons of plastic waste per year that are ending up somewhere other than the recycler. Where does the rest go? As we've seen, about 10 percent ends up in the world's waterways, and as we'll see in the next chapter, most of the rest will take up residence in our landfills. What becomes of the 8 percent that does get recycled varies widely depending on the type of plastic. According to the American Chemistry Council, the plastic in your curbside recycling bins typically goes to a material recovery facility, where it is sorted by type, baled, and sent to a reclaiming facility. There, it is washed and ground into small flakes. The flakes are then dried, melted, filtered, and formed into pellets. Finally, the pellets are shipped to product manufacturing plants, where they are made into new plastic goods.[17]

How much of your plastic actually gets reused in new products depends on its type. You're probably familiar with the "following arrows" symbol found on many plastic products, and the numbers inside that symbol indicating the type of plastic. Type 1, for instance, is polyethylene terephthalate, or PET. PET is the most recyclable plastic—almost 30 percent of the bottles and jars made with it are recycled. In the process, they are broken down into their primary polymers to be reborn as clothing, plastic lumber, and a host of other consumer products. About one-third of all high-density polyethylene (HDPE) bottles, those marked with the number 2, are recycled into new bottles.[18]

Other plastics are not so easily recycled, and some can't be economically recycled at all. Packaging, the main source of waste plastics, typically cannot be recycled. Recycling rates for polyvinyl chloride (PVC), the hard plastic used in plumbing pipes and other products, are less than one-quarter of 1 percent. And less than 1 percent of the one billion plastic bags used in

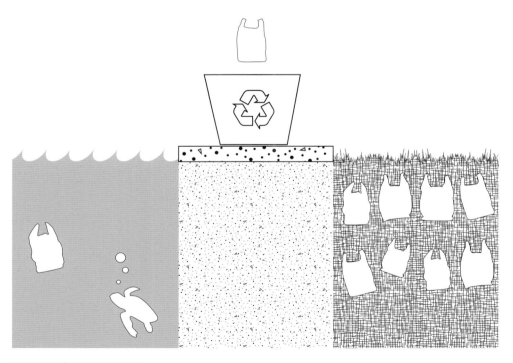

Figure 5.2: Where Our Plastic Goes
About 10 percent of our plastic waste ends up in the world's waterways. Another 10 percent gets recycled, and 80 percent ends up in landfills. Illustration by Maria Meza.

America every year get recycled. Added up, the overall recycling rate for all plastics in the U.S. is just 8 percent.[19,20,21]

But recycling plastic is, not surprisingly, better for the environment than burying it in a landfill or burning it. Compared to using virgin plastics, recycling a ton of plastic saves about 3.8 barrels of crude oil and 7.4 cubic yards of landfill space. An average American family can reduce their carbon dioxide emissions by up to 340 pounds per year by recycling their plastic waste. But even those plastics that can be recycled can't go on being recycled forever. Plastics degrade as they're used, resulting in "downcycling." For most polymers, recycling reduces performance, so they need to be recycled into lower performance specification products, or used as only a percentage of material in plastic products. As the authors of the book *Polymers* put it, "It is generally accepted that a maximum of 15%–30% of recycled material can be added to the virgin material without seriously affecting its mechanical properties. … For instance, the properties of virgin PET can be retained for up to five reprocessing cycles, after which the flexibility of the material becomes substantially diminished."[22,23]

Another obstacle to recycling is the growing number of "mixed plastic" products on the market. Materials like composite lumber, combining a variety of plastic types with other materials such as wood or glass, make separation into distinct plastic types for recycling impossible.

Life in the Landfill

> It is an environmental paradox that the United States is digging up new oil fields in
> pristine areas and, at the same time, continues to convert greenfields to brownfields
> by burying nearly 20 million tons of plastic fuel annually.
>
> (Nickolas J. Themelis and Claire E. Todd, Columbia University)[24]

On a chilly autumn morning in 1989, University of Arizona Professor of Archaeology Bill Rathje stood on one of the highest points on the Atlantic coast. Rising 225 feet above sea level, the Fresh Kills landfill on Staten Island is the world's largest dump, covering an area three times the size of Central Park. Rathje and his Garbage Project team were sorting through the detritus pulled up by a drilling rig as it bored down through 40 years of garbage.

"At present we have more reliable information about Neptune than we do about this country's solid-waste stream," lamented Rathje. But by applying the archaeological dig methods he developed excavating Mayan ruins to U.S. landfills, Rathje and the Garbage Project have advanced our understanding of what goes on inside our landfills and, even more importantly, what doesn't go on there.

"The notion that much biodegradation occurs inside lined landfills is largely a popular myth," he said. Exploring a landfill layer dating from the 1950s, he added, "Almost all the organic material remained readily identifiable. … Whole hot dogs have been found in the course of every excavation."[25]

Figure 5.3: "Garbologist" William Rathje
Applying methods he developed excavating Mayan archaeological digs to U.S.
landfills, Professor Rathje discovered that plastics and other waste are breaking down
much more slowly than previously thought. Corbis image; photo by Louie Psihoyos.

Burial in landfills, his team learned, blocked the light, air, and moisture garbage needs to break down. And if hot dogs remain intact in our landfills for over 50 years, how long will plastic last there? In the landfill, the durability that makes plastic so attractive becomes a liability, and most of the 66,000 tons of plastic that has gone into U.S. landfills today will still be there hundreds of years from now. "The majority of polymers manufactured today," according to a report published in the journal *Philosophical Transactions of the Royal Society*, "will persist for at least decades, and probably for centuries if not millennia."[26]

Between 1973 and 1992, the Garbage Project exhumed and analyzed over 14 tons of landfill garbage. Plastic, they found, made up 12 percent of the total volume, meaning there might be as much as 12 million tons of it in the Fresh Kills landfill alone. No one knows how long it will be there. It's also unclear how much of the toxins contained in those buried plastics will leach out over time. The absence of light, air, and water in the landfill may slow the process, but we know that leaching is taking place. For example, half of the "probable human carcinogen" cadmium in U.S. landfills comes from plastics.[27,28]

Notes

1   Weisman, Alan, "Polymers Are Forever," Orion, May/June 2007, www.orionmagazine.org/index.php/articles/article/270/

2   U.S. Environmental Protection Agency, "Plastics," www.epa.gov/osw/conserve/materials/plastics.htm

3   Myers, Todd, "Should Cities Ban Plastic Bags?" *Wall Street Journal*, October 8, 2012, http://online.wsj.com/article/SB10000872396390444165804578006832478712400.html; Clean Air Council, "Why Plastic Bag Fees Work," May 2009, www.cleanair.org/program/waste_and_recycling/recyclenow_philadelphia/waste_and_recycling_facts

4   Del Signore, John, "Here's the 'Suspicious Package' that Brought Bedford Avenue to a Standstill," May 18, 2012, http://gothamist.com/2012/05/18/suspicious_package_taped_to_tree_sh.php

5   Moore, Charles, and Phillips, Cassandra, *Plastic Ocean*, New York: Avery Books, 2011.

6   Mallos, Nick, "On Alaskan Beaches, More Foamed Plastic than Sea Foam," The Blog Aquatic, Ocean Conservancy, September 6, 2012, http://blog.oceanconservancy.org/2012/09/06/on-alaskan-beaches-theres-much-more-foamed-plastic-than-sea-foam/

7   Elvin, George, "Anna Cummins of 5Gyres: What Designers Can Do About Ocean Plastic Pollution," February 22, 2012, Green Technology Forum, http://gelvin.squarespace.com/green-technology-forum/2012/2/22/anna-cummins-of-5gyres-what-designers-can-do-about-ocean-pla.html

8   Hyrenbach, David, Nevins, Hannahrose, Hester, Michelle, Keiper, Carol, Webb, Sophie, and Harvey, James, "Seabirds Indicate Plastic Pollution in the Marine Environment: Quantifying Spatial Patterns and Trends in Alaska," Marine Debris in Alaska Workshop, February 14–15, 2008.

9   "Plastic Bags Kill Crocodile Found in Australian Tourist Zone," *Telegraph*, November 3, 2008, www.telegraph.co.uk/news/worldnews/australiaandthepacific/australia/3374894/Plastic-bags-kill-crocodile-found-in-Australian-tourist-zone.html

10 "Polluting Plastic Particles Invade the Great Lakes," National Meeting and Exposition of the American Chemical Society, April 8, 2013, http://portal.acs.org/portal/acs/corg/content?_nfpb=true&_pageLabel=PP_ARTICLEMAIN&node_id=222&content_id=CNBP_032565&use_sec=true&sec_url_var=region1&__uuid=80ee059b-20ff-4fc2-9fe1-b4c13f1b67f5

11 Andrady, Anthony, ed., *Plastics and the Environment*, Hoboken, NJ: John Wiley, 2003, 389.

12 U.S. Environmental Protection Agency, "Marine Debris Impacts," http://water.epa.gov/type/oceb/marinedebris/md_impacts.cfm

13 Ibid.

14 Scientific and Technical Advisory Panel (STAP), "Marine Debris as a Global Environmental Problem," Global Environment Facility, Washington, DC, November 2011, www.thegef.org/gef/sites/thegef.org/files/publication/STAP%20MarineDebris%20-%20website.pdf

15 Cima, Roseann, "How Much Recycling Actually Gets Recycled," *Stanford Magazine*, http://alumni.stanford.edu/get/page/magazine/article/?article_id=47701

16 Themelis, Nicholas J., and Todd, Claire E., "Recycling in a Megacity," Technical Paper, *Journal of the Air & Waste Management Association*, Volume 54, April 2004, 389–395, www.seas.columbia.edu/earth/wtert/sofos/Themelis_Recycling_in_a_Megacity.pdf

17 U.S. Environmental Protection Agency, "Plastics."

18 Ibid.

19   Hopewell, Jefferson, Dvorak, Robert, and Kosior, Edward, "Plastics Recycling: Challenges and Opportunities," *Philosophical Transactions of the Royal Society B*, Volume 364, Number 1526, July 27, 2009, 2115–2126, http://rstb.royalsocietypublishing.org/content/364/1526/2115.full

20   Edwards, Katie, "Waste and Recycling Facts," Clean Air Council, www.cleanair.org/Waste/wasteFacts.html

21   U.S. Environmental Protection Agency, "Plastics".

22   Jefferson et al., "Plastics Recycling: Challenges and Opportunities"; U.S. Environmental Protection Agency, Report, "Municipal Solid Waste Generation, Recycling, and Disposal in the United States: Facts and Figures for 2008," Washington, DC, www.epa.gov/osw/nonhaz/municipal/pubs/msw2008rpt.pdf

23   Azapagic, Adisa, Emsley, Alan, and Hamerton, Ian, *Polymers: The Environment and Sustainable Development*, Hoboken, NJ, John Wiley, 2003, 109.

24   Themelis and Todd, "Recycling in a Megacity."

25   Rathje, William, and Murphy, Cullen, *Rubbish!: The Archaeology of Garbage*, New York: Harper Collins, 1992, 114.

26   Hopewell et al., "Plastics Recycling: Challenges and Opportunities."

27   Rathje, William, "Rubbish!" *The Atlantic*, December 1989, 1–10, http://infohouse.p2ric.org/ref/30/29559.pdf

28   Aucott, Michael, "The Fate of Heavy Metals in Landfills: A Review," Report, New York Academy of Sciences, New York, February 2006.

6

Toxicity

Drilling and Spilling

Eventually, all of the world's five billion tons of plastic will release their toxins into the environment. Some will be neutralized over time and some will cause harm. How much harm is hard to say because almost all of the plastic ever produced is still intact and degradation tests conducted in laboratories can't perfectly reproduce long-term environmental conditions. But we don't have to wait for plastic to decay before it releases toxins into the environment. While oil companies, plastics manufacturers, disposers, and recyclers spend billions every year trying to prevent toxins from escaping, their efforts aren't foolproof. As a result, oil spills, oil refining, plastic manufacturing, use, disposal, and recycling all provide opportunities for the environmental release of toxins. Every year in the U.S., over a quarter million gallons of oil and chemicals are spilled, and oil refineries alone pour over half a million tons of pollutants into the air.[1]

How much our plastics factories produce is not so clear. But consider, for example, that there are currently 16 major polyvinyl chloride (PVC) production facilities in the United States. Each one, according to the EPA, "emits or has the potential to emit 10 or more tons per year of any single air toxic, or 25 tons per year or more of any combination of air toxics." That's a potential 400 tons of toxins per year, just from the manufacture of one type of plastic in one country. Let's proceed through the life cycle of today's plastics and see how these toxic particles can get there, and how they can get out.[2]

The plastic life cycle begins underground in the world's oil fields, and oil extraction can be harmful, especially if what's extracted spills into our waterways. When spills occur, crude oil is released that contains "hydrocarbon fractions." These naturally occurring components can include benzene, xylene, toluene, and ethyl benzene. The good news is that all four of these toxins usually evaporate within the first 48 hours of a spill and do not persist in the body for long periods of time. The bad news is that all four, according to the Center for Disease Control, "can produce neurological impairment, and exposure to benzene can additionally cause hematological effects including aplastic anemia and acute myelogenous leukemia."[3]

Even the chemicals used to disperse oil spills can be toxic. These dispersants don't really "clean up" oil spills at all. They simply break oil into smaller particles. They can reduce the impact of spilled oil on wildlife, but dispersed particles can recongeal and sink, actually increasing the exposure of deeper-dwelling aquatic life. The quantities of dispersants deployed in an oil spill can be staggering. BP reportedly dumped almost two million gallons into the Gulf of Mexico following the Deepwater Horizon disaster. The dispersant they used, called Corexit, has been in use since the *Exxon Valdez* oil spill in 1989. A 1997 study of Corexit by Exxon found it to have "low to moderate toxicity to most aquatic organisms" and "moderate toxicity to early life stages of fish, crustaceans, and mollusks." According to the National Institutes of Health, Corexit 9527 contains the toxin 2-Butoxyethanol (EGBE), "a petrochemical solvent readily absorbed through the skin," and warns that, "prolonged and/or repeated exposure through inhalation or extensive skin contact with EGBE may result in damage to the blood and kidneys."[4,5,6,7]

Workers exposed to Corexit during the cleanup of the BP oil spill recounted a variety of disturbing symptoms. Jamie Griffin, chief cook on one of the "floating hotels" set up to accommodate the cleanup crews, complained, "My throat felt like I'd swallowed razor blades." "It felt like the nerves were coming out of my skin. It was so painful. My right leg swelled—my ankle would get as wide as my calf—and my skin got incredibly itchy." Her symptoms were by no means unique, according to Michael Robichaux, a Louisiana physician who treated Griffin and over 100 other patients with similar complaints. "[I have] never seen this grouping of symptoms together: skin problems, neurological impairments, plus pulmonary problems." "These are the same symptoms experienced by soldiers who returned from the Persian Gulf War with Gulf War syndrome," he concluded.[8]

The harm done by chemical dispersants after the Deepwater Horizon disaster may well be less than the effects of 185 million gallons of undispersed crude oil reaching our shores, but it should make us think twice about calling the use of toxic dispersants a "cleanup." In fact, a study published in *Environmental Pollution* found that while Corexit 9500 and crude oil were of equal toxicity, combining the two increased toxicity 52-fold.[9]

Plastic, Refined

To turn crude oil into plastic, gasoline, and other useful materials, oil refineries must separate the hundreds of different hydrocarbons found in it. Distilling crude is a complex process involving dozens of separate stages, each with its own unique equipment. Refineries cost billions to build, and some can process nearly a million barrels of crude per day. And while today's refineries release far fewer harmful emissions than their twentieth century predecessors, petroleum refining remains a major source of toxic waste. According to the 2008 National Emissions Inventory (NEI) produced by the EPA, refineries pump nearly half a million tons of pollutants into our air every year, adding, "We believe the NEI likely underestimates oil and gas emissions."[10]

Regardless of the exact numbers, harmful outputs from the refineries pose a serious threat to our health. As the NEI explains,

> Harmful pollutants emitted from this [the oil and gas production] industry include air toxics such as benzene, toluene, ethylbenzene, and xylene; criteria pollutants

and ozone precursors such as nitrogen oxide and volatile organic compounds; and greenhouse gases such as methane. These pollutants can result in serious health impacts such as cancer, respiratory disease, aggravation of respiratory illnesses, and premature death.

Elsewhere, the EPA points out that hazardous emissions from petroleum refineries can also include sulfur dioxide, carbon monoxide, naphthalene, hydrogen fluoride, hydrogen cyanide, and hydrogen sulfide.[11]

The situation is improving, however. According to the NEI, oil refinery air toxics emissions (a portion of their total harmful emissions) fell by 91 percent between 1990 and 2002. And yet cause for concern remains. Between 2009 and 2013, for instance, "emission events" (events resulting in unauthorized emissions) at just 20 Texas oil and gas refineries were said to total nearly 50,000 tons, according to a complaint filed with the EPA by a coalition of community and public interest organizations. Hilton Kelley, Director of Community in Power and Development in Port Arthur, Texas, said: "Too many people are being subjected to toxic fumes and are becoming ill; one out of every five households in my hometown has someone who suffers from respiratory problems or other illnesses related to chemical exposure."[12,13]

Another concern is that the current rise in oil production means more refining, and therefore more emissions. Natural gas and oil production are already the second-biggest source of U.S. greenhouse gases, behind power plants, and the EPA expects onshore crude oil production to increase 30 percent by 2025. With plastic production also rising, the toxic emissions resulting from petroleum refining for plastics aren't going away anytime soon.[14]

Manufacturing's Most Wanted List

NINETEEN of the EPA's 31 Priority Chemicals, a Most Wanted List of toxic chemicals, can be found in plastic, its waste, or emissions from its manufacture. Once crude oil is refined into polymers, it is combined with plasticizers, stabilizers, and softeners. These additives help make plastic light, strong, flexible, rigid, hard or soft; but they can also introduce toxins like bisphenol A, phthalates, ethylene oxide, and a variety of heavy metals. Processing these chemicals can also add toxins to the air, as can burning some of the plastics made from them. Fortunately, in any single piece of plastic, they are present, if at all, only in trace amounts. But, as the EPA warns, "Even when released in very small amounts, they accumulate and can cause environmental problems." Self-reported toxic emissions from U.S. plastics manufacturing plants total over 85 tons per year.[15]

Phthalates—32,562 pounds per year
Phthalates, pronounced THAL-ates, are plasticizers added to the petroleum polymers that form the basis of plastics to make them more flexible. They appear in a wide array of consumer products including building materials, children's toys, detergents, and even medicines. Unlike

many plasticizers, phthalates do not form a chemical bond to the plastics that contain them. This allows them to be more easily released into the environment and our bodies. They are "generally believed to be even ingested routinely along with food." They have been found to cause cancer in animals, and they can act as disruptors to human endocrine and immune systems. The Consumer Product Safety Improvement Act of 2008 banned three types of phthalates in children's toys and certain childcare articles. However, they remain the number one plasticizer for polyvinyl chloride (PVC), the third most common type of plastic.[16,17]

Bisphenol A—1,823 pounds per year

Remember phenol, the petroleum-based ingredient in Leo Hendrick Baekeland's Bakelite? When combined with acetone, it creates bisphenol A (BPA), a chemical compound used to make a variety of plastic products from baby bottles and CDs to food containers and plumbing pipes. The National Toxicology Program has, "Some concern for effects on the brain, behavior, and prostate gland in fetuses, infants, and children at current human exposures to bisphenol A."

The EPA is more specific, stating that, "Because BPA is a reproductive, developmental, and systemic toxicant in animal studies and is weakly estrogenic, there are questions about its potential impact particularly on children's health and the environment." They go on to assure consumers that, "Studies … indicate that the levels of BPA in humans and the environment are below levels of potential concern for adverse effects."

"However," they add, "results of some recent studies … are potentially of concern for the environment because the concentration levels identified with effects are similar to some current environmental levels to which sensitive aquatic organisms may be exposed." These concerns have led China, Canada, the European Union (EU), and other world governments to ban BPA in some products or, as in California, to require a warning label. The EPA has indicated it intends to list BPA as a "chemical of concern" under the Toxic Substances Control Act.[18,19]

Dioxins—71 pounds per year

PVC is also the primary plastic source of dioxins, a group of toxic endocrine and immune system disruptors suspected of causing cancer. They can enter the environment through the burning of certain plastics and other waste. They are extremely slow to break down in the environment, and most people have detectable amounts of them in their bodies. Thanks to EPA regulations, government ordinances, and industry self-regulation, air emissions of dioxins are just 10 percent of what they once were. However, the EPA cautions that current exposures levels remain a concern.

The authors of a report from the University of Buffalo explain those concerns this way:

> What makes dioxins so toxic is that they accumulate in the body and once in the body, the molecules attach themselves to specific receptor molecules in the cell. This is similar to the lock and key biological process for natural enzymes in the body to react with receptors of cells, the only problem is that dioxins are not naturally found in the body. When a dioxin molecule attaches itself to the receptor, it changes the regulation of genes and alters cell function. When a cell's function is altered, it will promote an undesired mutation in that cell. Because of this the EPA has

recognized dioxin as a potential cancer-causing agent. The dioxins act as hormones. These hormones impair the reproductive development of not only fish, but also all mammals. This, in turn, causes them not to reproduce as often or as prolifically as they should. Slowly their population will decrease if these chemicals are continuously dumped into waterways. Perhaps the most notorious dioxin is 2,3,7,8-tetrachlorod-ibenzo-p-dioxin or (TCDD). This was the toxic contaminant found in Agent Orange and at Times Beach, Missouri.[20,21]

Ethylene Glycol—48,198 pounds per year
Ethylene glycol is used as a plasticizer and stabilizer, and can be found in polyester fiber, polyethylene terephthalate (PET) bottles, latex paint, and a host of other common goods. According to the Centers for Disease Control and Prevention, "Ethylene glycol is chemically broken down in the body into toxic compounds. It and its toxic byproducts first affect the central nervous system, then the heart, and finally the kidneys. Ingestion of sufficient amounts can be fatal." They report, however, that "systemic toxicity" is unlikely as a result of contact or inhalation.

However, the American Association of Poison Control Centers reported "more than 4,800 and 6,000 exposures to ethylene glycol in 1997 and 1998 respectively. Although the majority of these cases were unintentional, 21 in 1997 and 22 in 1998 were fatal. These reports are based on a surveillance system that underestimates the actual number of exposures." The Centers added that most plastics users shouldn't have to worry about acute or chronic exposure to ethylene oxide, since it breaks down quickly in the environment.[22,23]

Methylene Chloride—quantity unknown
Methylene chloride (dichloromethane) is a solvent most frequently used in making polyurethane foam boards. According to the EPA, it "poses health risks to anyone who breathes the air when this compound is present." The Occupational Safety and Health Administration considers methylene chloride "a potential occupational carcinogen. Short-term exposures to high concentrations may cause mental confusion, lightheadedness, nausea, vomiting, and headache. Continued exposure may also cause eye and respiratory tract irritation. Exposure to methylene chloride may make symptoms of angina more severe. Skin exposure to liquid methylene chloride may cause irritation or chemical burns."[24]

Heavy Metals—quantities vary
Heavy metals are toxic, naturally occurring metals. Heavy metals including lead (76,343 pounds per year), barium (1,024 pounds per year) and cadmium (194 pounds per year) can be used as stabilizers in the production of PVC, and can cause kidney damage, sterility, and cancer. *Lead* is used as a plastic stabilizer, and is a probable human carcinogen. It can affect every organ and system in the body. Long-term exposure can result in decreased performance in some tests that measure functions of the nervous system; weakness in fingers, wrists, or ankles; small increases in blood pressure; and anemia. Exposure to high lead levels can severely damage the brain and kidneys and ultimately cause death. In pregnant women, high levels of exposure may cause miscarriage. In men, it can damage the organs responsible for sperm production.

Barium sulfate is used as a filler in plastics. Short-term exposure to barium can cause vomiting, abdominal cramps, diarrhea, difficulties in breathing, increased or decreased blood pressure, and muscle weakness. Large amounts of barium intake can cause high blood pressure, changes in heart rhythm, or paralysis and possibly death.

Cadmium, used as a stabilizer in PVC, is known to cause cancer. Severe damage to the lungs may occur through breathing high levels of cadmium. Ingesting very high levels severely irritates the stomach, leading to vomiting and diarrhea. Long-term exposure to lower levels leads to a buildup in the kidneys and possible kidney disease, lung damage, and fragile bones. Based on these concerns, the EU is considering a ban on cadmium in all plastics, having already banned it in certain ones. [25,26]

In addition to these toxins, the EPA's list of 31 Priority Chemicals found to be toxic contains 16 other chemicals found in plastic or its waste. But the above list makes clear the effects they can have on living things. How much of any one toxin might be found in any given piece of plastic or in the emissions from its manufacture varies widely, and some plastics contain none of them. But even small amounts of these toxins can accumulate in the environment and in our tissues.

U.S. plastic factories release over 65,000 tons of toxic emissions every year. That's enough to fill a line of pickup trucks stretching from Boston to Baltimore. Over half of these emissions are released into the air; the rest are transferred to public sewage treatment plants. How many toxic particles are contained in any given plastic product is unclear; some contain no toxins at all, while others have been banned due to dangerously high levels. It is known that plastic products can transfer toxins to humans by contact or ingestion, eating and drinking from plastic containers being the primary means. Another pathway is inhalation. For every ton of polystyrene (the most common plastic) produced, over 100 pounds of particulates are released into the atmosphere. And while safeguards to reduce the amount of toxins released during plastic production have increased since 2002, plastic production has risen 40 percent, making it likely that toxic emissions have increased.

Use and Exposure

WHILE inhalation and skin contact are a concern, ingestion is the main route for plastic particles to enter our bodies. Plastic is the most common food packaging material, and toxins can migrate from plastic containers into our bodies. But according to American Chemistry Council spokesperson Kathryn Murray St. John, "All materials intended for contact with food must meet stringent FDA safety requirements before they are allowed on the market." Governmental safety requirements, however, are no guarantee that our food and drink will be free of toxins. For example, when the Natural Resources Defense Council tested over 100 samples of bottled water, they found that nearly a quarter of them contained contaminants exceeding state or federal limits. Another study, published in *Environmental Health Perspectives*, sampled 72 common foods and found phthalates in every one of them. The authors concluded that, "While

Table 6.1

Top 10 Toxic Chemicals and Compounds Released Annually by the Rubber and Plastics Industry

Toxin	Amount (tons)	Effects
Styrene	12,718	Short-term exposure results in mucous membrane and eye irritation, and gastrointestinal effects. Long-term exposure results in effects on the central nervous system (CNS), such as headache, fatigue, weakness, and depression, CNS dysfunction, hearing loss, and peripheral neuropathy.
Carbon Disulfide	3,969	Short-term exposure can cause headache, dizziness, fatigue, and irritation of eye, nose, and throat. Exposure to high concentrations may result in trouble breathing or respiratory failure. Contact with skin can cause severe burns. Long-term exposure to high levels in excess of regulatory standards may result in peripheral nerve damage and cardiovascular effects. A few studies contend that chronic exposure may also result in potential reproductive effects.
Toluene	3,674	Inhalation or ingestion can cause headaches, confusion, weakness, and memory loss. Toluene may also affect the way the kidneys and liver function. Some studies have shown that unborn animals were harmed when their mothers inhaled high levels of toluene, although the same effects were not seen when the mothers were fed large quantities of toluene. These results may reflect similar difficulties in humans.
Methyl Ethyl Ketone	2,205	Breathing moderate amounts for short periods of time can cause adverse effects on the nervous system ranging from headaches, dizziness, nausea, and numbness in the fingers and toes to unconsciousness. Its vapors are irritating to the skin, eyes, nose, and throat and can damage the eyes. Repeated exposure to moderate to high amounts may cause liver and kidney effects.
1-Chloro-1, 1-Difluoroethane	1,964	A chlorofluorocarbon refrigerant listed due to its impact on the ozone layer.
Xylene (Mixed Isomers)	1,595	Xylenes are rapidly absorbed into the body after inhalation, ingestion, or skin contact. Short-term exposure to high levels of xylenes can cause irritation of the skin, eyes, nose, and throat, difficulty in breathing, impaired lung function, impaired memory, and possible changes in the liver and kidneys. Both short- and long-term exposure to high concentrations can cause effects such as headaches, dizziness, confusion, and lack of muscle coordination.

Toxin	Amount (tons)	Effects
Zinc Compounds	1,519	Zinc is a nutritional trace element; toxicity from ingestion is low. Severe exposure might give rise to gastritis with vomiting due to swallowing of zinc dusts. Short-term exposure to very high levels is linked to lethargy, dizziness, nausea, fever, diarrhea, and reversible pancreatic and neurological damage. Long-term zinc poisoning causes irritability, muscular stiffness and pain, loss of appetite, and nausea. Zinc chloride fumes cause injury to mucous membranes and to the skin. Ingestion of soluble zinc salts may cause nausea, vomiting, and purging.
Methanol	1,370	Methanol is readily absorbed from the gastrointestinal tract and the respiratory tract, and is toxic to humans in moderate to high doses. In the body, methanol is converted into formaldehyde and formic acid. Observed toxic effects at high-dose levels generally include central nervous system damage and blindness. Long-term exposure to high levels of methanol via inhalation can cause liver and blood damage in animals.
Dichloromethane (Methylene Chloride)	1,021	Short-term effects of inhalation in humans consist mainly of nervous system effects including decreased visual, auditory, and motor functions, but these effects are reversible once exposure ceases. Effects of long-term exposure suggest that the central nervous system is a potential target in humans and animals. Human data are inconclusive regarding methylene chloride and cancer. Animal studies have shown increases in liver and lung cancer and benign mammary gland tumors following the inhalation of methylene chloride.
1,1-Dichloro-1-Fluoroethane	973	Exposure can have an anesthetic effect on the central nervous system, irritate the eyes, and cause asphyxiation and defatting of the skin. Inhalation may cause dizziness, weakness, fatigue, nausea, and headaches. Ingestion may cause gastrointestinal irritation, nausea, vomiting, and diarrhea. Overexposure may result in impaired cardiovascular functions.

Note: The U.S. Environmental Protection Agency's *Profile of the Rubber and Plastics Industry*, 2nd Edition, lists 110 toxic substances released by Rubber and Miscellaneous Plastics Products manufacturers.

Sources

U.S. Environmental Protection Agency, *Profile of the Rubber and Plastics Industry*, 2nd Edition, Washington, DC, February 2005, www.epa.gov/compliance/resources/publications/assistance/sectors/notebooks/rubplasn.pdf

U.S. Environmental Protection Agency, "Styrene," www.epa.gov/ttnatw01/hlthef/styrene.html

U.S. Environmental Protection Agency, "Methylene," www.epa.gov/ttnatw01/hlthef/methylen.html

estimated intakes for individual phthalates in this study were more than an order of magnitude lower than EPA Reference Doses, cumulative exposure to phthalates is of concern."[27,28]

For their part, while the EPA says they see "no causal link" between phthalate exposures and human health, they are "concerned about phthalates because of their toxicity and the evidence of pervasive human and environmental exposure to them." Because of these concerns, the EPA has said it intends to add eight phthalates to its "chemicals of concern" list (a list of chemicals it finds present or may present an unreasonable risk of injury to health or the environment) under the Toxic Substances Control Act.[29]

As for bisphenol A (BPA), the EPA says that, "Humans appear to be exposed primarily through food packaging manufactured using BPA." Because of this, as well as BPA's toxicity and abundance (over a million pounds per year are released into the environment), the EPA has indicated it intends to list BPA as a chemical of concern under the Toxic Substances Control Act. The U.S. Food and Drug Administration, however, is not convinced. In denying a 2012 petition to ban BPA, they concluded that while "some studies have raised questions as to whether BPA may be associated with a variety of health effects, there remain serious questions about these studies, particularly as they relate to humans and the public health impact."

Plastic Doesn't Go Away

FIVE of the six chemicals that create the most hazardous waste are used in making plastic. And with current recycling rates running at just 8 percent, plastic accounts for a lot of waste—about 20 million tons per year. Almost all of it is piling up in our nation's landfills, and, as we've seen, it isn't breaking down anytime soon. That may be good news for now, since it could mean that tons of toxins including phthalates, bisphenol A, and toluene are not yet degrading into the environment. But just because the polymers that make up our plastics are degrading at a snail's pace in our landfills doesn't necessarily mean their toxins aren't leaching out.[30]

Modern landfill design strives to reduce leaching by requiring plastic liners and leachate collection systems. Even so, dissolved toxic chemicals can move through porous materials in the landfill, eventually contaminating surrounding groundwater. In fact, the EPA has concluded that all landfills will eventually leak into the environment. There are also as many as 100,000 unlined landfills throughout the United States. One that the U.S. Geological Survey calls typical is the Norman Landfill in Norman, Oklahoma. Closed in 1985, its subterranean toxic leachate "plume" has reached a tributary of the Canadian River, which stretches over 900 miles through Oklahoma, Texas, and New Mexico.

But how many of the toxins leaching from our landfills are from plastic? The New Lyme Landfill in Ohio, a former EPA Superfund site, gives some indication. A detailed analysis of the hazardous substances released at the site found a dozen chemicals used in plastics. A similar study of Wisconsin landfill leachate found the plastic solvent, toluene, to be the most common contaminant, present in 95 percent of the state's landfills. Another study found phthalates in the majority of landfills tested in Europe, and called out polyvinyl chloride as one of the likely sources.[31]

Heavy metals from plastic may be the greatest concern. U.S. landfills receive over half a million tons of heavy metals every year, including one thousand tons of cadmium, half of which is from plastic pigments or stabilizers. Leachate from a number of U.S. landfills has been found to contain levels of cadmium more than 40 times the maximum contaminant levels allowed by state drinking water regulations.[32]

One way to reduce the amount of plastic in our landfills is to burn it. Every year, enough municipal solid waste is burned in the U.S. to fill a line of semis stretching from the Atlantic to the Pacific Ocean, and over 2.5 million tons of it is plastic. Because plastic is made from high-energy sources like oil and natural gas, burning it can produce more energy than any other type of municipal solid waste. If it is burned in waste-to-energy facilities, plastic produces steam that can heat buildings or generate electricity. But heat and electricity aren't the only things being produced when plastic is burned. Hazardous emissions can include carbon oxides, sulfur oxides, nitrogen oxides, dioxins, and furans. One study found 21 individual atmospheric pollutants in the waste from burning plastic. And while burning plastic can reduce its bulk to just 10 percent of its original volume, the remaining ash usually ends up in landfills. As waste-to-energy facilities improve their efficiency, burning plastic may become a viable disposal option. But for now, it's not hard to see why less than 1 percent of our plastic waste goes up in smoke.[33]

Plastic and Climate

THE 90 million barrels of oil we burn every day in the U.S. produce over 40,000 tons of carbon dioxide (CO_2), enough to fill Yankee Stadium more than 27,000 times. But when we think of CO_2 emissions, we tend to think of cars and power plants, not plastic. With over a quarter billion vehicles registered in the U.S. and each one spewing about one pound of CO_2 per mile, cars are one of the top sources of CO_2. Power plants release about one pound of CO_2 per kilowatt generated, making them an even greater source than cars. But producing one pound of common plastics like polyethylene (HDPE, LDPE, and PET) generates about 2 pounds of CO_2. Most of the emissions at plastic manufacturing plants come from the equipment used to create chemical reactions, blend solvents, heat resins, and introduce additives. Other sources include storage tanks, equipment leaks, wastewater treatment, combustion sources, and cleaning and surface coating operations.[34]

Plastic also releases its CO_2 content when burned. Every ton of polyethylene incinerated emits about 1.3 tons of CO_2. One study published in *Energy & Environmental Science* found that burning plastic can release up to 18 times the CO_2 resulting from landfilling. Emissions from landfilled plastics are quite low (0.04 tons per ton of polyethylene) but eventually all 5 billion tons of the world's plastic will release its embodied CO_2, adding roughly 10 billion tons of CO_2 to the atmosphere.[35]

Petroleum-based plastic production generates nearly a trillion pounds of CO_2 every year, enough to perpetuate global climate change even if we were to switch transportation, heating, cooling, manufacturing, and electrical power generation to clean energy today. If we want to slow the pace of global climate change, we must do something about plastics. Stemming the skyrocketing proliferation of petroleum-based plastic in our world will reduce our CO_2 output from a trillion-pound-per-year-emitting industry and make the U.S. less dependent on foreign fossil fuels.

Plastic has many benefits. Plastic packaging and products, for example, typically weigh less than alternatives, reducing fuel consumption and, in some cases, CO_2 emissions. But petroleum-based plastic also has impacts on our health and environment that make us question its value. And since it is made from non-renewable fossil fuels, eventually we will have no choice but to give it up. Given its environmental and health concerns, wouldn't we be better off reducing our dependence on plastic today, rather than waiting until we run out of the oil to make it with?

Notes

1 Levin, Alan, "Oil spills escalated in this decade," *USA Today*, June 8, 2010, http://usatoday30.usatoday.com/news/nation/2010-06-07-oil-spill-mess_N.htm; U.S. Environmental Protection Agency, "2008 National Emissions Inventory, Draft version 2," Report, Washington, DC, June 2012, www.epa.gov/ttnchie1/net/2008neiv2/2008_neiv2_tsd_draft.pdf

2 U.S. Environmental Protection Agency, Fact Sheet: Proposed Air Toxics Standards for Polyvinyl Chloride and Copolymers (PVC) Production," Washington, DC, 2011, www.epa.gov/ttn/oarpg/t3/fact_sheets/pvcpropfs20110415.pdf

3 U.S. Agency for Toxic Substances and Disease Registry, "Interaction for Benzene, Toluene, Ethylbenzene, and Xylenes," www.atsdr.cdc.gov/interactionprofiles/ip-btex/ip05-c1.pdf

4 U.S. National Library of Medicine Toxicology Data Network, "Corexit 9500," http://toxnet.nlm.nih.gov/cgi-bin/sis/search/r?dbs+hsdb:@term+@na+corexit+9500

5 Hertsgaard, Mark, "The Worst Part about BP's Oil-spill Cover-up: It Worked," April 22, 2013, http://grist.org/business-technology/what-bp-doesnt-want-you-to-know-about-the-2010-gulf-of-mexico-spill/

6 George-Ares, Anita and Clark, James R., "Acute Aquatic Toxicity of Three Corexit Products: An Overview," International Oil Spill Conference Proceedings, 1997, 1007–1008, http://ioscproceedings.org/doi/pdf/10.7901/2169-3358-1997-1-1007

7   U.S. National Library of Medicine Toxicology Data Network, "Corexit 9527," http://toxnet.nlm.nih.gov/cgi-bin/sis/search/r?dbs+hsdb:@term+@na+corexit+9527

8   Hertsgaard, "The Worst Part about BP's Oil-spill Cover-up: It Worked."

9   Rico-Martinez, Roberto, Snell, Terry, and Shearer, Tonya, "Synergistic Toxicity of Macondo Crude Oil and Dispersant Corexit 9500A to the Brachionus Plicatilis Species Complex (Rotifera)," *Environmental Pollution*, Volume 173, February 2013, 5–10, www.sciencedirect.com/science/article/pii/S0269749112004344

10 U.S. Environmental Protection Agency, "2008 National Emissions Inventory, Draft version 2."

11 U.S. Environmental Protection Agency, "EPA Needs to Improve Air Emissions Data for the Oil and Natural Gas Production Sector," Report, Washington, DC, February 20, 2013, www.epa.gov/oig/reports/2013/20130220-13-P-0161.pdf; U.S. Environmental Protection Agency, "Improvements in Air Toxics Emissions Data Needed to Conduct Residual Risk Assessments," Washington, DC, October 31, 2007, www.epa.gov/air/tribal/pdfs/presentationpetroleumrefineries14Dec11.pdf

12 Ibid.

13 "Groups: Texas Groups Ask EPA Inspector General to Investigate Thousands of Tons of Pollution Released During 'Upsets' at Texas Gas and Petrochemical Plants," Houston, Texas, April 23, 2013, www.environmental-integrity.org/news_reports/documents/042313EIPTXUpsetEmissionsEPATCEQletterreleaseFINAL1.pdf

14 Drajem, Mark, "Oil, Gas Production among Top Greenhouse-Gas Sources," *Bloomberg News*, February 8, 2013, www.bloomberg.com/news/2013-02-05/greenhouse-gas-emissions-fall-in-u-s-power-plants-on-coal-cuts.html; U.S. Environmental Protection Agency, "EPA Needs to Improve Air Emissions Data for the Oil and Natural Gas Production Sector."

15 U.S. Environmental Protection Agency, "Priority Chemicals," www.epa.gov/osw/hazard/wastemin/priority.htm

16 U.S. Environmental Protection Agency, *Profile of the Rubber and Plastics Industry*, 2nd Edition, Washington, DC, February 2005, www.epa.gov/compliance/resources/publications/assistance/sectors/notebooks/rubplasn.pdf

17 U.S. Environmental Protection Agency, "Phthalates," www.cpsc.gov/phthalates

18 National Institute of Environmental Health Sciences, "Bisphenol A (BPA)," www.niehs.nih.gov/health/topics/agents/sya-bpa/

19 Ibid.; Lee, Stephanie M., "California Decides Chemical BPA Is Toxic," April 12, 2013, www.sfgate.com/bayarea/article/California-decides-chemical-BPA-is-toxic-4428719.php; Beveridge & Diamond, P.C., "Update on TSCA Developments in Congress and at EPA," March 22, 2012, www.bdlaw.com/assets/attachments/BD%20Client%20Alert%20-%20Update%20on%20TSCA%20Developments%20in%20Congress%20and%20at%20EPA.pdf

20 U.S. Environmental Protection Agency, "Dioxin," Environmental Assessment, http://cfpub.epa.gov/ncea/CFM/nceaQFind.cfm?keyword=Dioxin; U.S. Environmental Protection Agency, "Dioxins and Furans," Persistent Bioaccumulative and Toxic (PBT) Chemical Program, www.epa.gov/pbt/pubs/dioxins.htm; U.S. Environmental Protection Agency, "Fact Sheet: Proposed Air Toxics Standards for Polyvinyl Chloride and Copolymers (PVC) Production."

21 Doyle, Matthew, et al., "Paper Versus Plastic," Course Material for Introduction to Polymers, Department of Chemical and Biological Engineering, University at Buffalo, www.eng.buffalo.edu/Courses/ce435/PvsP1/PvsP.html

22 Centers for Disease Control and Prevention, "Ethylene Glycol: Systemic Agent," Emergency Response Safety and Health Database, www.cdc.gov/niosh/ershdb/EmergencyResponseCard_29750031.html

23 Scalley, Robert D., Ferguson, David, Piccaro, John, Smart, Martin, and Archie, Thomas, "Treatment of Ethylene Glycol Poisoning," *American Family Physician*, Volume 66, Number 5, September 1, 2002, 807–813. www.aafp.org/afp/2002/0901/p807.html

24 U.S. Environmental Protection Agency, "Brief Summary: New EPA Regulations for Flexible Polyurethane Foam Production," 40 CFR, Part 63, Subpart OOOOOO, August 2008, www.epa.gov/ttn/atw/area/foamprodbs.doc; Agency for Toxic Substances & Disease Registry, "ToxFAQs for Methylene Chloride," February 2001, www.atsdr.cdc.gov/toxfaqs/tf.asp?id=233&tid=42; U.S. Department of Labor, "Methylene Chloride," Occupational Safety & Health Administration, 2003, www.osha.gov/Publications/osha3144.html

25 Martin, Sabine, and Griswold, Wendy, "Human Health Effects of Heavy Metals," Center for Hazardous Substance Research, Kansas State University, Environmental Science and Technology Briefs for Citizens, Issue 15, March 2009, https://www.engg.ksu.edu/chsr/outreach/resources/docs/15HumanHealthEffectsofHeavyMetals.pdf

26 "Europe Mulls Total Ban on Cadmium in Plastics," *PlasticNews*, January 15, 2013, www.plasticsnews.com/article/20130115/NEWS/301159995/europe-mulls-total-ban-on-cadmium-in-plastics

27 Freinkel, Susan, "Trace Chemicals in Everyday Food Packaging Cause Worry over Cumulative Threat," *Washington Post* online, April 17, 2012, www.washingtonpost.com/national/health-science/trace-chemicals-in-everyday-food-packaging-cause-worry-over-cumulative-threat/2012/04/16/gIQAUILvMT_story.html; Natural Resources Defense Council, "Bottled Water: Pure Drink or Pure Hype?" Updated July 2013, www.nrdc.org/water/drinking/bw/bwinx.asp

28 Schecter, Arnold, et al., "Phthalate Concentrations and Dietary Exposure from Food Purchased in New York State," *Environmental Health Perspectives*, Volume 121, Issue 4, April 2013, http://ehp.niehs.nih.gov/1206367/

29 U.S. Environmental Protection Agency, "Phthalates Action Plan," Revised March 14, 2012, www.epa.gov/oppt/existingchemicals/pubs/actionplans/phthalates_actionplan_revised_2012-03-14.pdf

30 U.S. Environmental Protection Agency, "Municipal Solid Waste Generation, Recycling, and Disposal in the United States: Facts and Figures for 2012," Washington, DC, www.epa.gov/osw/nonhaz/municipal/pubs/2012_msw_fs.pdf

31 U.S. Environmental Protection Agency, "New Lyme Landfill," Updated January 2012, www.epa.gov/R5Super/npl/ohio/OHD980794614.html; Jonssona, Susanne,, Ejlertsson, Jörgen, Ledin, Anna, Mersiowsky, Ivo, and Svensson, Bo H., "Mono- and Diesters from O-phthalic Acid in Leachates from Different European Landfills," *Water Research*, Volume 37, 2003, 609–617, http://wri.wisc.edu/Downloads/Projects/Final_WR03R006.pdf

32 Aucott, Michael, "The Fate of Heavy Metals in Landfills: A Review," Report, New York Academy of Sciences, New York, February 2006.

33 Andrady, Anthony, ed., *Plastics and the Environment*, Hoboken, NJ: John Wiley, 2003, 693; Cho, Renee, "What Happens to All That Plastic?" The Earth Institute, Columbia University, January 31, 2012, http://blogs.ei.columbia.edu/2012/01/31/what-happens-to-all-that-plastic/; Clariter, "Incineration," www.clariter.com/global-challenges/plastic-waste-management/incineration/; Li, Chun-Teh, Zhuang, Huan-Kai, Hsieh, Lien-Te, Lee, Wen-Jhy, and Tsao, Meng-Chun, "PAH Emission from the Incineration of Three Plastic Wastes," *Environment International*, Volume 27, Number 1, July 2007, 61–67, www.ncbi.nlm.nih.gov/pubmed/11488391; Rathje, William, "Rubbish!" *The Atlantic*, December 1989, 1–10, http://infohouse.p2ric.org/ref/30/29559.pdf

34 U.S. Environmental Protection Agency, "Plastics," Waste Reduction Model, www.epa.gov/climatechange/wycd/waste/downloads/plastics-chapter10-28-10.pdf; U.S. Environmental Protection Agency, "Preferred and Alternative Methods for Estimating Air Emissions from Plastic Products Manufacturing," Report, Emission Inventory Improvement Program, December 1998, www.epa.gov/ttnchie1/eiip/techreport/volume02/ii11.pdf

35 U.S. Environmental Protection Agency, "Plastics"; Eriksson, Ola, and Finnveden, Göran, "Plastic Waste as a Fuel—CO2-neutral or not?" *Energy & Environmental Science*, Volume 2, 2009, 907–914, www.ecolateral.org/plasticasafueirschem0709.pdf; U.S. Environmental Protection Agency, "Plastics."

PART THREE

Post-Petroleum Design

– 7 –

What Is Post-Petroleum Design?

The Post-Petroleum Era

Future generations will inherit a post-petroleum world whether they like it or not, simply because the wells are running dry. The question is, will we choose to be proactive and begin now to design a positive post-petroleum world, or will we continue to stall and find ourselves unprepared for the end of oil? Consider the consequences if we don't adopt post-petroleum design today. In this very likely scenario, we continue our oil-dependent ways and suffer potentially massive global shock and social disruption as supplies dwindle. Particularly in the U.S., where we are especially dependent on oil, the trauma could be severe. Rapidly rising prices resulting from scarcity will not reduce demand enough to cushion the blow, and no amount of green incentives, taxes, or regulations are going to reduce consumption fast enough to pull us out of our dependency on oil; the wells are simply running dry too fast.

Over 95 percent of our vehicles run on petroleum. Can you imagine commerce without trucks and trains? While these, along with individual auto travel, will not stop overnight, imagine the impact ten dollar per gallon gas will have on our transportation, commerce, and everyday life.

As supplies run down, global demand is expected to increase nearly 10 percent by 2040. Growth in industrializing nations like Brazil, India, and China will more than make up for reductions in the U.S. and Europe. And cars won't be the only things using oil. By 2024 there will be twice as much plastic on Earth as there is today. In that year, we will produce almost 430 million tons of it. That rate of increasing consumption, coupled with declining oil production, means we could need half of our current oil production to make plastics in 2100. The problem is that, by most estimates, there won't be any appreciable oil production in 2100.[1]

Unless we find a way today to drastically cut back on our use of oil, and that includes plastic, we appear headed for the "economic shock and social unrest" that former Energy Secretary James Schlesinger warned Congress about in 2005. Finding alternative energy sources and new modes of transportation are vital to avoiding that scenario. Conservation is critical; but conservation, even in concert with new oil discoveries and alternative fuel technologies, will not be enough. What follows is about the surprisingly large role that design will play as we transition to a post-petroleum world that doesn't rely on oil and plastic.

Why Design Matters

> In many ways, the environmental crisis is a design crisis. It is a consequence of how
> things are made, buildings are constructed, and landscapes are used.
>
> (Sim van der Ryn and Stephen Cowan, *Ecological Design*)[2]

Why is design so important to our post-petroleum future? After all, almost 70 percent of U.S. petroleum consumption goes to transportation. Well, transportation is a design problem. How do we engineer electric cars that people will want to drive? How do we redesign our infrastructure to support them? What even greener transportation options lie beyond the current trend toward electric vehicles? Everything is designed—our vehicles, our homes, our products—and these three aspects of our lives account for 99 percent of U.S. petroleum consumption. But before we ever use these things, someone has to design them.[3]

The world we've made with petroleum and plastic has brought us power and convenience beyond our ancestors' dreams, but at a heavy cost to our health and environment. Recognizing this, we now design with greater awareness. Buildings and vehicles today must conform to ever-stricter energy conservation standards, and products are scrutinized for their impacts on planet and people. Still, no single material has as much impact on our environment and our health as petroleum. Burning fossil fuels, for example, accounts for ten times the carbon dioxide emissions of all other sources combined. The intersection of petroleum and design therefore may be the biggest single determinant of our future quality of life. Can we create a new breed of vehicles, homes, and products less reliant on oil, and less harmful to people and planet than their oil-dependent predecessors? The answer is yes, and my purpose in writing this book is to share the inspiring stories of the designers who are leading the way to a positive, post-oil future.[4]

Post-Petroleum Design

POST-PETROLEUM design is about people taking action to create a world free of the harmful effects of petroleum-based products, free of our current dependence on oil. My company, Gone Studio, is practicing it by making its products plastic-free, using no electricity and producing no waste in its manufacturing. Patagonia is doing it by offering an organic cotton alternative to conventional polyester outdoor gear. Tesla and other electric carmakers are doing their part by putting cars on the road that don't burn gas. And many other post-petroleum pioneers are emerging to lead a movement that says no to petroleum and yes to clean, renewable alternatives.

But this book isn't just about "green" companies or alleviating climate change. It points specifically to the end of the oil era and argues that even if we are able to dodge the climate change bullet, we are still going to have to face a world without oil. And we will face it sooner than most of us think. The question is, will we allow it to blindside us, creating untold turmoil as our oil-dependent economy comes screeching to a halt, or will we plan ahead, easing our inevitable transition into renewable energy sources and creating a healthier, more livable planet as a result?

By the end of this century, we will be in the post-petroleum era whether we like it or not. The world's oil supply is declining, and the cost of extracting what remains will increase rapidly as reserves dwindle. Eventually, we will only use it for special needs, but in its most common applications—fuel for transportation and heating, packaging and consumer products—it will be replaced. One day, biofuels and bioplastics will replace fossil fuels and petroleum-based plastics. But with biofuels representing just 2.5 percent of global fuel production and bioplastics making up less than 1 percent of today's plastics market, that day appears to be a long way off. Certainly, more packaging and products will be made from recycled plastic. But current plastic recycling is energy-intensive, produces considerable carbon emissions, and can be toxic to workers and the environment.[5]

Post-petroleum design offers a low-energy, low-emission, less toxic alternative based on naturally renewable materials. And while not all of the designs profiled here are plastic-free, some of their creators are adamant about avoiding it. Eric Strebel, head of Botzen Design, expresses the urgency that some designers feel about avoiding plastic. "We cannot continue to make products out of plastic," he said, "or we will destroy this planet. We have to try as a society to make and consume products that are not made out of petroleum or plastic. We have to come up with different materials."[6]

Through post-petroleum design, we can make a much cleaner, healthier, more sustainable world than the one we've created with petroleum-based design. Working in design studios, startups, labs, and rural villages around the world, post-petroleum designers are saying no to fighting for the last drops of oil, saying no to the environmental harm it has wrought, and crafting a new world of goods and technologies designed to free us from our dependence on non-renewable energy and materials. While some are adapting preindustrial methods to modern conditions, many others are exploring innovative technologies to find new ways of creating petroleum-free, environmentally friendly products.

This book defines the shift from the oil-dependent era to the post-petroleum one as not only a technological transformation, but as a design movement. It is a firsthand account by someone who has witnessed the damage done by our dependence on oil and sought a better way. It draws on my own experience as the founder and owner of Gone Studio, the post-petroleum design company making plastic-free goods with zero waste and zero energy. But it weaves the Gone Studio experience together with interviews and profiles of over 40 other designers and products. From their work and mine, it distills larger principles and practices of post-petroleum design to present a vivid manifesto for designing a world free of oil and its harmful environmental legacy.

Notes

1   U.S. Energy Information Administration, "International Energy Outlook 2014," Report, Washington, DC, 2014, www.eia.gov/forecasts/ieo/more_overview.cfm; Lemstra, Piet, "Petro- versus Biobased Polymers," Presentation to the Summer School Catalysis for Sustainability: Exploring Resource Diversity for Energy and Materials Supply, June 23–26, 2013, Rolduc Abbey, the Netherlands.

2   van der Ryn, Sim, and Cowan, Stephen, *Ecological Design*, Washington, DC: Island Press, 1996.

3   U.S. Energy Information Administration, "International Energy Outlook 2014."

4   U.S. Environmental Protection Agency, "GHGRP 2013: Reported Data," Greenhouse Gas Reporting Program, www.epa.gov/ghgreporting/ghgdata/reported/index.html

5   U.S. Energy Information Administration, "International Energy Outlook 2014." Vidal, John, "'Sustainable' Bio-plastic Can Damage the Environment," *The Guardian*, April 25, 2005, www.guardian.co.uk/ environment/2008/apr/26/waste.pollution; Slavin, Chandler, "Recycling Report: The Truth about Recycling Clamshells and Blisters in America with Suggestions for the Industry," October 16, 2012, www.dordan.com/ blog/bid/231946/Recycling-Report-The-Truth-about-Recycling-Clamshells-and-Blisters-in-America-with-Suggestions-for-the-Industry

6   Author interview.

– 8 –

Transportation

T**HE** average new car contains more than a thousand plastic parts. But all that plastic makes up just 17 percent of a car's total weight. If that plastic were metal then in the U.S. alone, it would take an additional 88 million barrels of oil per year to haul the extra weight. But that plastic is not without impact on the environment, and a number of post-petroleum designers are exploring alternatives. From Ford Motor Company's plans for a "compostable car" to the cardboard bike developed by Israeli designer Izhar Gafni, innovations are emerging that address the difficulty of recycling plastic auto parts as well as their non-renewable resource consumption and carbon emissions.[1]

Plastic's low recycling rates are about to become a big issue in auto design. Only 8 percent of all plastic used in the U.S. gets recycled, and European rates aren't much higher. But a European Union auto recycling directive set to take effect in 2015 requires 60 percent of all auto plastics to be recycled. The 100 different types of plastic in today's cars, however, can't be easily separated or recycled. With similar laws coming worldwide, the plastics industry is in a quandary over how to meet these tighter regulations.[2]

One option is to substitute biodegradable materials. Bamboo, hemp, cardboard, and even seaweed are just some of the materials being experimented with. Not only the materials but the design as well is revolutionary in some of them. Others seek to be more evolutionary, like the Toyota 1/x, made from seaweed bioplastic but sporting a Prius look. All are concept vehicles, and most will require some refining to meet safety regulations. But they all have one thing in common—they radically reduce or even eliminate plastic from the design. Most use electric engines to reduce oil consumption, but so much has been written elsewhere about alternative fuels that our focus here will be on the materials the cars are made from. As Mike Kimberley, CEO of Group Lotus acknowledged, "Fuel efficiency is probably the most important factor in greening the road, but we mustn't forget how we are making these vehicles. With tens of millions of cars manufactured annually, production also has a huge impact on the environment."[3]

Lotus Eco Elise: "A Different Perspective on 'Green'"

H**EMP** and driving don't mix, unless the hemp is used as an alternative to plastic auto parts, as in the Lotus Eco Elise. The car's seats, rear spoiler, and body panels are all made of hemp grown in East Anglia, U.K. "We used hemp instead of fiberglass because it's grown locally and it's a strong material," said Group Lotus environmental manager Lee Preston in a BBC interview. "It's also a beautiful material to look at."

"We decided to focus on the environmental benefits of using sustainable materials," he explained. "This is why the Eco Elise promotes a different perspective on 'green'—one not directly tied to tailpipe emissions, but rather looking at the materials in the building process."

In the Eco Elise, hemp body panels replace the fiberglass panels used in some other Lotus models. And although these incorporate a typical polyester (plastic) resin, the company hopes to use a fully recyclable composite resin in the near future. Hemp roof panels integrate flexible solar panels, and natural wool and sisal give the car's interior an organic touch. Even the car's finish is a green innovation. Collaboration with DuPont led to a water-based, solvent-free system for the primer, color coat, and clear coat, an industry first.

As unconventional as hemp cars may seem today, Lotus isn't the first to try it. "Why use up the forests which were centuries in the making and the mines which required ages to lay down, if we can get the equivalent of forest and mineral products in the annual growth of the hemp fields?" Those were the words of none other than Henry Ford, who in 1941 unveiled a car made from hemp/soy bioplastic that even ran on hemp biofuel. Unfortunately, despite his vow to "grow automobiles from the soil," the car never advanced past prototyping.[4]

Toyota 1/x: Seaweed Sedan

As if making cars from hemp isn't surprising enough, Toyota plans to make one from seaweed. The seaweed-based 1/x (pronounced "one-xth" because its carbon footprint is a fraction of that of other cars) is an evolution of an earlier 1/x Toyota concept car made from carbon fiber.

"We used lightweight carbon fiber reinforced plastic throughout the body and frame for its superior collision safety," said project manager Tetsuya Kaida. "But that material is made from oil. In the future, I'm sure we will have access to new and better materials, such as those made from plants, something natural, maybe something like paper. In fact, I want to create such a vehicle from seaweed."

Rajendran Narasimmalu, biology professor at Hiroshima University, thinks seaweed's day will come. "Seaweed based bioplastics play a vital role as an environment friendly and biodegradable alternative compared to conventional plastics," he and his co-authors write in "Seaweeds Can Be a New Source for Bioplastics," a study published in the *Journal of Pharmacy Research*. "Seaweeds are cost effective, minimize the impact on the food chain and are chemical-independent. Bioplastics from seaweeds are reported to be more resistant to microwave radiation, less brittle, and durable."

The 1/x concept car is leading the charge with some impressive numbers. It weighs about one-third as much as the Prius and gets over 100 mpg. But don't expect to see seaweed in auto showrooms before 2025, according to Toyota. "In reality," said David Buttner, Senior Executive Director of Sales and Marketing, "the seaweed car is another decade away. However, it shows where we're going. It's a concept car of post-2020. It is ultra-light and ultra-strong. Our thinking is that post-2020, cars like the 1/x will be made of plant-based plastic."[5]

Ford's Better Idea: Petroleum-Free Cars

"One day I hope to see the automotive world go totally compostable, removing the use of petroleum-based parts 100 percent." That's not a quote you would expect to hear from a director at Ford Motor Company, but that's what Debbie Mielewski, Director of the company's Plastics Research Group, hopes to achieve. Ford already uses soy-based foam for seat cushions and other parts in nearly all its vehicles, cutting petroleum use by over 1,500 tons and reducing carbon dioxide emissions by more than 5,500 tons. In an interview with hybridcars.com, Mielewski said, "The objective of my group is to develop alternative materials to limited, traditional petroleum-based plastics. Some of the materials are compostable, eliminating the landfill of plastics. Plastics are certainly a huge part of the automotive process—and we are quick to recognize that—so the more sustainable we can make these plastics the better."

Ford is also turning to some very imaginative sources to reduce plastic in its cars. "Rising oil prices," the company said in a press release, "have Ford upping the ante in its push to reduce petroleum dependence and use more sustainable materials—including retired U.S. paper currency—to make parts."

The first steps to reducing petrochemical plastic have already been taken, as Ford, Mazda, Toyota, and other automakers already use bioplastics made from soy, corn, and wheat in their cars. And Ford plans to convert 100 percent of its fleet to use biofoam in the future. "Automotive is one of the several market segments driving toward greater use of high-performance bio-based materials to meet their sustainability challenges," said Richard Bell, Global Development Manager for renewable materials at DuPont Automotive Performance Polymers. The move to bioplastics is motivated as much by economics as environmentalism. "The pricing of bio-based chemicals and plastics has been less volatile than petroleum-based products," said Craig Crawford, President and CEO of the Ontario BioAuto Council. "And in the longer term, they are expected to become cheaper as the technologies mature and production achieves economies of scale."[6,7]

Mercedes-Benz Biome: Growing Greener Cars

To meet the Los Angeles Auto Show Design Challenge, the engineers at the Mercedes-Benz Advanced Design Studios created a concept car that's not built, but grown. "The Mercedes-Benz Biome symbiosis vehicle," they said, "is made from an ultralight material called BioFibre grown from proprietary DNA in the Mercedes-Benz nursery."

The designers envision growing the car's interior from the DNA in the Mercedes star on the front of the car, while the exterior grows from the star on the rear. The Biome would be genetically engineered according to each customer's preferences. And while this is not a car that you're going to be able to buy today or tomorrow, it's telling that the future of automotive transportation as Mercedes-Benz sees it is plastic- and petroleum-free. "We wanted to illustrate the vision of the perfect vehicle of the future, which is created and functions in complete symbiosis with nature," said Hubert Lee, head of the Mercedes-Benz Advanced Design Studios.

The BioFibre the company envisions would be lighter than metal or plastic, yet stronger than steel. It could also be easily composted or used as a building material. And while it may sound like a material for the twenty-second century, rather than the twenty-first, the nanotechnology already used in today's cars is not to so different. Almost all car bumpers, for example, are made from carbon nanotube composites that are lighter and stronger than steel. The carbon nanotubes used in these nanocomposites are grown in that they self-assemble under electrochemical stimulus. Still, it will be a while before you can pick your car from a local auto grower instead of a dealer's lot.[8]

Phoenix car: Rattan Roadster

POST-PETROLEUM vehicles don't have to rely on bioplastics and look like a Prius. The Phoenix car, by product designers Kenneth Cobonpue and Albrecht Birkner, breaks the mold of conventional car design with a body made of bamboo and rattan. Cobonpue frequently uses rattan, a material common in his native Cebu, an island of the Philippines. The Phoenix car

Figure 8.1: Phoenix car
Designers Kenneth Cobonpue and Albrecht Birkner teamed to create this concept car, which features the innovative use of rattan and other post-petroleum materials. Image courtesy of Kenneth Cobonpue.

shows Cobonpue's respect for craft, elegantly shaping rattan into a flowing form unlike anything else. And while you won't see it on the roads anytime soon because it's a one-of-a-kind prototype, its innovative design and materials may very well inspire the vehicles you drive in the future. Kenneth Cobonpue explains:

You're famous for your innovative use of rattan, a natural material, to carry out your cutting-edge design ideas. How does this "traditional" material help you achieve your very modern design goals?

After returning to Cebu from design school abroad, not only was I truly re-inspired by the wealth of natural materials and incredibly skilled craftsmanship around me, I also really respected the challenge of working with the unique structural properties of each type of natural material. I love to take the materials I've selected and just experiment with them, almost like a couturier with fabric. Sometimes the inspiration I have taken from the material dovetails beautifully with what it allows me to do. Other times, my ideas change and develop from this hands-on experimentation.

You also incorporate other materials like wood and steel, but I rarely see any plastic in your work. Is that an intention on your part?

As with everything I do, I keep to a very responsible ecological tenet. I think we all need to be very aware of our environment and minimize our negative impact upon it as much as possible. To that end, we work very hard to use sustainable natural options with very little manufacturing footprint, and working with such skilled artisans who create magic with their hands makes that goal ultimately so achievable.

How do your clients respond to your emphasis on natural materials?

Well, first of all, I think that the accessibility of good design has increased everyone's ability to appreciate it. Much like with a piece of art, or music, beauty is internationally understandable in all its forms, regardless of its origin. I would like to think that the beauty of my work is equally relatable and understandable worldwide, and something about the purity of the natural materials resonates.

Your products often use not only natural materials, but low-energy handcrafting techniques as well. How do the two complement each other? What are some of the advantages of using less energy-intensive machinery and hand artistry in the production?

The one common factor in all of my pieces, regardless of material, is the production process, which is primarily handmade. The inspiration I find in the strength of the human spirit is one commonality that will never change. I have a tremendous drive to preserve that heritage of crafts-manship in our region for generations to come. I hope that by introducing that talent through my work to every corner of the globe, I will help ensure its future. I think the purity of craft somehow humanizes all of us and reminds us of the splendor of humanity, and the grace of creativity, and it continually inspires me to create new designs. It also enables us to maintain the ability to customize, in contrast to Europe or China, where almost everything is done in such large volume by machines. Finally, it's important to me to continue my efforts to show to the world that there is an environmentally friendly solution to absolutely everything that we do, and that we don't have to look far to find it.

What other materials and production techniques would you like to work with as you move forward?

I believe that design is a living process, forever transforming in response to the changing world. Because of that, I work hard to avoid getting boxed in to a personal esthetic, because it has a tendency towards repetition. Sticking to a winning formula, while safe, can only kill creativity and innovation. I design very instinctually, according to my taste, which evolves along with what inspires me, so I never know what the future will bring. We are, however, constantly trying to evolve and refine the techniques we use, but it is all within the framework of respecting the craft.[9]

Notes

1   Weill, David, Rouilloux, Gaël, and Klink, Götz, "Plastics: The Future for Automakers and Chemical Companies," June 2012, www.atkearney.com/automotive/featured-article/-/asset_publisher/S5UkO0zy0vnu/content/plastics-the-future-for-automakers-and-chemical-companies/10192; Azapagic, Adisa, Emsley, Alan, and Hamerton, Ian, *Polymers: The Environment and Sustainable Development*, Hoboken, NJ, John Wiley, 2003.

2   Andrady, Anthony, ed., *Plastics and the Environment*, Hoboken, NJ: John Wiley, 2003; Weill et al., "Plastics: The Future for Automakers and Chemical Companies."

3   Malnati, Peggy, "Lotus Elise Concept: Eco Enhanced," *Composite Technologies*, 46–48, www.compositeshelp.com/resources/CT+AUG+09+EI-Lotus+ECO+Elise+with+cover.pdf

4   Ibid. "Lotus Announces Hemp-based Eco Elise: A New Type of 'Green' Car," *Transport 2.0*, July 10, 2008, www.transport20.com/uncategorized/lotus-announces-hemp-based-eco-elise-a-new-type-of-green-car/

5   Mack, Ben, "Toyota Wants to Build Car From Seaweed," Wired.com, February 4, 2009, www.wired.com/autopia/2009/02/toyota-makes-pl/; Rajendran, Narasimmalu, Puppala, Sharanya, Sneha, Raj M., and Angeeleena, Ruth, "Seaweeds Can Be a New Source for Bioplastics," *Journal of Pharmacy Research*, Volume 5, Issue 3, March 2012, 1476–1479, www.specialchem4polymers.com/resources/latest/displaynews.aspx?id=7952; McDonald, Neil, "Kelp Is On the Way for Toyota," February 24, 2009, www.heraldsun.com.au/news/kelp-is-on-the-way-for-toyota/story-e6frf7jo-1111118942824

6   "Higher Oil Costs Could Speed Up the Use of New 'Green' Materials Such as Old U.S. Paper Money in Future Fords," April 17, 2012, https://media.ford.com/content/fordmedia/fna/us/en/news/2012/04/17/higher-oil-costs-could-speed-up-the-use-of-new-green-materials-s.html

7   Berman, Brad, "Ford Aims for 100-Percent Petroleum-Free Compostable Cars," hybridcars.com, June 24, 2010, www.hybridcars.com/environment/ford-aims-petroleum-free-compostable-cars-28147.html; de Guzman, Doris, "The Use and Development of Renewable Chemicals in Automotive Parts Is Rising," June 2, 2010, www.icis.com/Articles/2010/06/07/9364336/use-of-bio-based-auto-parts-is-increasing.html

8   "Mercedes-Benz BIOME: An Ultralight Vehicle at One with Nature," November 12, 2010, http://media.daimler.com/dcmedia-ca/0-981-710708-1-1349695-1-0-1-0-0-0-13003-710708-0-1-0-0-0-0-0.html

9   Author interview.

– 9 –

Electronics

VIRTUALLY every electronic device on the planet contains plastic parts. Plastic is non-conductive and insulating, making it an excellent material for circuitry, batteries, and anything carrying electrical charge. But e-waste adds millions of tons to our landfills every year, much of it plastic. While plastics in electronics aren't going away anytime soon, alternatives are emerging, especially for the casings of our electronic paraphernalia. Electronic products made with traditional materials like wood and cardboard are capturing an increasing share of the market. Experiments with more radical innovations, from electronic paper to cellular computing, show that we can meet our electronic needs in a future less dependent on oil.[1]

E-Paper: Print Your Own Electronics

PAPER may not seem like a very high-tech material, but nanoscientists are finding ways to make it outperform plastic in electronic applications. Researchers at the Max Planck Institute of Colloids and Interfaces in Germany have created conductive paper that can be shaped into three-dimensional electrically conductive structures. "Using a commercial inkjet printer, we print a solution of the catalyst in a fine pattern on a sheet of paper," said the Institute's Stefan Glatzel. The catalyst is iron nitrate, which converts the cellulose of the paper into graphite. The printed areas can then conduct electricity, while the unprinted ones remain neutral. After printing, the team then discovered they could shape the paper into any form and it would retain its conductivity. Glatzel showed some artistic flair by folding the paper into an origami crane.

But the significance of e-paper goes far beyond the curiosity of conductive origami. Thin, flexible electronics have tremendous potential in clothing, implants, consumer electronics, packaging, and more. Plastic can have limitations in these applications, but paper—light, flexible, renewable, and inexpensive—may prove to be a better fit for many of them.

Mark Hersam, a professor at Northwestern University in the U.S., is developing inks for printing circuitry on paper. "By formulating an inkjet-printable ink based on graphene," he said, "we now have an inexpensive and scalable path for exploiting these properties [of high electrical conductivity, mechanical flexibility, and chemical stability] in real-world technologies." If researchers like Hersam and Glatzel are successful in developing graphene ink and electronic paper further, it may not be long until you hear the question, "Paper or plastic?" not only at the supermarket, but also at the electronics store.[2]

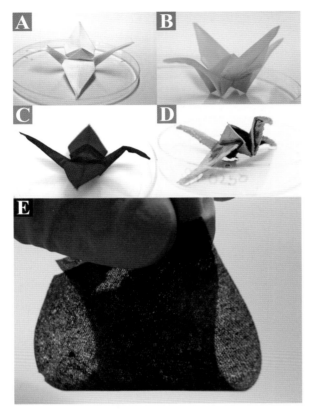

Figure 9.1: E-Paper
"Paper is becoming a high-tech material," especially at the Max Planck Institute of Colloids and Interfaces in Potsdam-Golm, Germany, where researchers are using it to create three-dimensional conductive structures using conventional inkjet printers. A) Untreated paper crane; B) Crane soaked in catalytic ink; C) Calcined crane; D) Calcined crane coated with copper; E) Final E-paper. Image courtesy of John Wiley and Sons.

Cellular Computing: Bringing Electronics to Life

I F electronic paper sounds far-fetched, imagine computing with living cells. That's what Drew Endy, a synthetic biologist at Stanford University, is creating. He's part of a growing, global research community exploring cellular computing. As the name suggests, cellular computing uses living cells instead of silicon and transistors to manage information. "Any system that's receiving information, processing information and then using that activity to control what happens next, you can think of as a computing system," Endy said. He's using the DNA of E. coli bacteria as living transistors, the on/off switches that all computing, no matter how complicated, is based on.

"For us, what's become exciting is the idea that we could get inside the cells in sort of a bottom-up fashion," he said. He hopes to program DNA to create logic circuits. The Massachusetts Institute of Technology (MIT) researcher Timothy Lu, who also works on cellular computing, sees great potential. "These cells could light up," he suggests, "and you could easily see whether the cell has computed if you may have early signs of cancer or not." So far, cellular computing only works for the simplest of logic circuits. But the proof-of-concept work by Lu, Endy, and others shows that plastic is by no means the only material our electronics can be made from.[3]

Bamboo Smartphone: Natural Material for Future Electronics

ROUGHLY 150 million cell phones are discarded every year. What if they were made of biodegradable materials instead of plastic? That's the challenge Kieron-Scott Woodhouse addressed in designing the ADzero, the world's first bamboo smartphone. The electronics of the razor-thin ADzero are housed in organically grown bamboo specially treated for durability and strength.

What inspired you to make the ADzero smartphone from bamboo?

We went through an extremely conceptual initial design process when we were first coming up with ideas for the ADzero. We experimented with all types of materials from Corian to copper. As a designer, my biggest priority was having a material that really told a story and developed with the user over time, whether that be because of its physical properties or the technology we used to create this story. Originally this design was in copper but I thought it lacked the story we were looking for to make the product truly individual. At first we tried normal hardwood and we realized this was the missing link; the initial concept renders looked amazing with such an organic material. From this point we looked into how we could make this commercially viable as well as ensuring we didn't have a detrimental effect on the environment. Bamboo was the perfect answer; not only is it extremely durable and strong, but it allowed us to create that story in a more environmentally friendly way.

The ADzero is certainly a radical departure from other smartphone designs; do you see design changing in the twenty-first century? If so, what forces do you see driving that change?

I think people are done with the mass-commoditization of everything around them and yearn for products that show individualism, be it small or obvious. The boom in open initiatives and communication has begun to change the way products come to market. Consumers have more power than ever before when it comes to supporting and deciding what comes to market. This is evident in websites such as Kickstarter and Quirky that actively involve the user throughout the development process of a product.

Figure 9.2: ADzero Bamboo Phone
Phone cases made from bamboo are common
enough, but designer Kieron-Scott Woodhouse
used it to make the entire body of this phone.
Image courtesy of Kieron-Scott Woodhouse.

What other designs do you have in progress, and how do environmental concerns fit in?

At present ADzero is my primary focus. Ours isn't necessarily a "green" company but one of our core values is that we are very much aware of the environmental concerns and ensure all of our products have this in mind, whether that be material choice or offsetting our carbon footprint. We feel this is a major responsibility.[4]

Craft Camera: Do-It-Yourself Sustainability

THE Craft Camera by Coralie Gourguechon and Stéphane Delbruel defies convention in its design, materials, and sales model. With its cardboard casing and textured patina, it stands out among ordinary plastic-clad cameras. And as for the sales model, there isn't one. Instead, the pair chose to make their plans available for free under a Creative Commons license. Do-it-yourselfers can download the plans and acquire the specified single-piece electronic system on their own. Building your own camera may not be for everyone, but the result is a simple yet fully functional digital camera with a plastic-free case.

"The objective was to counter the planned obsolescence and complexity of electronic products," said Gourguechon. In their place, the Craft Camera offers accessibility, repairability, and sustainability.[5]

Figure 9.3: Craft Camera
Eschewing plastic, Coralie Gourguechon and Stéphane Delbruel forged this affordable camera from cardboard. Image courtesy of Coralie Gourguechon.

Figure 9.4: Craft Camera Cutout Sheet
The Craft Camera's parts come on a single cardboard sheet, and plans are available for free under a Creative Commons license. Image courtesy of Coralie Gourguechon.

IKoNO Wooden Radio: Local Artistry, Local Materials

WHEN Singgih Susilo Kartono, a native of Kandangan, Indonesia graduated college, he wasn't sure what he wanted to do, so he followed his heart. Returning to his hometown, Kartono started Magno Design, his company which now employs dozens of local artisans. Today, Magno Design combines local artisanry, Kartono's design experience, and sustainably grown wood to make innovative consumer products. Beautiful local hardwoods, readily available and yet in danger of overharvesting, have become a focal point of Kartono's work.

Figure 9.5: Singgih Susilo Kartono with IKoNO Wooden Radio
Javanese designer Singgih Susilo Kartono employs local wood and local artisans to make his IKoNO Wooden Radio. Image courtesy of Magno Design.

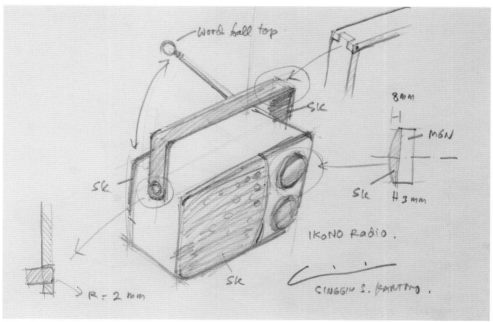

Figure 9.6: IKoNO Wooden Radio Sketch
Local wood influences the design of the IKoNO Wooden Radio. Designer Singgih Susilo Kartono even plants a tree for every one used to make his products. Image courtesy of Magno Design.

"I consider wood as a balance material," he said. "Compared to synthetic materials, I feel that wood is a material with soul inside. The beautiful texture and grain actually tell the story of its life. Wood is a kind of perfect material, perfect because of its imperfectness. Its character teaches us about life, balance, and limits." And Kartano follows through on his words, planting a new tree for every one used in his products.[6]

iZen Bamboo Keyboard: Tough, Beautiful, Sustainable

T<small>HE</small> notion that wood is for old-fashioned, rather than high-tech, products has been laid to rest by Robin Behrstock and Ryan Stecher, creators of the iZen Bamboo Keyboard. The Bluetooth keyboard works with a wide range of devices and is 92 percent bamboo. The casing is completely recyclable and will biodegrade should it end up in the landfill. Robin Behrstock talked about why the company chose bamboo, and the role it could play in post-petroleum design.

Of all the materials you could have chosen to make a keyboard out of, what made you choose bamboo?

Bamboo is a perfect combination of strength and sustainability. It grows extremely fast without help from pesticides and other resources. It's tough enough to be used for bridges and scaffoldings that hold thousands of pounds, so it's tough enough to be used for a keyboard too. And the obvious answer: it's beautiful.

Figure 9.7 iZen Bamboo Keyboard
Designers Ryan Stecher and Robin Behrstock chose bamboo for its strength and sustainability; it makes up 92 percent of their iZen Bamboo Keyboard. Image courtesy of iZen Bamboo.

Consumer electronics and plastics seem almost inseparable. Is the iZen keyboard a sign that we can expect more variety in the materials our electronics are made from in the future?

Definitely. Plastic is manufactured using non-renewable natural resources like crude oil. As we continue to deplete the earth's supply of crude oil, it will become more and more important for us to use other renewable materials, and bamboo is one of the most renewable materials available.[7]

Notes

1   U.S. Environmental Protection Agency, "eCycling: Frequent Questions," www.epa.gov/epawaste/conserve/materials/ecycling/faq.htm#howmuch

2   Hergersberg, Peter, "Electronics Comes to Paper," Max-Planck-Gesellscahft, May 8, 2013, www.mpg.de/7239441/paper-electronics?filter_order=LT&research_topic=MT; "Opening Doors to Foldable Electronics with Inkjet-Printed Graphene," May 20, 2013, http://nanotech2day.blogspot.com/2013/05/opening-doors-to-foldable-electronics.html; "Paper Electronics," May 16, 2013, http://mumbaimirror.com/others/sci-tech/techtalk/Paper-electronics/articleshow/20080091.cms

3   Brumfiel, Geoff, "Tiny DNA Switches Aim to Revolutionize 'Cellular' Computing," March 29, 2013, www.npr.org/2013/03/29/175604770/tiny-dna-switches-aim-to-revolutionize-cellular-computing

4   Author interview.

5   Gourgechon, Coralie, Craft Camera, http://cargocollective.com/craftcamera

6   Kartono, Singgih Susilo, Magno Design, www.magno-design.com/

7   Author interview.

10

Packaging

Packaging is the number one use of plastic. It can reduce transportation costs and save energy because it weighs less than glass or metal. And, according to the Plastics Industry Trade Association, "Plastic packaging, which constitutes less than 4% of all municipal solid waste by weight, also can be disposed of safely in landfills." The EPA, meanwhile, reports plastic packaging as over 5 percent of municipal solid waste by weight. And, as we've seen, plastics that leach toxic chemicals into our landfills are far from safe. Plastic packaging is also one of the least recycled types of plastic because so much of it is thin film that defies recycling.[1]

While packaging is the most common use of plastic, plastic accounts for less than 20 percent of all packaging. Paper dominates the packaging field and is used more than all other materials combined. And while about 8 percent of plastic is recycled every year, the recycling rate for paper is eight times that.[2]

But paper packaging is by no means the only alternative to plastic. Bioplastics made from plant material, while less than 1 percent of total plastic sales, are growing at a rate of 20 percent per year. Currently, 70 percent of all bioplastics are used for packaging, and even mainstream plastic producers are seeing opportunities in future bioplastic packaging. Dow Chemical and Mitsui, for example, recently bought a $200 million Brazilian sugarcane plantation, with plans to spend even more to create what will be the largest bioplastics production plant in the world. "The flexible packaging market is currently booming, not only in Brazil but throughout Latin America," said Luis Cirihal, Dow's Business Director for Green Alternatives and New Business Development for Latin America. "At the same time, consumers are increasingly turning to sustainable solutions. For these reasons, we are certain that there is ample market demand and growth potential for biopolymers, particularly within the high-performance flexible packaging, hygiene, and medical markets."[3,4]

Bioplastics can also help reduce our energy use and emissions. Ingeo bioplastic from NatureWorks, for instance, produces 60 percent less carbon dioxide than petroleum-based plastic and requires 30 percent less energy to manufacture. But bioplastics aren't perfect. For one thing, the name has been somewhat compromised, and some products marketed as made from it contain only a small amount of plant-based polymers mixed with mostly petrochemical polymers. There is also a misconception that all bioplastics are biodegradable. Not all are, especially when landfilled. Bioplastic feedstocks can include crops like corn and sugar, and, like with corn-based ethanol, the question of using crops to feed industry rather than people is a controversial one.

Bioplastics don't have to be made from plants that feed people, however. Metabolix and some other bioplastic makers use switchgrass as a feedstock. Instead of harvesting switchgrass and then processing it, Metabolix actually grows bioplastic particles in the switchgrass itself. Using a process called multi-gene expression, their engineers are able to boost the plants' production of polymers. "It's a matter of changing the genetic makeup of the plant so that it takes carbon and turns those plants into a plastics factory," said Metabolix Chief Executive Rick Eno. "The benefit of the switchgrass approach is the plant does all the work. It's basically just taking CO_2, sunlight, and water and producing plastics and chemicals." While still in the proof-of-concept phase, their technology suggests a future where plastic is produced in plants and not just factories.[5,6,7]

Mushroom Material Packaging: A Growing Business

WHILE plants like switchgrass may become tomorrow's bioplastics factories, a company in New York state is making today's packaging from an unlikely source: mushrooms. "We don't manufacture materials," Ecovative's co-founder Eben Bayer is fond of saying, "we grow them." The company's facility in Green Island, New York is filled with mycelium, a growth stage of fungus that produces a network of threadlike cells so dense there are eight miles of them per cubic inch. Growing in the dark, these mycelia digest agricultural waste to form packaging and other materials. In other words, the mushrooms don't grow into raw materials that are harvested and processed into packaging; they're actually grown in the shape of the packaging. Towering racks of mycelium fill the 40,000 square foot facility, growing without water, light, feed crops, or petrochemicals. The result is packaging that's plastic-free, low-energy, and compostable.[8]

Eben Bayer explained the company's technologies and philosophy:

The versatility of your technology is remarkable; you're already marketing or exploring packaging, building insulation, even padding for ocean buoys that will warn us of tsunamis. Its versatility reminds me of plastic, but without all the environmental ill effects. Do you see the synergy of natural materials and innovative processes like yours reducing our reliance on petroleum-based products?

Companies like Dow and Dupont have been leading the way in material design for the past 100 years by turning petroleum and natural gas into plastics and other materials. These materials can take millions of years to break down and are therefore filling up our landfills and waterways. Ecovative aims to resolve this issue by becoming this century's material leader. Unlike plastics and foams, our materials are bio-based, sustainable, and are actually good for the environment. As long as people continue to be concerned about their environmental impact, there is no end to the applications of our materials. In the future, Mushroom Materials might be found in the bumper of your car, the walls of your home, or even inside your desk.

Figure 10.1 Eben Bayer and Gavin McIntyre
Ecovative co-founders Eben Bayer and Gavin McIntyre stand
amid towering racks of the mushroom mycelium they grow
their products from. Image courtesy of Ecovative Design.

You use agricultural byproducts like plant stalks and seed husks as opposed to the feed stocks like corn and soybeans that most bioplastics rely on. Do you think that non-food stocks like yours will eventually replace edible feed stocks as the raw materials for bioplastics?

One of the main advantages of our product is that we can grow our mycelium around and through almost all natural products. By using agricultural byproducts, our material gains a competitive advantage over other bioplastic companies that use feed stocks to create their materials. Ideally, we will see more companies take the approach of upcycling materials, rather than creating a material that is level with its starting point.

Products and technologies as far ahead of their time as yours often face resistance from consumers who may not understand or be ready for them yet. Insulation made from mushrooms, for example, undoubtedly raises some fears of mold growth. How do you overcome that resistance and help move society and its thinking about new materials and their benefits forward into such uncharted territory?

Thankfully, most people recognize the damage humans have been doing to the Earth and want to help in some way. Our product is a viable alternative to many of the materials that are contributing to this damage. Once people find out that our materials are cost-competitive, fire resistant, tunable in performance, continually pass quality testing, and are free of spores, allergens, and mold, using our product just makes sense. The push from government agencies to steer away from Styrofoam and plastic reliance has also been tremendous in the success of our company.[9]

Natralock Security Packaging: Reducing Wrap Rage

THE frustration of trying to open plastic clamshell packaging has become so widespread it now has a name—wrap rage. But it may not be wrap rage that ends plastic's prevalence in clamshell packaging. "With the instability in petroleum-based materials, people said we need an alternative to the clamshell," said Jeff Kellogg, Vice President for Consumer Electronics and Security Packaging at MeadWestvaco (MWV). His company's Natralock packaging is a paper-based alternative that reduces plastic content by 60 percent. Clients like Eastman Kodak are finding it a welcome option that retains the best qualities of the plastic clamshell without its drawbacks. "The Natralock solution from MWV offers in-store security without excessive packaging materials or compromising consumer friendliness," said Donna Cirella, a Kodak packaging manager. "It is an excellent solution that supports our brand and the environment."

And it's not just Kodak that is looking for alternatives. As the *New York Times* reports, "High oil prices have manufacturers and big retailers reconsidering the use of so much plastic, and some are aggressively looking for cheaper substitutes." Wal-Mart, for example, pledged in 2008 to cut its packaging by 5 percent by 2013. That may not sound like a lot, but when you go through as much packaging as Wal-Mart does, the savings add up; the company says it is now saving $3.4 billion per year.[10]

Figure 10.2 Natralock Security Packaging
Packaging is the main use of plastic, but
MeadWestvaco's Natralock Security Packaging
reduces plastic content by 60 percent. Image
courtesy of MeadWestvaco Corporation.

Amazon Frustration-Free Certified Packaging: Less Plastic Means Happier Customers

ECOGNIZING that reducing plastic packaging saves time, frustration, money, and the environment, Amazon established its Frustration-Free Certified Packaging program in 2008. Because the program is aimed at reducing wrap rage, its packages come without the plastic clamshell casings, bindings, and ties that infuriate shoppers. And because Amazon sells online, they don't have to worry about shoplifters—one of the main reasons for bulky, hard-to-open packaging.

While only a few hundred of Amazon's millions of products are currently available plastic-free, the program has cut customer complaints by 73 percent. And because of that success, Amazon's Vice President for Global Fulfillment, Nadia Shouraboura, expects the program to grow. "We don't expect to make a miracle in a week," she told the *New York Times*, "but I think over time it's going to happen."[11]

PlantBottle: Things Go Better with Plant-Based Packaging

"This is the beginning of the end of petroleum-based plastics," said Allen Hershkowitz, a senior scientist with the Natural Resources Defense Council. He was referring to plans by Pepsi to sell their drinks in bottles made entirely of plant-based plastic. Current versions of their bottles are made from switchgrass, pine bark, and corn husks, with plans to also use orange peels, oat hulls, and potato scraps in the future. Meanwhile, Coca-Cola, Ford, Heinz, Nike, and Procter & Gamble have joined forces to move toward 100 percent plant-based packaging for their products as well. Calling their alliance the Plant PET Technology Collaborative, the group will build on Coke's established PlantBottle packaging technology, also licensed by Heinz, which is made from 30 percent Brazilian sugarcane. Since launching them in 2009, Coke has used more than 15 billion PlantBottles, saving an estimated 140,000 tons of carbon dioxide emissions.

The PET part, polyethylene terephthalate, is a plastic used by all member companies in a variety of products and materials including plastic bottles, apparel, footwear, and automotive fabric and carpet. While plant-based PET isn't a silver bullet—the main ingredient in PlantBottles is still petroleum-based plastic—it has demonstrated a lower environmental impact as compared to conventional PET plastic bottles. As for when we'll see them offering 100 percent plant-based packaging, "We have committed publicly to convert all of our PET plastic bottles to PlantBottle packaging by 2020," said Scott Vitters, Coke's General Manager for their PlantBottle packaging platform. To achieve that goal, the company has partnered with biotech companies Virent, Gevo, and Avantium to develop new bioplastics from plant waste like barks, stems, and peels instead of food sources such as corn and soybeans. They've even partnered with Ford to explore using the same renewable material used to produce PlantBottle packaging in the interior fabric of an experimental Ford Fusion Energi.[12,13]

Ooho! The Water Bottle You Can Eat

ONE way to cut down on water containers is to eat them. As far-fetched as that may sound, it's exactly the idea behind the Ooho! edible water bottle by Skipping Rocks Lab. Company founders Rodrigo García González, Pierre Paslier, and Guillame Couche conceived of the Ooho as a container that's "simple, cheap, resistant, hygienic, biodegradable, and even edible." Made from calcium and brown algae, "Ooho challenges the way we think about packaged water. While plastic offers a convenient solution, it generated enormous amount of waste and health hazard," as Guillame Couche explained. Others apparently agree that the Ooho is good enough to eat; it received a Lexus Design Award in 2014.[14]

Vivos Edible Delivery Systems: "Have Your Film and Eat it Too"

WHILE they may not win the award for best tag line, the Vivos Edible Delivery Systems by MonoSol are disappearing off the shelves. In fact, the clear pouches disappear when dropped in hot or cold water, making them a unique, plastic-free way of portioning and preparing a wide variety of foods and drinks.

"The uses in some ways are only constrained by our imagination," Media Manager Matt Scearce told Co.Design. "Examples include oatmeal, cereals, instant teas/coffees, sweeteners, soups, drink sticks, gravy and sauces, hot chocolate, back of the kitchen applications, pre-portioned spice packs, pre-portioned dry ingredients, workout proteins and supplements (that are currently scooped out from huge bulk containers), etc." The Vivos system points to a future where food and its packaging may become one, eliminating the need for plastic waste and potential leaching of toxins from packaging into our food.[15]

Edible Burger Wrapper: "Não Dá Pra Controlar"

"You can't control yourself," is the tag line of Bob's, the South American burger chain founded by Brazilian-American tennis star Bob Falkenberg in the 1960s. To prove their point, Bob's set aside one day in 2012 to sell all their burgers in edible wrappers. Employees could be heard explaining to somewhat perplexed customers, "Se estiver com muita fome, come com papel e tudo." ("If you're hungry, you can eat the paper and everything.") For one day, customers could lose control and tear into their meals without stopping to unwrap them. And while it was a one-time promotional event, it could mean that one day fast food customers will have nothing to throw away.[16]

Libig G Bottle: Preserving the Classics

OVER one-third of consumers say they are "extremely or very concerned about the health and safety of plastics used in food and water packaging." Because of these concerns, a growing number are looking to an old friend, glass, to hold their drinks. A classic example is the Libig G bottle designed by OMC². The company describes it as "a very elegant bottle design in glass; it is a perfect fit for food related packaging such as olive oils, vinegar etc." Produced using blow molding techniques, the Libig is slightly oval in cross section, creating variety in profile as it is turned. Its

Figure 10.3 Ooho! Edible Water Container
The plastic container goes away completely in the Ooho edible "blob" by Skipping Rocks Lab. Image courtesy of Rodrigo García González.

Figure 10.4 Libig G Bottle
Unlike most plastics, glass can be recycled multiple times, with just a fraction of the greenhouse gas emissions and water consumption in manufacturing. Image courtesy of OMC² Design Studios.

flowing form is reminiscent of seedpods and other natural forms. One hundred percent reusable and recyclable, the Libig shows how a natural material like glass can be a work of art and yet perform a utilitarian function, and be cherished rather than discarded after a single use.

Consumers may also prefer glass to plastic for what it doesn't contain. Glass contains fewer toxins than many plastics. It's also more inert than plastic, which can leach toxins into its contents and the environment. Glass can also be recycled more easily than plastic. Plastic is lighter and therefore uses less fuel and produces fewer greenhouse gases during transport, but during their manufacturing, PET plastic jars produce five times more greenhouse gas emissions than glass and use 17 times as much water. When you consider that the average household buys 4,000 packaged products per year, those numbers add up.[17]

Pure Safe-Shell Bottle: Safer Glass

EVERY year, Americans send about 38 billion plastic bottles to the landfill. But it doesn't have to be that way. Glass bottles are reusable and recyclable, and they don't require the 21 million barrels of oil all those plastic bottles are made from. But glass has one big drawback—it breaks. Scientist turned entrepreneur Walt Himelstein, however, has created a reusable glass bottle that's hard to break and won't shatter if broken. The Pure Safe-Shell is made from tough Borosilicate glass that can withstand high impact. Like the safety glass used in car windshields, the Safe-Shell keeps shards contained and away from human touch.

"No other reusable glass bottle offers the advantages of a clear non-removable coating that is BPA free and a safety coating that protects the consumer should the glass break," says Marc Heinke, President and Chief Executive of Precidio Design, the Canadian company marketing the bottle. Safety, sterility, and convenience converge in the Pure Safe-Shell, and because it's 100 percent recyclable, you can simply recycle it when you're done.[18]

Figure 10.5 Pure Safe-Shell Bottle
A glass water bottle isn't much use if it breaks easily, but the Pure Safe-Shell Bottle is made from tough Borosilicate glass that's hard to break and won't shatter if broken. Image courtesy of Precidio Design Inc.

Figure 10.6 Conventional Water Bottle Shattering
Regular glass water bottles can shatter into shards when broken. Image courtesy of Precidio Design Inc.

Notes

1   Plastics Industry Trade Association, "Plastics in Packaging," www.plasticsindustry.org/AboutPlastics/content. cfm?ItemNumber=636&navItemNumber=1118; U.S. Environmental Protection Agency, "Plastics," www.epa. gov/osw/conserve/materials/plastics.htm; Truth Studio, "Material Flows Visualization," www.truthstudio.com/ viz_material_flows.html

2   U.S. Environmental Protection Agency, "Paper Recycling: Frequent Questions," www.epa.gov/osw/conserve/ materials/paper/faqs.htm

3   "Global Bioplastics Market Analyzed by Transparency Market Research," November 23, 2012, www.prweb.com/ releases/2012/11/prweb10164424.htm; Swamy, J.N. and Singh, Balaji, "Bioplastics and Global Sustainability," Society of Plastics Engineers, October 13, 2010, www.4spepro.org/view.php?article=003219-2010-09-13

4   Smock, Doug, "Dow & Mitsui Plan Brazil Bioplastics Plant," *DesignNews*, August 22, 2011, www.designnews. com/document.asp?doc_id=231613&dfpPParams=aid_231613&dfpLayout=article&dfpPParams=aid_231613 &dfpLayout=article

5   "Metabolix to Test Feasibility of Producing Bioplastics from Switchgrass Post the Receipt of US Patent," SpecialChem, August 26, 2013, www.specialchem4bio.com/news/2013/08/26/metabolix-to-test-feasibility-of- producing-bioplastics-switchgrass-post-the-receipt-of-us-patent#sthash.bDpWgHY9.dpuf

6   "Ingeo Eco-Profile," NatureWorks, www.natureworksllc.com/The-Ingeo-Journey/Eco-Profile-and-LCA/ Eco-Profile; Andrady, Anthony, ed., *Plastics and the Environment*, Hoboken, NJ: John Wiley, 2003, 158–159.

7   "Crop-based Technologies," Metabolix, www.metabolix.com/Products/Crop-based-Technologies

8   "About Ecovative," www.ecovativedesign.com/about

9   Author interview.

10 Mohan, Anne Marie, "Kodak Opts for Paperboard Package over Clamshell for Digital Camera," *Greener Packaging*, January 7, 2010, www.greenerpackage.com/source_reduction/kodak_opts_paperboard_package_ over_clamshell_digital_camera; Clifford, Stephanie, "Devilish Packaging, Tamed," *New York Times*, June 1, 2011, www.nytimes.com/2011/06/02/business/energy-environment/02packaging.html?_r=0

11 "Amazon Certified Frustration-Free Packaging," www.amazon.com/b?ie=UTF8&node=5521637011; Clifford, Stephanie, "Packaging Is All the Rage, and Not in a Good Way," *New York Times* online, September 7, 2010, www.nytimes.com/2010/09/08/technology/08packaging.html?_r=0

12 "Beyond the Bottle," Coca-Cola Company Press Center, www.coca-colacompany.com/press-center/ image-library/look-inside-fords-new-fusion-energi#TCCC

13 "PepsiCo Unveils 100 Percent Plant-based Bottle," *Washington Post* online, March 15, 2011, www. washingtonpost.com/wp-dyn/content/article/2011/03/15/AR2011031501022.html; Kaplan, Andrew, "Awaiting PlantBottle 2.0," *Beverage World*, October 1, 2012, www.beverageworld.com/articles/full/15300/awaiting- plantbottle-2.0; Elvin, George, "Major Companies Join to Create 100% Plant-based Packaging," August 2, 2012, http://gelvin.squarespace.com/green-technology-forum/2012/8/2/major-companies-join-to-create-100- plant-based-packaging.html; Hsu, Tiffany, "Coke, Ford, Nike, Others Back Petroleum-free, Plant-based Plastics," *Los Angeles Times* online, June 5, 2012, www.latimes.com/business/money/la-fi-mo-coke-ford-nike- plant-20120605,0,1139461.story?track=rss&utm_source=feedburner&utm_medium=feed&utm_campaign=F eed%3A+MoneyCompany+%28Money+%26+Company%29

14 Couche, Guillaume, "Ooho!" Design Portfolio, www.guillaumecouche.com/208492/3422259/gallery/ooho

15 "Vivos Films," MonoSol, www.monosol.com/brands.php?p=117

16 "So Hungry You Could Eat the Wrapper: Brazilian Fast Food Joint Launches Edible Burger Packaging," *New York Daily News*, December 19, 2012, www.nydailynews.com/life-style/eats/brazilian-fast-food-chain-edible-burger-packaging-article-1.1223509

17 Strom, Stephanie, "Wary of Plastic, and Waste, Some Consumers Turn to Glass," *New York Times* online, June 20, 2012, www.nytimes.com/2012/06/21/business/more-consumers-choosing-reusable-glass-bottles.html?_r=0; "Libig G Glass Bottle," Design by OMC², www.omcdesign.com/?design=1635&type=Glass+Bottle; Siegle, Lucy, "Are Plastic Jars Worse for the Environment?" *The Guardian* online, May 12, 2013, www.theguardian.com/environment/2013/may/12/are-plastic-jars-better-than-glass

18 Himelstein, Walt, "Pure Growth," January 3, 2013, http://pureglassbottle.com/; Strom, Stephanie, "Wary of Plastic, and Waste, Some Consumers Turn to Glass."

11

Services

D ESIGN isn't just about objects. Events and processes can be designed as well, and how we design them can have an even bigger environmental impact than how we design our objects. For example, a building's operation consumes more than ten times as much energy as its construction. The flow of materials through the building during its lifetime—things like cleaning supplies, light bulbs, and water—are of critical importance too. Reducing the amount of plastic and petroleum we use in our buildings and products is good, but we can't overlook the great potential of the choices we make in the services we provide—how a building is maintained, for instance. Other services like healthcare, tourism, and entertainment are a largely untapped opportunity to reduce our use of petroleum.

Jack Johnson: Making Little Changes

G ROWING up in Hawaii, singer-songwriter Jack Johnson witnessed firsthand the growing heaps of plastic washing up on the island's beautiful beaches. "The Hawaiian Islands are like a filter for floating debris in the Pacific," he said. "The east side is just a wall of plastic bottles and bags and junk." Not content to simply lament his native state's growing plastic pollution problem, Johnson has become the frontman for the fight against it. His 2008 and 2010 tours were not only not-for-profit, with 100 percent of profits going to charity, they were models for plastic-free living. Hydration stations provided concertgoers filtered tap water without plastic bottles, recycling stations accepted plastic that fans brought with them, and tour trucks, buses, and on-site generators ran on biodiesel. His efforts to reduce plastic on tour saved over 55,000 single-use water bottles, diverted 460 tons of waste from landfills, and saved over 200,000 pounds of carbon dioxide.

Johnson carries the same attitude into the studio. His fifth album, *To the Sea*, was recorded in early 2010 at a solar-powered studio. Debuting at number one and ultimately selling over a million copies, the CD was printed on 100 percent recycled Forest Stewardship Council (FSC)-certified paper and was the first to use a 100 percent recycled plastic tray. And it seems Johnson won't rest until all the plastic is purged from his releases. Subsequent CDs have been packaged in Ecopac 100 percent recycled paper foam cases that can be recycled like ordinary paper. He has even challenged his distributor to develop biodegradable corn-based shrink wraps and soy-based inks.

Figure 11.1 Jack Johnson
Jack Johnson saved 55,000 plastic water bottles, 460 tons of waste from landfills, and over 200,000 pounds of carbon dioxide through a variety of strategies on his 2008 and 2010 tours. Image courtesy of Brushfire Records.

He's also conscious of plastic waste in his personal life, saying he feels embarrassed if he leaves a store with a plastic water bottle in one hand and a single-use bag in the other. But he also sees his efforts and the efforts of others like him paying off. "Right now a lot of people are thinking about the little changes they can make—there's a subtle shift happening in our social consciousness."[1]

Near Field Communication: Reading the Future

IF you ask digital artist Anthony Antonellis to show you his artwork, he'll extend his hand out, not to shake, but for you to swipe you smartphone over. Doing so will automatically pull up an animated image on your screen. It works thanks to a microchip implanted in Antonellis's hand

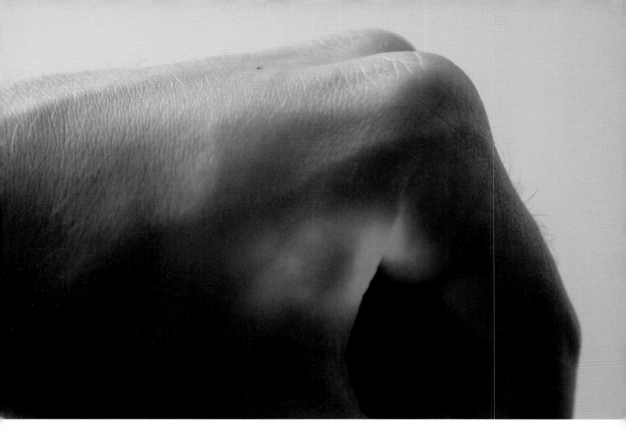

Figure 11.2 Anthony Antonellis Implant
The microchip implanted in artist Anthony Antonellis's hand activates
software in compatible smartphones, delivering his latest artwork to its user.
Image courtesy of Anthony Antonellis.

that activates software in compatible smartphones. "The artwork will be rotated out to exhibit new artists and artworks on a regular basis," Antonellis said. Near field communication (NFC) implants are, to the surprise of many, an established technology. In fact, it was back in 2006 that an Ohio surveillance company made headlines by "chipping" some of its employees. Employees could only gain access to the company archives if a scanner recognized the microchip implanted under their skin. Today, chipping is common in pets, and even in newborn babies, to deter kidnappers.[2]

NFC technology can be applied anywhere, not only under our skin. The Google Wallet app, for instance, employs NFC to enable in-store purchases without cash or credit cards. And a technology that could eliminate credit cards could have a big impact on our plastic consumption. The average American carries eight credit and identity cards, adding up to over 2.5 billion in circulation today. Many more are in our landfills. But if near field communication continues to catch on, it may make credit cards obsolete in the near future. Unlike today's cards that need to be swiped through a machine, an NFC card uses a tiny radio frequency identification (RFID) transmitter to send data over a short distance to a reading device. Jason Whigham and Jose Mendoza envision how an NFC-enabled phone could work:

7:30 a.m. To board the train for his morning commute, Eric takes out his NFC-enabled phone and taps a reader, easily opening the turnstile.

7:32 a.m. Seeing a poster announcing a free concert that evening, he touches his phone to it. Details about the show are transferred to his phone.

8:15 a.m. Arriving at work, Eric touches his phone to the office gate to unlock it.

12:00 p.m. At lunch, a swipe of his phone transfers money from his credit card to pay for his meal.

1:00 p.m. At his afternoon meeting, participants exchange business cards by touching phones.

6:00 p.m. After work, Eric meets his wife for the concert. A touch of his phone opens the turnstile, reservations are confirmed, and they enjoy the show.

10:00 p.m. Arriving home, Eric realizes he left his phone on the train. But he's quickly able to deactivate its NFC services with a call from his wife's phone to his mobile service provider. Later, when his phone is returned, he's able to just as easily reactivate those services with another call.

While proponents suggest that NFC and RFID will make our transactions more secure, others aren't so sure. "The dark side of RFID is surreptitious access," said Bruce Schneier, a security expert with Counterpane Internet Security. "When RFID chips are embedded in your ID cards, your clothes, your possessions, you are effectively broadcasting who you are to anyone within range. The level of surveillance possible, not only by the government but by corporations and criminals as well, will be unprecedented."

Whether NFC will make transactions more or less secure, it appears likely to replace credit cards thanks to its ease of use; no more taking the card out of your purse or wallet and swiping it. In fact, it may mean no more interacting with cashiers at all. MasterCard has already introduced MasterPass, which allows customers to make purchases by simply tapping their smartphone against an in-store terminal.[3]

Notes

1   Frampton, Scott, "Local Hero: Singer Jack Johnson Is Making Rock 'N' Roll Go Green," *O. The Oprah Magazine*, June 2010, www.oprah.com/world/Singer-Songwriter-Jack-Johnsons-Eco-Friendly-Efforts#ixzz2HE3zD2Pz; "Asda CD Series to Be Sold in Recycled Foam Packaging," *PackagingNews*, June 22, 2007, www.packagingnews.co.uk/sectors/retailers/asda-cd-series-to-be-sold-in-recycled-foam-packaging/

2   Antonellis, Anthony, "Net Art Implant," www.anthonyantonellis.com/news-post/item/670-net-art-implant

3   NFC Forum, "NFC in Action," http://nfc-forum.org/what-is-nfc/nfc-in-action/; Whigham, Jason, and Mendoza, Jose, "Near-Field Communication Chip," November 20, 2013, https://prezi.com/kohwulgqmujz/near-field-communication-chip/; Sieberg, Daniel, "A Company Requires Employees to Have RFID Chip Implanted Under Skin," CNN, www.gvsu.edu/cms3/assets/2D085406-FC80-AE2E-7233BDF30DCE3642/

electronicmonitoringofemployees/employees_required_to_be_rfid_chipped.pdf; Kelly, Samantha Murphy, "Mobile Payments May Replace Cash, Credit Cards by 2020," *Mashable*, April 17, 2012, http://mashable.com/2012/04/17/mobile-payments-2020/; Gerdes, Geoffrey R. et al., "The 2007 Federal Reserve Payments Study," Report, Washington, DC, December 10, 2007, www.frbservices.org/files/communications/pdf/research/2007_payments_study.pdf

12

Sports and Recreation

PLASTIC is ubiquitous in sporting goods. Fishing rods and tennis racquets once made from wood are now made from plastic, as are high-end bike frames, bowling balls, and a multitude of other equipment. Plastic has replaced traditional materials because it's often stronger, lighter, and cheaper. But there are alternatives that combine traditional materials like metal, wood, and even cardboard with innovative design. The results are groundbreaking new products that can replace the environmental and health concerns of plastic with positive impacts while also achieving peak performance.

Grain Surfboards: Reinventing the Surfboard

SURFING is a bit of an environmental oxymoron. Its adherents are out to become "one with the wave" and spend their days immersed in nature. But the boards they ride are typically made from environmentally unfriendly polystyrene foam and fiberglass. Grain Surfboards is out to change that. Its founders, Mike LaVecchia and Brad Anderson, make surfboards from local woods, but with a high-tech twist. Their studio is equipped with computer numerical control (CNC) machines capable of cutting intricate framing struts like the ones used to make airplane wings. The CNC machines cut wood using LaVecchia and Anderson's computer-based 3D drawings as input. The system allows them to create hollow boards, reducing cost and weight, by veneering the engineered struts with local woods.

Whereas conventional boardmaking shops are filled with the toxic dust from carving polystyrene foam, Grain Surfboards' studio is filled with the smell of freshly milled cedar. Step outside their studio, and you find yourself in an unlikely surfer's paradise: York Beach, Maine.

"York is a great town; it's a beautiful place," said Mike LaVecchia. "Starting building surfboards here wasn't really a plan," he continued, "it just happened pretty naturally. I had probably built about three boards here when a local New England outdoor magazine published a little article about us, and that led to a story that the Associated Press put out that wound up being spread all over the world. The next day we had six board orders. And here we were working in my basement with zero tools."

"It was pretty fun," he added with a touch of both sarcasm and sincerity. "It was a disaster, almost," Brad Anderson chimed in as he recalled wondering how they were going to make six boards.

Figure 12.1 Grain CAD Drawing
Data from 3D computer-aided design (CAD) files are cut by CNC machines to make the internal frames of Grain surfboards. Image courtesy of Grain Surfboards.

I understand there are something like ten million surfers in the world. What can you tell me about the environmental impact of all the foam used to make their boards?

Mike: Most of the foams used to make surfboards are non-recyclable. And foam boards are almost, in a sense, designed to fail; surfers get them and after the first session in the water they expect them to show wear. So most surfboards are retired after just a few years. That's just what's expected—it's part of the consumer's picture that what they're going to have to do is buy a new surfboard every few years. We're trying to build ones that are much longer lasting—lifetime boards. We had a 13-year-old kid come in and build a ten-foot longboard and we were laughing about it because he's such a tiny little guy. And we asked him, "Why are you building the biggest board we have?" And he just looked at us and said, "Well, I'm going to have it for the rest of my life."

When you're working with foam, you're almost always wearing a respirator and using power planers and loud machines that throw a lot of dust all over the place or you're sanding, which also throws a lot of dust. But here one of the things that's so great about wood is that we can use hand tools like spokeshaves and draw knives. They're quiet, and you can be working away without creating dust and making loud noises.

Brad: It's such a pleasure to use those kinds of tools, with the sounds they make and the shavings coming off and the smell of the wood. It's meditative and pleasant. People get so addicted to it that sometimes in the classes they can't stop and will actually overcut into their wood. We have to warn them, "If you need to get a piece of wood and just stroke it then do that, but don't get carried away on your board."

Can you tell me more about the relationship between the traditional techniques of boatbuilding that you use and the more contemporary ones like CNC milling from designs created on the computer?

Figure 12.2 Dave Rastovich
Professional freesurfer Dave Rastovich puts the finishing touches on a Grain surfboard. Image courtesy of Grain Surfboards; photo by Nick LaVecchia.

Brad: The whole thing is kind of a strange amalgam of old and new. Obviously, a thousand years ago surfboards were all wood and all handmade. Then after World War II they started using these "advanced" materials that were all petroleum- and chemical-based and using power tools to shape them. Today a lot of surfboards are what they call pop-out surfboards that are barely touched because they're cut out by machine. So the traditional surfboard industry has moved from handcraft to almost total mechanization. We embrace technology in designing on the computer, which allows us to be very deliberate about it and create a design that we can replicate every time. Then once it comes out of the computer it goes to a guy who cuts the frames out for us with a CNC machine. So they're a very precise shape, a shape that can be replicated not only by our own builders but also by kit builders or people who take our classes. Then it's all handwork from there. You could probably say that it's more of a handmade surfboard than almost any board in the world. It's something we're very pleased about, that we're able to put advanced materials technology and advanced computer design technology together with this very traditional, almost spiritual act of building a board, trimming it, feeling it, and making sure it's perfect on the outside.

I understand you're committed to using local woods in your boards, even when you give classes in distant places.

Mike: The use of local materials is definitely something that, almost from day one, has been a really high priority for us. In fact, the whole way we design our boards was designed around Northern White Cedar, which grows here in Maine.

Brad: We also make an effort to use found or recycled wood. We got a call one time from somebody in Massachusetts who said, "I have a pile of California Redwood from an old fence, and you guys are welcome to come down and get it." We picked it up and used it for two years in all our details. It was great for us because California Redwood is a traditional surfboard building wood. We had another instance where we were in Hawaii and met a luthier who was making very high-end ukuleles out of a Hawaiian wood called koa, which is a very traditional Hawaiian wood for surfboard building. He gave us a couple boxes of scraps that we were able to use to make details for over a year. Being able to use waste stream woods like that is great for us, especially when it has some kind of homage to surfboard history.

A lot of sustainable products are expensive, but you've come up with a system of kits and workshops to help make yours more affordable.

Brad: Some people think it's an idiotic business model—developing this intricate way of building a surfboard and then going out and showing everybody how to do it. But our motivation when we began Grain Surfboards was to build our own boards, and that's kind of at the root of the kits and classes. To not give other people the tools and capability to build their own surfboards and take them out on the water would be selfish, I think.

Mike: Most of the classes we do are seven days, and everybody comes in and basically starts from scratch. But all of our boards are designed in the computer, so people aren't coming in and coming up with their own shapes; they're taking one of ours, and we've got 20 different ones for them to choose from. And we give them the internal structural frame, just like on a boat, that's already cut out for them so they're taking that frame and assembling a board around it. Then they build a board and take it home with them. It's a good way to build a community and offer experience to people.[1]

Cardboard Bike: Thinking Outside the Box

CARS can only be so green. They require an engine that, even if it runs on electricity or biofuel, comes with a hefty carbon footprint. But a bike requires no petroleum and produces no carbon emissions. In fact, it's the most efficient machine ever created, getting the equivalent of 3,000 miles per gallon if you convert its rider's exertion to calories. The most high-tech models can reach speeds in excess of 150 mph and are made from plastic composites like carbon fiber. But to create an inexpensive, efficient bike for everyday use, Israeli engineer Izhar Gafni turned to a surprisingly ordinary alternative: cardboard.

Figure 12.3 Cardboard Bike
Strong, affordable, and resistant to fire and water, the Cardboard
Bike from Cardboard Technologies weighs just 27 pounds. Image
courtesy of Cardboard Technologies.

   Challenged by engineers who told him an affordable cardboard bike was "impossible,"
Gafni spent three years refining his. "I almost felt like the Wright Brothers going into unknown
territory," he said, alluding to the pair of bike builders better known for another invention.

His invention is made primarily from recycled cardboard. And while it can support riders up to 300 pounds, it weighs just 27 pounds. That's in part because you won't find any metal on this bike. Its spokes, rims, and frame are made from cardboard, and its puncture-proof wheels are made from used auto tires. The cardboard itself is a far cry from reused shipping boxes. It's treated with an organic compound to make it strong, as well as fire- and water-resistant. With a recent Invention Award from *Popular Science* providing momentum, Gafni has teamed with CEO Nimrod Elmish to create Cardboard Technologies, with plans to roll the bike onto the market in 2016.[2]

Notes

1   Author interview.
2   Choi, Charles, "2013 Invention Awards: Cardboard Bike," *Popular Science* online, June 7, 2013, http://www.popsci.com/technology/article/2013-04/transportation-cardboard-bike

13

Buildings and Building Materials

CONSTRUCTION accounts for one-quarter of the raw materials removed from the Earth. Oil accounts for a large percentage of that, and much of that oil goes to make plastic. But when it comes to architecture, alternatives to plastic abound. Wood is the most widely used material on Earth by volume, and concrete is the most widely used by weight. But plastic's use in non-structural materials like plumbing, insulation, and wiring make building its second most common use after packaging. Wiring is one area where we're not likely to see alternatives to plastic. Plumbing and insulation, however, are two areas where alternatives are being eagerly investigated because of concerns about the plastics currently used in them.

Most drainpipes, and many water supply lines, are made from polyvinyl chloride (PVC). It's cheap, durable, and easy to cut and glue. But it has also come under fire recently for health reasons. Specifically, the phthalates used to make flexible PVC have been cited as bronchial irritants and potential asthma triggers. The authors of a study published in *Environmental Science and Pollution Research International* found that leachates from all the plasticized PVC products they tested were toxic. And when researchers put five San Francisco families on a three-day diet of food that hadn't been in contact with plastic, they found that the participants' levels of bisphenol A (BPA) dropped by two-thirds. PVC production is also the world's largest consumer of chlorine gas, using about 16 million tons of chlorine per year worldwide. The chlorine embodied in PVC pipe can also be released as toxic hydrogen chloride gas if the pipe should catch fire.[1]

ArboSkin: Building with Bioplastic

THE snake-like structure of the ArboSkin pavilion at the University of Stuttgart not only combines skin and structure in a single, innovative system, it's also biodegradable. The building's façade, developed by students and professors at the university's Institute of Building Structures and Structural Design (ITKE), consists of 388 three-dimensionally triangulated panels made from a specially developed bioplastic.

"The goal of the project," the university declared in a press release, "was to develop a maximally sustainable yet durable building material while keeping petroleum-based components and additives to a minimum." To accomplish that goal, they turned to the German firm, Tenarco, which combined different biopolymers such as lignin, a wood pulping byproduct, with natural reinforcing fibers. The resulting "Arboblend", as Tenarco called it, was then extruded into sheets

Figure 13.1 ArboSkin Building
The ArboSkin pavilion at the University of Stuttgart is made from
388 biodegradable bioplastic panels. Image courtesy of University
of Stuttgart Institute of Building Structures and Structural Design.

that were in turn formed into the triangular panels that make up the façade. Waste from the process was even recycled back into new panels.

"Thermoforming sheets of bio-based plastics can be a resource-efficient alternative in the future," explained professors and project leaders Carmen Köhler, Manfred R. Hammer, and Thiemo Fildhuth. "We linked the moldability of thermoplastics with the environmental benefits of materials made from over 90% renewable resources."[2]

House of Tree: Rising above the Ordinary

"It feels like it's always been there," said designer Scott Constable of his House of Tree, a unique and exquisitely crafted cabin perched 20 feet off the ground among the redwoods of Northern California. Its timeless beauty is a direct result of Constable's design philosophy, which integrates materials, site, and sustainability. In House of Tree you'll find no plastics, very few inorganic

Figure 13.2 House of Tree

The plastic-free House of Tree by Wowhaus uses materials from the local bioregion to create an arboreal oasis in Northern California. Image courtesy of Wowhaus.

materials, and no electricity. You'll also find extensive use of local materials and an implacable attention to craft and detail. The focus on materials and site is consistent with the rich portfolio of work Constable has built up across the country together with his wife, Ene Osteraas-Constable.

What aspects of your design helped you achieve the feeling that House of Tree has "always been there"?

Having a building feel like it has emerged from the site, or is somehow obviated by the site's conditions, is always a goal for me, especially in a natural setting like House of Tree.

What role did the materials you chose play in achieving it?

Materiality is a big part of this—using materials that are from within the bioregion leads to a visual integration with a site, and how these materials are ordered and arranged can lead to a functional integration with the site's conditions—weather, seasonal variation, light, moisture, etcetera.

What about the siting and integration with the site?

Approached this way, buildings can be highly site-specific, even site-generated to some degree, and their "look" is as much a result of cumulative local knowledge about materials and the forces that affect them as it is about a client's functional requirements. You might say that each bioregion suggests a specific building style.

What role do materials play in your concept of "the luxury of the essential"?

For the client, or for anyone who experiences this building, knowing that many of the materials grew where the building stands creates a feeling of connectedness with the place. This is reinforced by the natural warmth of wood, both visually and to the touch, and to its changing character over time, gaining patina and polish where worn. Darks get darker and lights get brighter with age and use, bringing out a natural beauty that is unique to that particular material and how one interacts with it. It's a haptic experience, like taking a bath, engaging all of the senses.

What were some of the other criteria for the materials you chose?

How a material is maintained and responds to maintenance is a major consideration for how I assess a material. I aim for a situation where maintenance equals improvement. I also try to design things to be easily repaired or adapted by people who use them. I give a lot of thought to the life cycle of a material when I consider how to use it—how readily available a material is should it need to be replaced, and how does the material's natural life cycle resonate with how it is being used in a structure.[3]

Figure 13.3 Shangri La Botanical Garden and Nature Center
Not only are the walkways at Shangri La Botanical Garden and Nature Center in Orange, Texas half recycled wood, the other half is recycled plastic, saving the equivalent of 3.6 million plastic bags from the landfill. Photo by Hester + Hardaway Photographers.

Shangri La Botanical Garden and Nature Centers: Focus on Nature

THE Shangri La Botanical Garden and Nature Center in Orange, Texas is a certified LEED (Leadership in Energy and Environmental Design) Platinum project, the highest level awarded by the U.S. Green Building Council. As building complexes of its size go, it is surprisingly plastic-free. The designers, Lake|Flato Architects, incorporated a variety of post-petroleum design features to make this Shangri La as sustainable as possible, including:

- Metal cisterns collect rainwater to irrigate the courtyard and flush the toilets.
- Metal roofing reflects heat, cutting energy usage by more than half.
- Floor coverings are made from renewable materials such as corn.
- Cypress trees felled by Hurricane Rita were milled on site to create benches, a boardwalk, and a rustic folly.
- Where plastic is used in walkways, it is made from 50 percent recycled plastic and 50 percent recycled wood. The amount of plastic recycled is equivalent to 1.1 million milk jugs or 3.6 million plastic bags.
- Soybean-based insulation is used in the walls and ceilings throughout the buildings.
- Bricks were salvaged from an old warehouse built in Arkansas in 1910.

I asked former director, now retired, Mike Hoke:

How does the sustainable aspect of the buildings (low or zero energy, natural materials) reinforce Shangri La's environmental education mission of "mentoring children of all ages to be kind to their world"?

We at Shangri La, from the beginning, knew it wasn't good enough just to preach sustainability. We wanted to practice what we preached and, more importantly, preach what we practice. All of this is wrapped in the overall mission of Shangri La, meaning that we also teach what we preach to more than 30,000 children and 20,000 adults every year. The word mentoring has a component involved in modeling. Good mentors must model behaviors, so this ties back to everything we do at Shangri La.

What do you find appealing, and what do you find challenging, about the buildings in your role as Director of Shangri La?

When you try to be on the cutting edge as we did back in 2005, you find out some things have inherent problems. For instance, if you are going to emphasize recycling, you must have a source to deliver your materials. There are no recycling centers within 35 miles of Orange. To solve this problem, I had to convince Waste Management Corporation to place a recycling center at Shangri La. Balancing the necessity of having a strong horticulture program with being sustainable is also a problem, since most horticulture students in the past weren't taught to develop sustainable gardens. It has been a learning curve for that department but they have adapted very well. Operating a garden using organic fertilizers and without using pesticides adds additional problems that at times we were not able to solve.

Are some of the structures plastic-free? If so, can you tell me how they're different? Does their plastic-free aspect affect maintenance, their relationship to the gardens and environment, or their "feeling"?

From the beginning we realized that recycling plastic is an excellent way to remove plastics from the waste-stream. We used 1.1 million milk jugs to make our more than one mile of boardwalk and outpost buildings. All of our plastic furniture is made from recycled plastic. In areas where plastic was not practical, we used recycled stainless steel and recycled aluminum. Since Shangri La had a lot of historical artifacts we also took advantage of these materials to make signage and other informative structures.[4]

UltraTouch Denim Insulation

BUILDING insulation is critical in our effort to reduce CO_2 emissions and climate change. In fact, it's the most cost-effective means of reducing CO_2 emissions available to us. In other words, a dollar spent on insulation will reduce CO_2 emissions more than a dollar spent on anything else. And today much of our insulation is plastic. Buildings are wrapped in it to reduce

Figure 13.4 UltraTouch Denim Insulation

UltraTouch Denim Insulation is made from used blue jeans, and scraps from
its manufacturing are cycled back into the raw material supply, resulting in
a "virtually zero waste process." Image courtesy of Bonded Logic Inc.

air infiltration and covered in rigid insulation most often made from polystyrene. But styrene is a
good example of why so many people are working to find alternatives to plastic in buildings. The
EPA has identified styrene as a possible carcinogen, and a study ranking four polymers for life
cycle environmental impact found polystyrene worst in every category.

But a Chandler, Arizona company has created an alternative that's a perfect fit. Blue jean
sales in the U.S. top 450 million per year, and the makers of UltraTouch building insulation
have found a way to put used ones to good use saving energy. "People have a lot of affection for
America's favorite fabric," said David Church, General Manager of Bonded Logic, UltraTouch's
parent company, "and UltraTouch gives those well loved jeans a second life and keeps them out
of the landfill."

Even the scraps from the insulation's manufacturing are reintroduced into the raw material
supply creating a "virtually zero waste process." And unlike many other insulation products,
UltraTouch contains no chemical irritants or harmful airborne particulates and requires no
carcinogenic warning labels. It also avoids the fire-retardant hexabromocyclododecane (HBCD),
a chemical used in many polystyrene insulation boards. The EPA says HBCD "presents potential
human health concerns based on animal test results indicating potential reproductive, developmental and neurological effects." Instead, UltraTouch is treated with borate, a material less toxic
than table salt.[5]

Figure 13.5 Ready for Recycling
Blue jean sales in the U.S. alone top 450 million per year, making
them a resource that will never wear out. Photo by Vladimir Dimitroff.

Hy-Fi Tower: A Building that Grows Itself

WHEN David Benjamin, principal architect at The Living, visited the facilities of Ecovative in Green Island, New York, he knew he wanted to use their Mushroom Materials (see Chapter 10) in his next building. Benjamin was designing the installation known as Hy-Fi Tower for New York's Museum of Modern Art (MoMA) as part of their Young Architects Program. As he examined row after row of mycelium, the growth stage of fungus that grows to become packaging, building materials, and other products at Ecovative, founders Eben Bayer and Gavin McIntyre explained their new "Grow It Yourself" program. The program allows designers, artists, educators, and other innovators to grow their own creations with Mushroom Materials, and Benjamin could imagine them forming the building blocks of the tower that would occupy

Figure 13.6 Hy-Fi Tower
The building blocks of the Hy-Fi Tower installation at New York's
Museum of Modern Art were grown from Ecovative's Mushroom
Material. Image courtesy of Ecovative Design; photo by Susan Shafer.

the courtyard of MoMA's PS1 complex. "One of the things that we're experimenting with in the project," Benjamin explained, "is a kind of local economy of materials."

"Everything from the project, in its entire life cycle, comes from within a 150 mile radius," he told The Creators Project. "Then at the end of the lifespan of the temporary structure, we're going to compost it, again, right here in New York City, and then return that raw material to local community gardens and tree planting."

It took three months to pile the project's 10,000 mycelium bricks to its full 40-foot height. And as Hy-Fi Tower rose up in the courtyard, MoMA apparently grew to like it too, declaring it the winner of their 2014 Young Architects Program.[6,7]

Microhouse, Big Impact

DID your home come with instructional videos, a complete materials list, and an online owner's instruction manual? Was it built in less than two weeks? These are just a few of the achievements of the Microhouse, a natural construction building made from compressed earth blocks. The house is the first architectural project by Open Source Ecology (OSE), a global network of engineers, farmers, and supporters building the Global Village Construction Set (GVCS). The GVCS is the vision of OSE founder and Executive Director, Marcin Jakubowski. Since starting in 2003, Jakubowski and his collaborators have completed more than a dozen different "industrial machines," including tractors, welders, and bioplastics extruders.

But you can't buy these machines in any store. Instead, you can build them yourself, using a continuously evolving set of free, online instructions from OSE. The Global Village Construction Set, however, is much more than an online database. It has brought together a fast-growing global community of people committed to breaking the chains of conventional production and commerce to create a new way of making everything.

Figure 13.7 Microhouse Complete
Not only is the Microhouse at Open Source Ecology's Factor e Farm in Missouri a showcase of natural construction building materials and technologies, its complete design and construction plans are available free of charge through OSE. Image courtesy of Chris Reinhart and Open Source Ecology.

Chris Reinhart is one of those people. With many years of experience designing and building homes from compressed earth blocks and other natural materials, he was the perfect choice to lead OSE's first foray into architecture. In 2013, he led the design development and then, in just two weeks, led the construction of the Microhouse using many of the industrial machines made with the GVCS and the help of a small cadre of volunteers. The project was so successful that more Microhouses are now in development, and Reinhart has become OSE's architectural creative director and construction manager. In a lecture at Ball State University immediately following the completion of the first Microhouse, Reinhart, founder and lead designer at Open Source House Studio, explained the project and the ideas behind it:

> The goals for the Microhouse were the same as for Open Source's other projects—that it be modular, incorporate parallel processing during construction, and design for tolerancing, making it easier for people of low skill to build. Design for tolerancing allows as many people as possible to do their own thing. The house is designed for a couple, so you could build the first four-meter by four-meter module for two people. Then it could grow as the needs, means or size of the family grows. The idea was to create a building that was natural in the sense that it used compressed earth block, passive solar design, and natural ventilation. But it was also to make something that was finished to a level that the average American can appreciate. I've worked on lots of earthen buildings that are beautiful but that you sort of have to be a special person to appreciate; some people would probably call them "hippie huts." We didn't want this to be a hippie hut; we wanted it to have the same level of finish as your typical middle class house.

Figure 13.8 Microhouse Construction
Chris Reinhart (left), founder and lead designer at Open Source House Studio, works with volunteers to assemble a compressed earth block wall on the Microhouse. Image courtesy of Chris Reinhart and Open Source Ecology.

It's all open source, so everything is on the web for people to access and use for themselves; there's no intellectual property involved. The entire design is on a wiki so anyone can access it. Because everything Open Source does is open source and they want people to learn from it, everything we did was documented rigorously. We took time-lapse photos of the construction and lots of still photos as well.

OSE does work all over the world—they're collaborators in lots of places. One thing they imagine doing is having their kit of parts that could be put inside a shipping container and shipped somewhere with the instruction manuals and maybe a teacher who could teach people how to assemble the tractor and build the brick press. Then, once they've built one house, they could teach each other.[8]

A New Twist on Green Roofing: Algae

FEW natural materials are as ubiquitous as algae, which spreads across the planet's waterways. Now it's spreading across another, unexpected surface—roofs. Algae is well recognized as a future energy source, particularly as a biofuel. But another, less recognized use is bitumen roofing. Because it's made from petroleum, conventional bitumen roofing contains large amounts of energy and embodied CO_2.

Now two Dutch companies—Icopal and Algaecom—have teamed with Hanze University to combine algae and bitumen roofing in a very unique way. At the Icopal roofing recycling plant in Groningen, the Netherlands, heat and CO_2 produced in the recycling process feed algae, which becomes raw material for new roofing material. In their pilot project, the team grew algae in giant 12-meter-long polymer sacks. Feeding off heat and CO_2 produced in the recycling process, the algae grew quickly, doubling their volume every two days. Oil from the algae was then harvested to make new roofing.

"Nowhere else in the world," according to Algaecom managing partner, Bert Knol, "is a recycling plant using harvested algae mass in roofing." Herman Schutte, Icopal's CEO, added, "It also plays a role in the impending shortage of bitumen. Oil companies which supply bitumen are increasingly opting for cracking to convert it into fuel." Using algae as the source material for roofing has the potential to free the industry from its dependence on oil, while at the same time converting waste energy, as well as reducing CO_2 emissions and energy use. Waste could also be reduced considerably, since most bitumen roofing ends up in the landfill. The savings could be considerable, since the U.S. alone manufactures and disposes of more than ten million tons of asphalt shingles per year.[9]

Notes

1   Lee, H.S., Yap, J., Wang, Y.T., Lee, C.S., Tan, K.T., and Poh, S.C., "Occupational Asthma Due to Unheated Polyvinylchloride Resin Dust," *British Journal of Industrial Medicine*, Volume 46, Issue 11, November 1989, 820–822, www.ncbi.nlm.nih.gov/pmc/articles/PMC1009875/; Lithner, D., Nordensvan, I., and Dave, G., "Comparative Acute Toxicity of Leachates from Plastic Products Made of Polypropylene, Polyethylene, PVC, Acrylonitrile-butadiene-styrene, and Epoxy to Daphnia Magna," *Environmental Science and Pollution Research International*, Volume 19, Issue 5, June 2012, 1763–1772, www.ncbi.nlm.nih.gov/pubmed/22183785; Rudel, R., Gray, J., Engel, C., Rawsthorne, T., Dodson, R., Ackerman, J., et al., "Food Packaging and Bisphenol A and Bis(2-Ethyhexyl) Phthalate Exposure: Findings from a Dietary Intervention," *Environmental Health Perspectives*, Volume 119, 2011, 914–920, http://ehp.niehs.nih.gov/1003170/

2   Institute for Building Construction and Structural Design, University of Stuttgart, "ArboSkin: Durable and Recyclable Bioplastics Facade Mock-Up," February 10, 2013, www.itke.uni-stuttgart.de/download.php?id=690

3   Author interview.

4   Author interview. "Green Design," Shangri La Botanical Gardens & Nature Center, http://starkculturalvenues. org/shangrilagardens/about/green-design

5   U.S. Environmental Protection Agency, "(Styrene) Fact Sheet: Support Document," December 1994, www.epa. gov/chemfact/styre-sd.pdf; Azapagic, Adisa, Emsley, Alan, and Hamerton, Ian, *Polymers: The Environment and Sustainable Development*, Hoboken, NJ, John Wiley, 2003, 138; "In 2009, Ingeo Plastic Made from Plants Achieves a New Eco Plateau Reducing CO2 Emissions by 35%," *NatureWorks*, October 9, 2009, www.nature-worksllc.com/News-and-Events/Press-Releases/2009/02-10-09-Ingeo-EcoProfile

6   "Hy-Fi: The Living's Local, Sustainable, 10,000 Brick Mushroom Tower at MoMA PS1," June 30, 2014, http://thecre-atorsproject.vice.com/blog/hy-fi-the-livings-local-sustainable-10000-brick-mushroom-tower-at-moma-ps1

7   "Your Product Ideas Come to Life with Ecovative's 'Grow It Yourself' Mushroom Materials," *Ecovative News*, July 22, 2014, www.ecovativedesign.com/news/?guid=8F0216CF2A036835311529B730C6AFE01A9E7E895C8 91E4AE5CCF579F128BF4B69270C5A0266ACB72F895D7AFE3EBEEF

8   "The Open Source Initiative," http://opensource.org/; Reinhart, Christopher, "Presentation at Ball State Alumni Symposium 2013," Ball State University, College of Architecture and Planning, Muncie, Indiana, October 25, 2013.

9   "Algae Tested for Use in Roofing Tiles," *Algae Industry Magazine* online, November 18, 2013, www.algaeindus-trymagazine.com/algae-tested-use-roofing-tiles/

14

Furnishings and Housewares

Housewares and home furnishings are of particular concern when it comes to plastic content because we are in constant contact with them. Toxic particles can enter our bodies through our skin after contact with furniture and other household surfaces, and we can ingest them by way of plastic food containers. But because furnishings and housewares are the domain of industrial designers worldwide, there is no shortage of brainpower being focused on finding alternatives to plastic. Whether working with traditional materials like wood or experimenting with new entrants into the arena (would you believe, chicken feathers?) post-petroleum designers are creating some competition for the plastic that fills our homes.

Cortiça Chaise Lounge: Inspiring Innovation, Preserving Tradition

"I think that we're all getting a little tired of shiny plastic," said New York furniture designer, Daniel Michalik, "and we're trying to retreat a little bit back to natural materials, and I think cork is ideal for that." But it's clear that he really sees his work with cork as more of an advance than a retreat.

"What I find so inspiring about this material," he continued, "is that I see it as a jumping off point. It's not just a material to design interesting objects, which it is, but it's also a model for a different way of thinking of how we use natural materials. And it's got huge potential for design, for furnishings, for objects, for interiors, for architecture; it's got just potential everywhere."

Why cork? "Cork is a sustainable material, regenerating every nine years for harvest. The Portuguese regions of cork production hold centuries-old farming and manufacturing traditions that can teach us how objects can be made more responsibly. The cork objects I design and make reflect a love for the origin and context of a material, and it has led to exciting collaborations with adherent cultures and industries."

"My studio in New York City," he added, "is a laboratory dedicated to unlocking new potentials for cork and other materials. In this space we explore the deepest potentials of cork as an unusual natural material, allowing it to perform in new ways, and as no other material can."

For Michalik, his Cortiça Chaise Lounge and other works in cork are the result of a vision combining innovative design with craft and natural materials. "Manufacturing," he said, "has new models that are being engaged now, using different kinds of materials and different kinds of manufacturing techniques that are healthier than what we've known before. And this work that I've done with cork is a great starting point."[1]

Figure 14.1 Cortiça Chaise Lounge
Cork is extremely renewable, regenerating itself every nine
years; in the hands of New York designer Daniel Michalik, it's
also extremely beautiful. Image courtesy of Daniel Michalik.

Zeer Pot: Electricity-Free Refrigeration

Every year, nearly 150,000 tons of polyurethane foam are used to insulate appliances. But Nigerian teacher Mohammed Bah Abba has come up with a low-tech, hi-innovation alternative. The zeer pot is a refrigerator made of clay. Musa Elkheir, Knowledge and Information Officer at the U.K.'s Intermediate Technology Development Group (ITDG), tells the story of this affordable appliance that's easily crafted from local materials:

> Hawa Osman is a farmer in Darfur, Sudan. She grows tomatoes, okra, carrots, and rocket lettuce, and also has a small orchard of guava trees. In the hot weather of Darfur, Hawa used to lose half of the crops she hoped to sell each day in the market of Al Fashir, the capital city of North Darfur, because of inadequate storage

Figure 14.2 Zeer Pot
The zeer pot, designed by Nigerian teacher Mohammed Bah
Abba, can keep produce that would typically rot in just 2 days
fresh for 20. Image courtesy of Rolex Awards for Enterprise.

facilities—and no electricity or refrigerator—in her small canteen, the shed made out
of wood and palm leaves in which she displays her products to clients.

But these days she is selling fresher produce and making a bigger profit. This is because of an
ingenious device—the zeer pot—that was invented by a Nigerian teacher, Mohammed Bah Abba,
and introduced to Darfur last year. The zeer is a large pot inside which fits another smaller pot
with a clay lid. The space between the two pots is filled with sand, creating an insulating layer
around the inner pot. The sand is then kept damp by adding water at regular intervals—generally
twice a day—reducing the temperature within the inner pot.

Each zeer can contain 12 kilograms of vegetables, and costs less than two dollars to
produce. Experiments assessing its ability to extend shelf life show that tomatoes and guavas can

Figure 14.3 Zeer Pot Construction
The $2 zeer pot uses locally available materials and craft
expertise to keep costs down. Image courtesy of Rolex Awards
for Enterprise.

be kept for 20 days, compared to just 2 without. Even rocket, which usually lasts only a day before wilting, can be kept for five days.

Amina Abas, who sells zeers in the Al Fashir marketplace, says she has found a high demand for the pot, as almost every family accommodates a family of refugees from the fighting in the region. "As a result, there is a need for zeer for keeping water and vegetables and preserving fruit to meet the needs not only of the host family, but also of the refugee family," she says. "It is really great."

Before getting her zeer, Hawa used to have to carry any unsold crops home each day. During the six-hour walk, the vegetables would end up rotting because of the heat. "This technology has helped me gain a suitable income to meet my family's daily needs. I see it as the most positive turning point in my life, in that it has allowed me to become self-sufficient."

The zeer is the brainchild of teacher Mohammed Bah Abba. Bah Abba passed his idea to the ITDG, which, with the assistance of researchers at the University of Al Fashir, carried out experiments to measure its value in maintaining nutrient content and extending the shelf life of vegetables. As a result, the Women's Association for Earthenware Manufacturing in Darfur, with the support of ITDG, is now producing and selling zeers for food preservation in the Al Fashir area.

Iman Mohamed Ibrahim of ITDG says women using the zeer to preserve their vegetables in the market can make an additional 25 to 30 percent profit on their income.[2]

Hemp Chair: Synergy of Old and New

HEMP is no longer a novelty material, but a mainstream alternative to plastic. It is renewable, strong, light, and biodegradable. And in the hands of German designer Werner Aisslinger, it takes on a new twist based on the latest technologies from auto manufacturing. Compression molding is already used to make car parts from both petroleum-based and plant-based plastics, and, working in his Berlin studio, Aisslinger has come up with a method of compression molding using a new natural fiber composite made from 70 percent natural hemp. The hemp fibers are bound together by Arcodur, a water-based acrylic resin developed by the chemical company, BASF. Arcodur releases no organic substances such as phenol or formaldehyde during the c linking process, and the only byproduct of the curing procedure is water. The res paper-thin chair that is strong and stackable.

"Design history," said Aisslinger, "is driven by new technologies a For us designers, the advent of these technologies has always been the s objects and typologies in design." But it is technology in the service of grow

focused consumer interest, he said. "Today's consumers are striving towards a well-balanced and
healthy lifestyle that is in harmony with the environment. They want innovative products such
as electric scooters and hybrid cars as well as new, environmentally compatible, light and durable
materials."[3]

Conversation Table Speaks Volumes

POST-PETROLEUM design often incorporates simple materials innovatively reimagined. New
processes and technologies can give new life to traditional, renewable materials. Cardboard is
a perfect example; while the humble cardboard box is its most familiar application, designer Leo
Kempf has reinvented it in dynamic 3D form. His Conversation Table plays on an iconic form to
create a playful piece with an environmentally sound message. Made primarily from corrugated
cardboard, Kempf's furniture takes a material that typically gets thrown out or, at best, recycled,
and turns it into a work of art. And, the designer points out, "The iconic 'speech bubble' shape
makes this unique table a great conversation piece."[4]

Figure 14.5 Conversation Table
Cardboard finds artistic expression in
the Conversation Table by Leo Kempf.
Image courtesy of Leo Kempf.

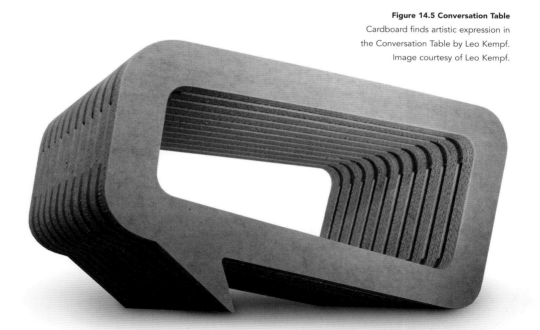

Meredith Vase: Elegant Twist on Ancient Tradition

Lᴵᴷᴇ cardboard, glass is an ordinary material that can become extraordinary in the hands of a talented designer. While glass is heavier than plastic (meaning more CO_2 emissions from transport), it is recycled almost three times as often. And unlike most plastics, it can be recycled again and again. Glass is also non-toxic, so it won't leach toxins if it should end up in the landfill. But one characteristic it does share with plastic is fluidity. Glass can be molded into almost any shape, and the only limitation is the designer's imagination. In the Meredith Vase by Peter Patzak of Patzak Design, it morphs into a simple but elegant twist on an ancient tradition. Bold lines and swooping curves combine in a prismatic form that makes the most of the transparency, light, and color inherent in glass.[5]

Figure 14.6 Meredith Vase

Glass is recycled three times more often than plastic, but when it takes as elegant a form as the Meredith Vase by Patzak Design, you'll want to keep it around a long time. Image courtesy of Peter Patzak.

Alessi Strawbowl: Closer to Nature

Pᴇᴛʀᴏʟᴇᴜᴍ-ʙᴀsᴇᴅ design too often takes non-renewables from the Earth, uses them to make products with short lifespans, and sends them to the landfill. Nature, in contrast, uses waste as the raw material for new processes and new life. That's the idea

Figure 14.7 Alessi Strawbowl

Designed for Alessi by Italian designer Kristiina Lassus, the Strawbowl combines organic ingredients including straw, dried grass, lime, and potato starch. Image courtesy Kristiina Lassus.

behind the Strawbowl by Italian designer Kristiina Lassus. Designed for Alessi, it combines straw or dried grass with a binder of water, lime, and potato starch. The result is a bowl that's thin yet strong, aglow with the earth tones of its natural components.

We don't see very many housewares made from straw. What made you choose that material?

Actually, Alessi was approached by a Finnish company who had invested in this material and technology. They suggested it as a packaging material but Alessi asked me to think if it could be used for some object. I decided for a centerpiece that is beautiful empty but can be used also for bread, fruit, and nuts. I felt that a simple and primitive form would give best visibility for the beautiful texture and associate nicely to indigenous cultures, very closely living with nature and using hay and straw.

You use a wide variety of materials in your work, from steel to recycled wood. How do you decide which material is right for your projects?

I love to use natural materials that are biodegradable and that don't therefore accumulate in nature forever when their product life cycle comes to an end. I choose the material for my designs mostly according to the purposefulness or according to client request and technological possibilities. Sometimes it is the other way round, a beautiful material fascinates and inspires me to think of a product in which it could be best used.[6]

Chicken Feather Flower Pot: New Life for a Wasted Resource

Y ou would expect horticulture to be one of the greenest industries, since it deals with plants. But Mark Teffeau, Director of Research at the Horticultural Research Institute in Washington, D.C., sees a contradiction. "We're supposed to be a green industry," he says, "but we have a lot of plastic pots." A lot as in 500 million

Figure 14.8 Chicken Feather Flower Pot
Proving that ingenuity can make almost anything out of anything, the Chicken Feather Flower Pot by Walter Schmidt of the USDA's Environmental Microbial and Food Safety Laboratory offers a biodegradable alternative to the 500 million plastic flower pots used every year. Image courtesy of U.S. Department of Agriculture.

per year, according to *Gardening* magazine. Most are discarded after only one use to avoid cross-contamination between plant species, ending up in the landfill.

But now Walter Schmidt, a research chemist at the U.S. Department of Agriculture's (USDA) Environmental Microbial and Food Safety Laboratory, has come up with an unlikely alternative. He has been studying chicken feathers for 20 years, and finds them to be a perfect material for flowerpots. Feathers are made from keratin, the same material as fingernails, and are eight times stronger than wood. Sledgehammers and blenders can't break them down. But when ground with the proper equipment and combined with a naturally occurring polymer, the result is a fully functional, 100 percent biodegradable flowerpot.

Interviewed by NPR at his lab in Beltsville, Maryland, Schmidt mused, "If you figure there are two-and-a-half billion pounds of feathers produced each year, and if their value is comparable to polypropylene, which is like 66 cents a pound, that's about $2 billion worth of natural resources that are not being harvested."

Not content to sit in his lab making flowerpots, Schmidt imagines feathers could be used to make building materials, fishing equipment, fertilizer, and BB pellets. And while he has yet to commercialize his feather pots, the prospects are good. Consumer demand for alternatives to petroleum-based pots is up, and a study out of Texas A&M University found that consumers would pay up to 10 cents more for pots made from poultry feathers.[7]

Flexible Footstool

LIGHT and springy aren't the first words that come to mind when most of us think of wood furniture. But French designer Franck Fontana has added some spring to this naturally flexible Tabouret stool made of fine French oak. While the wood is extremely hard, the overall form is springy thanks to the S-shaped laminations designed by Fontana. His creation shows that traditional materials can be reinvented without always relying on new technologies.[8]

Figure 14.9 Tabouret Sketch
French designer Franck Fontana explored a wide range of possibilities to achieve the flexibility of his Tabouret stool. Image courtesy of Franck Fontana.

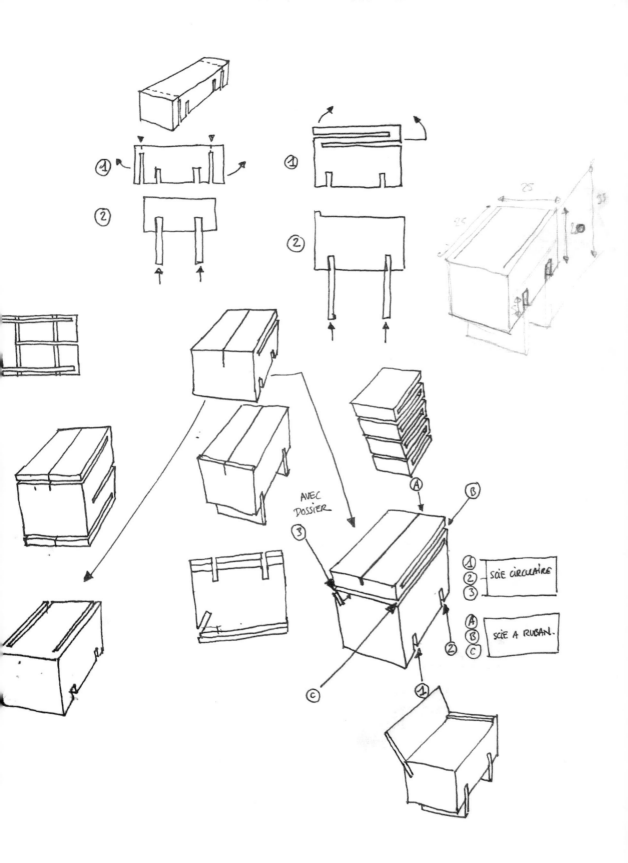

④

②

①

②

25
25
35

AVEC
DOSSIER

A

B

③

C

①

②

①	
②	SCIE CIRCULAIRE
③	

A	
B	SCIE A RUBAN.
C	

Figure 14.10 Tabouret Stool

Both wood's flexibility and its strength are optimized in the
Tabouret stool. Image courtesy of Franck Fontana.

Notes

1 Michalik, Daniel, "Cork Design," uploaded February 14, 2011, www.youtube.com/watch?v=0gmVxvGH_SY; Morgan, Helen, "DMFD's Amazing Curved Chaise Lounge Is Made from 100% Recycled Cork," inhabitat. com, February 21, 2012, http://inhabitat.com/recycled-corks-arranged-into-amazing-curved-chaise-lounge-by-dmfd/; "Daniel Michalik, Furniture Design," http://danielmichalik.com/about/

2 Elkheir, Musa, "Refrigeration, the African way," SciDev.Net, www.scidev.net/en/features/refrigeration-the-african-way.html

3 "Hemp Chair & Hemp House," Studio Aisslinger, 2012, www.aisslinger.de/index.php?option=com_project&view=detail&pid=121&Itemid=1; LaBarre, Suzanne, "High Chair: A Lounger Made of Hemp for Stylish Stoners," March 14, 2011, www.fastcodesign.com/1663409/high-chair-a-lounger-made-of-hemp-for-stylish-stoners

4 "Leo Kempf Conversation Table," November 16, 2010, www.leokempf.com/blog/?p=141#sthash.rCaYcuis.dpuf

5 "Patzak Design," www.patzak-design.com/

6 Author interview; www.kristiinalassus.com

7 Berman, Emily, "Building the Next Big Thing with Chicken Feathers?" January 11, 2013, http://wamu.org/programs/metro_connection/13/01/11/building_the_next_big_thing_with_chicken_feathers; Yue, Chengyan, Hall, C., Behe, B., Campbell, B., Dennis, J., and Lopez, R., "Investigating Consumer Preference for Biodegradable Containers," *Journal of Environmental Horticulture*, Volume 28, Issue 4, December 2010, 239–243, http://aggie-horticulture.tamu.edu/faculty/hall/publications/jeh_10-11.pdf

8 "Le Tabouret—Design: Franck Fontana," Design Pyrenees, www.designpyrenees.com/produits/tabouret.html; www.franckfontana.com/www/FranckFontana.html

– 15 –

Clothing

A LOT goes into our clothing before it reaches the racks at the department store. The textile industry uses over a million tons per year of chemical surfactants—chemicals used as detergents, foaming agents, and emulsifiers, 70 percent of which end up in wastewater. In addition, it takes over 250 pounds of water to produce a single pound of dyed and finished textile fabric. Most textile plants are classified as major sources of hazardous and toxic air emissions by the EPA, mainly because of nitrogen and sulfur oxide emissions from their boilers. "It is not uncommon to find tens and even hundreds of thousands of pounds of methyl ethyl ketone, methyl isobutyl ketone, toluene, xylene, and dimethyl formamide emitted from coating processes in a large facility," according to Brent Smith, a professor of textile chemistry at North Carolina State University. We even use chemicals to counteract the effects of other chemicals during textile production—things like defoamers and bath stabilizers.

The same chemicals, surfactants and coating processes can be used to process natural fabrics as well as synthetics. One-quarter of the insecticide produced in the world, for instance, is used in cotton farming. The most common fabric in the world, however, is not natural but synthetic. Polyester, specifically polyethylene terephthalate (PET), is the same material used to make plastic water bottles. But plastic water bottles are not the largest use of PET; twice as much is used to make textiles. With petroleum used as a feedstock, chemical additive and energy source, PET production consumes 70 million barrels of oil per year.

A study by the Stockholm Environment Institute determined that it takes nearly five times more energy per ton to produce polyester fabric than to cultivate and produce cotton. Yet only one-third of the oil needed to make polyester is feedstock; the rest is processing energy and petrochemicals. Carbon dioxide emissions tell a similar story. Cotton produces less than two-thirds of the CO_2 emissions associated with polyester production. From an environmental perspective, the primary difference between synthetics and natural fibers may be that synthetics use petroleum as a feedstock. "Production of polyester," concludes the Stockholm report, "even if the energy requirements are met by renewable sources, cannot be sustained indefinitely. The raw material, oil, is a non-renewable resource which will, in time, run out."[1]

Armadillo Merino: Personal Protective Clothing, Plastic-Free

"In time," said Armadillo Merino founder Andy Caughey, "we will look back on this period of wearing synthetics in disbelief." Why? As Caughey explains, "We have a major health and safety issue on our hands with the extensive use of synthetic next-to-skin garments being worn in high risk professions. We have soldiers, firemen and police with severe injuries inflicted onto them because the petrochemical garments have melted, dripped or caught fire and have melted into their skin."

Military medical experts seem to concur. "Burns can kill you," said Navy Captain Lynn E. Welling, head surgeon for the 1st Marine Logistics Group, "and they're horribly disfiguring. If you're throwing (a melted synthetic material) on top of a burn, basically you have a bad burn with a bunch of plastic melting into your skin, and that's not how you want to go home to your

Figure 15.1 Armadillo Merino Shirt
Armadillo Merino is creating an alternative to petrochemical-based clothing with its wool protective clothing for professionals in high-risk environments. Image courtesy of Armadillo Merino.

family." The problem is that synthetic fabrics like nylon, acrylic, and polyester melt when ignited, producing a hot, sticky, molten goo that can fuse to the skin, adding to the severity of burns. The Marine Corps considers the danger so great that it prohibited Marines conducting operations outside forward operating bases in Iraq from wearing athletic clothing containing polyester or nylon. "The policy is good because it's designed for safety and is about keeping Marines in the fight," said Corporal Jason Lichtefeld, a military policeman with the 1st Marine Logistics Group.

While the ban, which went into effect in 2006, had mainstream athletic clothing manufacturers like Under Armour and Nike scrambling to cope, one man believed he had an answer. Andy Caughey was raised on a sheep ranch in South Island, New Zealand. That meant he was very familiar with the properties of merino wool. Merino is a particularly soft wool that's comfortable against the skin. It's excellent at regulating body temperature, retains warmth when wet, and is biodegradable and naturally fire-resistant.

Caughey, who also has experience in the clothing industry, established Ministry of Wool and began marketing a line of athletic wear he called Armadillo Merino, "body armour for professional risk takers." The company was recently named Product Business of the Year by the U.K.'s Startups Awards. "These are no longer just T-shirts but items of personal protective clothing," said Caughley, who has already inked a deal to equip the Italian Navy's special forces. His Armadillo Merino wool shirts can even be found on astronauts in the International Space Station. But the battle for the petroleum-free underwear market is heating up; Nike and Under Armour now make cotton garments that are outselling their synthetic predecessors.[2]

Dominique Duval Handbag: Algae Goes Hi-Fashion

Luxury accessories brand Dominique Duval has created a handbag collection made with algae-based bioplastics from Cereplast, the company recently acquired by Trellis Earth Products. The company's Biopropylene 109D, made with 20 percent post-industrial algae biomatter, reduces both the carbon footprint of the final product and its petroleum-based plastic content. Dominique Duval founder, Jane Gauthier, explained what drew her to Cereplast's bioplastic in an interview with the company:

Cereplast: Why did you decide to use bioplastics?

Jane Gauthier: As a designer, I am always looking for ways to improve the carbon footprint of my products without sacrificing quality. Bioplastics are more environmentally friendly than traditional plastics, and that's important to me and to my customers. The first products I made with Cereplast were hair accessories from algae bioplastics for The Barrette Factory. It's funny to think that as a child I used to scoop up algae and other sea flora while running down the beach alongside the ocean out at Stinson Beach, and now I'm harnessing algae through Cereplast. My customers love the algae collection. They think it's really neat that plastic can be made from algae and other plants.

Figure 15.2 Algae Handbag
This handbag from fashion firm Dominique Duval is made with a bioplastic composed of 20 percent post-industrial algae biomatter. Image courtesy of Dominique Duval LLC.

Cereplast: What do you like about the material?

Jane Gauthier: I love that the designs look delicate, but are actually extremely durable and eco-friendly. The algae has a wonderful grip and silky texture. The material I am using for the bags is very unique too because it's soft, flexible and strong, which makes it great for bags, all while being a better choice for the environment![3]

Tencel Fabric: Fashion from Waste

ONE-QUARTER of the world's insecticides are used to grow cotton, bamboo fiber "presents environmental hazards and harmful health effects," and petroleum-based synthetics raise the host of environmental concerns discussed throughout this book. Clothing made from wood is the unexpected alternative from textile-maker Lenzing AG. The Austrian manufacturer makes its

Figure 15.3 MILCH Tencel Fabric Shirts
Doubly sustainable, this line of clothing by Viennese designer Cloed
Baumgartner uses upcycled shirts originally produced by Lenzing from
their biodegradable Tencel fabric, which is made from wood pulp
cellulose. Image courtesy of MILCH; photo by Christina Leurer.

Tencel fabric out of lyocell, a biodegradable material made from wood pulp cellulose. In Lenzing's case, that wood is eucalyptus sourced from sustainably managed forests.

Tencel is versatile enough to create textures described as silky, peach skin, or moleskin, and it can be blended with other fibers like wool, cotton, and linen. Because of its versatility, it's used to make clothing, bedding, carpet, upholstery, and more. To make Tencel, Lenzing uses what it calls a "closed-loop production cycle," recycling 99.7 percent of all solvents back into the manufacturing process. In addition, the entire process uses 95 percent less water than cotton cultivation and production.

And as if Tencel isn't a sustainable enough material in its own right, Lenzing recently collaborated with Viennese designer Cloed Baumgartner on her project to upcycle the manufacturer's retired men's shirts into women's fashion wear. Baumgartner's design firm, MILCH, is dedicated to what she calls 100 percent upcycling. "We pay attention to environmental and social aspects throughout the production chain," explained Baumgartner. "The raw material (put away men's suits, shirts) comes from Vienna and is processed in socially and economically responsible companies." Her special edition collection takes upcycling to a whole new level, and it was a fashion success too, wowing audiences on the Paris runways in early 2014.[4,5]

Ethletic Shoes: Sneakers for People and Planet

Wнen it comes to footwear, plastic-free is hard to find. Even shoes with leather, canvas, or hemp uppers almost invariably have synthetic, petrochemical-based soles. But Ethletic, the European-based brand founded by Dr. Martin Kunz, has created 100 percent plastic-free sneakers. Ethletic shoes are made with organic, Fairtrade-certified cotton canvas tops and 100 percent natural rubber soles. What's more, the rubber is sourced from responsibly managed forests certified by the Forest Stewardship Council (FSC). Ethletic also pays a Fair Trade premium that provides education and healthcare programs to its rubber tappers and manufacturers. Ethletic's Nordic distributor, Ulrika Mensch, talked about why these social and environmental initiatives are so important to the company.

Why do you insist on natural materials like organic cotton and natural rubber for your sneakers?

The whole idea behind the sneakers is to take great responsibility regarding the environmental and social aspects—choosing Fairtrade-certified and organic cotton and FSC-certified natural rubber is one way, the Fair Trade premiums is another.

Why is certification important?

People want to feel certain that they buy the right thing, and certifications like Fairtrade and FSC are well known and are sort of a guarantee that they have made the right choice and get what they are looking for. And also for us as distributors it is important to be sure that the production chains are correct; it would take too much time and be too expensive to do the monitoring ourselves.

Why no plastic?

Plastic contains unnecessary chemicals that can harm people and the environment. And we are supporting small producers that work with natural latex.

You buy your natural rubber from responsibly managed plantations in places like Sri Lanka, and a portion of the cost pays for health and welfare facilities for the workers there. Why is the social aspect of your work so important to you?

Well, we do not want to look good at someone else's expense, and since we charge market prices for our products we just think it's fair that the producers should receive their share.

Is it possible for all companies to achieve this level of social and environmental good? If so, why aren't they doing it, and how can they make the change?

Actually, I think most companies can do more; it just takes a bit more work and creativity to find good alternatives regarding materials and labor sourcing. I think that the companies also lack the knowledge about the impact within branding, and how positive the association with the company can be if they communicate that they are a responsible company and actually act that way. I also believe one needs to create a demand among the customers and awareness that there are good alternatives in order to put pressure on the companies.

Returning to the plastic-free aspect, do you think we will see more plastic-free goods in the future? What can designers and manufacturers do to reduce our reliance on plastic?

Yes, we will absolutely see more products. We have, for example, flip-flops, footballs, caps, etcetera, all made from natural rubber. Regarding other designers and companies, again they just have to look for alternatives and have an ambition to change.[6]

Figure 15.4 Ethletic Shoes
Ethletic footwear is made without plastic, combining Fairtrade-certified and organic cotton with FSC-certified natural rubber. Image courtesy of Ethletic.

Notes

1   Andrady, Anthony, ed., *Plastics and the Environment*, Hoboken, NJ: John Wiley, 2003, 273; ibid., 283; "World Cotton Production," Cotton Incorporated, Monthly Economic Letter, October 2014, www.cottoninc. com/corporate/Market-Data/MonthlyEconomicLetter/pdfs/English-pdf-charts-and-tables/World-Cotton-Production-Bales.pdf; Barrett, John et al., "Ecological Footprint and Water Analysis of Cotton, Hemp and Polyester," Report prepared for and reviewed by BioRegional Development Group and World Wide Fund for Nature, Stockholm Environment Institute, 2005, www.sei-international.org/mediamanager/documents/ Publications/Future/cotton%20hemp%20polyester%20study%20sei%20and%20bioregional%20and%20 wwf%20wales.pdf; "Global Textile Manufacturing Industry," ReportLinker Textile Manufacturing Industry Market Research & Statistics, www.reportlinker.com/ci02126/Textile-Manufacturing.html

2   Author interview; Holt, Stephen, "Synthetic Clothes Off Limits to Marines Outside Bases in Iraq," *U.S. Department of Defense News*, April 12, 2006, www.defense.gov/News/NewsArticle.aspx?ID=15478; Astley, Oliver, "Why Wool is Andy's Secret Weapon on the Battlefield," *Derby Telegraph*, December 5, 2012, www. thisisderbyshire.co.uk/wool-Andy-s-secret-weapon-battlefield/story-17502707-detail/story.html

3   "Eco-Conscious Handbag Collection Made from Cereplast Bioplastics," http://investorshub.advfn.com/boards/ read_msg.aspx?message_id=83828744

4   "Tencel: The New Age Fiber," Lenzing Group, www.lenzing.com/en/fibers/tencel/tencelr.html

5   www.milch.tm/en/; "Upcycling Action: Tencel Shirts in a New Light," February 14, 2014, www.priscillaandpat. com/blog/upcycling-aktion-tencel-hemden-erstehen-im-neuen-glanz/

6   Author interview.

PART FOUR

Building a Post-Petroleum World

16

Post-Petroleum Manufacturing

Material Sourcing

POST-PETROLEUM designers are changing the way we make our world—creating plastic-free products with little or no petroleum or waste. As we have seen, products like Izhar Gafni's cardboard bike (Chapter 12), Werner Aisslinger's hemp chair (Chapter 14), and the Mercedes-Benz Biome (Chapter 8) point the way to a post-petroleum future less dependent on fossil fuels and less damaged by their side effects. But post-petroleum designers face considerable challenges in rebuilding a world that runs on oil. Take distribution, for instance. At Gone Studio, we design and manufacture products with zero plastic, zero waste, and zero electricity. But when it comes time to put those products in the hands of our customers, we have no choice but to rely on vehicles that burn oil. Mike LaVecchia and Brad Anderson of Grain Surfboards (Chapter 12) host build-your-own workshops around the country and source local woods, but even then, Mike and Brad, along with their students, tools, and materials, have to get to the workshop. Scott Constable, the designer of the House of Tree (Chapter 13), has toyed with the idea of hand-delivering his products by boat around the San Francisco Bay, but that doesn't leave much time for design and production.

Whether it's distribution, material sourcing, manufacturing energy, or waste management, post-petroleum designers are continuously stretching their creative powers to find new ways to minimize their fossil fuel footprint in a world that depends on oil. In distributing their products, the primary obstacles are shipping, which requires gas-powered vehicles, and plastic packaging. Most post-petroleum designers say no to plastic packaging, and some even produce their own alternatives.

As we saw in Chapter 10, MeadWestvaco, for example, gives customers the benefits of clamshell packaging with less than half the plastic in their Natralock paper-plastic hybrid. Ecovative grows their own packaging, and does a brisk business providing customers with all kinds of environmentally friendly options made from their Mushroom Material. Bob's Brazilian burger restaurants and MonoSol, with their Vivos Edible Delivery Systems, have even come up with packaging you can eat. And people outside the design professions are having an impact too, like Jack Johnson, whose CDs are distributed in plastic-free packaging (Chapter 11).

When it comes to sourcing raw materials, post-petroleum designers have a lot more options than they do for distribution. As we saw in Chapter 9, some take a new technology and employ a familiar, natural material. Kieron-Scott Woodhouse's ADzero smartphone housed in bamboo, iZen's bamboo keyboard, and Singgih Susilo Kartono's IKoNO wooden radio are examples from electronics. And, as we saw in Chapter 8, automotive design shows the wide range of options and innovations possible when designers look for materials to create their post-petroleum solutions. Mercedes-Benz's Advanced Design Studios employed bioengineering to design the Biome, a petroleum-free car designed to be grown from genetically engineered seeds. Toyota brought the petroleum-free concept closer to reality with its 1/x made from seaweed-based bioplastic. Lotus, meanwhile, used a hemp-polymer hybrid material in its Eco Elise. Ford's petroleum-free car project showed how even the world's largest automakers are looking beyond plastic. And in their Phoenix car, Kenneth Cobonpue and Albrecht Birkner opted for a natural alternative as well, choosing rattan for its beauty and to reinvigorate a local craft tradition.

The diversity of approaches to material acquisition taken by post-petroleum designers shows that there is a lot more to the movement than simply a resurgent interest in natural materials. Biohybrid materials combining bio-based and polymer-based ingredients represent a stepping stone toward completely petroleum-free products, a transition technology for companies easing their way (and their customers) into post-petroleum design. Werner Aisslinger's hemp chair, made from 70 percent natural hemp and Arcodur, the water-based acrylic resin developed by BASF, is a perfect example of the kind of partnerships emerging to bridge the worlds of petroleum-based and post-petroleum design by creating new hybrid materials (Chapter 14). Cellular computing, which uses living cells instead of silicon and transistors to manage information, points to a future where biomaterials—like those proposed in the Mercedes Biome (Chapter 8)—use DNA and other aspects of living organisms to create new materials that blur the boundaries between living and non-living objects.

Natural materials are thoroughly covered in other books, so I will not discuss them here in detail. But clearly, the post-petroleum designers featured in this book frequently turn to proven materials like wood and cotton as well as twenty-first-century organics like algae and bacteria.

Organic Materials from Post-Petroleum Design Profiles

Wood	Glass
Seaweed	Cotton
Rattan	Clay
Bamboo	Chicken feathers
Paper	Straw
E. coli bacteria	Cork
Cardboard	Rubber
Cellulose fiber	Hemp
Mushrooms	Wool
Corn husks	Algae

Bioluminescent Billboards: Illuminating Ecotourists in the Galapagos Islands

In this design for a tourism control station on the Galapagos Islands, designer Octave Perrault used bioluminescent bacteria to help visitors understand their impact on the fragile ecosystem. "The continuous flow of tourists and the economic vitality of the area threatens its own survival," said Perrault. "The project provides the Galapagos with purpose-built biological customs to improve the sustenance of its incredible biological diversity. The customs are overhung by a hundred bacteria-filled panels. Through the variation of the bacteria density, each panel conveys the state of a certain Indicator of Sustainable Development defined by the United Nations. Altogether, the panels give the visitors an overview of the social, economic and environmental situation of the archipelago."[1]

Figure 16.1 Bioluminescent Billboard
This Biological Gateway project for the Galapagos Islands by designer Octave Perrault incorporates 100 panels filled with bioluminescent bacteria. Image courtesy of Octave Perrault.

Natural or bio-based materials face stiff competition from petrochemical plastic because of its low cost. But as oil supplies thin out, the price of petroleum-based plastics will rise. Growing demand should also make bio-based materials more cost-competitive. But growing demand for bio-based materials raises some interesting concerns as well. As one questioner at one of my talks put it, "What happens when we start making everything from cork? Will we plant all our land with cork trees?" In other words, as demand for bio-based materials grows, will we face an overwhelming need for land to produce them on? European Bioplastics reports that bioplastic feedstocks take up less than one one-thousandth of the world's agricultural land, but that will change as they replace petroleum-based plastics. The key to providing natural raw materials in quantities sufficient to replace plastic is sustainable farming. Massive quantities of wood and other materials can be grown sustainably if we avoid large-scale monoculture and other harmful agricultural practices. We are also learning to use billions of tons of agricultural waste like corn stover as raw material for future bio-based materials. And ocean-based materials like algae and seaweed offer nearly unlimited room to grow, although these are currently grown more efficiently in land-based aquatic farms.[2]

Palm Oil: A Sustainable Material?

The only talk I ever gave under armed guard was at the opening of a biofuel plant in Bogotá, Colombia. At that time, refineries were still a target for terrorists looking to disrupt the country's growing economy. But this refinery wasn't for petroleum; it was the first of its kind in the country to convert palm oil to fuel for cars. Palm oil, however, has since developed a bad reputation because of large-scale monoculture farming. Some large companies have resorted to burning or clearcutting large tracts of land to farm endless rows of palm trees. But the problem isn't with palm oil, which has a lower carbon footprint and less harmful emissions than petroleum; it's with how we grow it.

Fortunately, concerns about monoculture farming have led to a blossoming sustainable palm oil industry. Several certification programs are now in place, and the number of sustainable farms is growing worldwide. Governments in many consumer nations are demanding that imported palm oil meet strict sustainability standards, as in the European Union's biofuel policy, and grower nations like Indonesia are establishing standards for sustainable farming practices as well.[3]

Manufacturing Energy

OIL is not only the main ingredient in the plastics we make our products from; it powers their making as well. In the U.S. alone, industry burns through nearly 2 billion barrels of oil per year. Plastic-free products are a big step toward reducing that number, but their sustainability is undermined when their manufacturing is powered by fossil fuels. And while clean energy alternatives like wind and solar will eventually power our manufacturing, they are still scarce in manufacturing. Looking at the products featured in this book, most are made using conventional, fossil fuel-based energy sources. Several, however, are powered by alternative energy. Some minimize or even eliminate the use of fossil fuel-based energy altogether. At one end of the industrial scale, some artisanal products are made with only human power. The zeer pot, manufactured in Sudan, requires only a hand-powered potter's wheel and the warmth of the sun (Chapter 14).

At Gone Studio, we sell hundreds of products every year made without electricity. We use natural raw materials like wool, some of which may use a small amount of electricity in their production, but all our manufacturing is done with human-powered tools.

But can a truly large-scale manufacturer like an auto assembly plant go oil-free? Automakers Lotus and BMW answer an emphatic "Yes!" Lotus has teamed with British clean energy company Ecotricity to power its Norfolk, U.K., assembly plant solely with wind turbines. "We're chuffed to bits," said Ecotricity's CEO Dale Vince, brandishing a bit of local dialect. "This is a great site for wind turbines and together with Lotus we're going to create something really special, the world's first car factory powered entirely from wind energy. This will be a massively influential project as the world starts to grapple with the energy crisis and climate change." But Lotus will have to outrace BMW to do it. The German automaker plans to power its Leipzig factory solely with wind as well. The project shows that it is possible to switch industrial production to clean energy, even in a factory producing 200,000 cars per year.[4]

Putting Wind to Work in Manufacturing

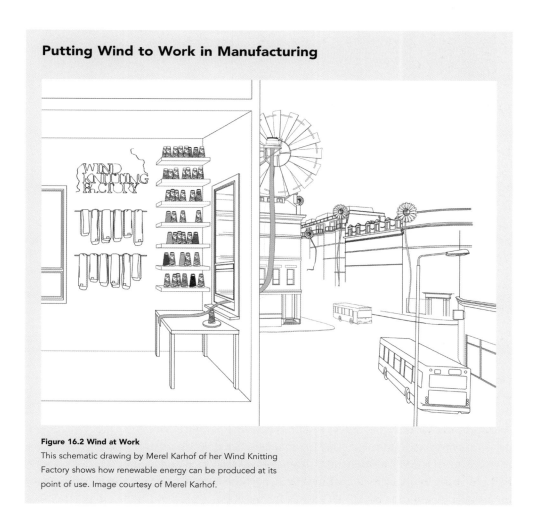

Figure 16.2 Wind at Work
This schematic drawing by Merel Karhof of her Wind Knitting Factory shows how renewable energy can be produced at its point of use. Image courtesy of Merel Karhof.

The Netherlands made windmills famous. Now one Dutch designer is taking them on the road to promote clean energy for manufacturing. Designer Merel Karhof created a mobile wind power unit she first used to run a loom for knitting scarves. Now she has scaled up to power an entire furniture factory with one. Karhof's home province of Noord Holland is home to historic windmills like De Kat (the Cat), that produce dyes, and Het Jonge Schaap (the Young Sheep), that saws lumber. Her furniture mill is a collaboration between a saw miller, a dye miller, and Karhof, a knitting miller. Their three different mills work together to cut the wood, weave the fabric for cushions, and dye it. "This mobile wind factory illustrates a production process and it visualizes what you can produce with the present urban wind," she said.[5]

Figure 16.3 Wind Knitting Factory
Scarves are knitted by the wind in Dutch designer Merel
Karhof's Wind Knitting Factory, where a small windmill
powers a knitting machine. Image courtesy of Merel Karhof.

Energy-intensive industries are also reducing their overhead by using a free energy source that's overhead. Solar power is becoming common in industry, running factories making everything from cheese to ukuleles. A ballet shoe factory in Lawrence, Massachusetts sports over 1,000 rooftop panels, claiming the title of world's largest solar-powered ballet shoe factory. But their panels are no gimmick; the company expects them to pay for themselves in four years, and to enjoy free energy from above after that. Their rooftop solar array will produce 273,000 kilowatt-hours of electricity annually, more than enough to power the production of over one million pairs of shoes per year.[6]

Apple Backs Up Data with Solar

Maiden, North Carolina may not sound like an alternative energy mecca, but this tiny town in the foothills of the Smoky Mountains just happens to be home to the nation's largest private solar power system. That's because it's also home to the main data center for Apple. Solar panels cover 100 acres and are augmented by the country's largest privately owned biogas-powered fuel cell plant on the same site. Together these two alternative energy systems produce over 100 million kilowatt-hours of power per year. All the company's data centers now run on 100 percent renewable power, as do 75 percent of their corporate offices.[7]

Other corporations are cutting back on oil, not by switching to renewables, but by developing manufacturing processes that drastically reduce energy consumption. Ecovative, the makers of mushroom-based surfboards, insulation, and packaging, reduces energy use at its 40,000-square-foot plant in New York by growing their products—just add water and their mycelium grows almost without energy input (Chapter 10). Mercedes-Benz cut energy use by 75 percent in painting some models using a cold curing nanocoating that's also scratch-resistant.

From individual efforts like wind-powered looms to million-kilowatt solar installations by the world's largest corporations, petroleum-free manufacturing is happening today. Its practitioners are overcoming obstacles like lack of capital, the high energy requirements of many industrial processes, and site limitations for solar and wind production. In time, factories will simply draw clean energy from a power grid fueled by renewable sources. But that time is still a long way off. In the meantime, post-petroleum leaders from individual entrepreneurs to industrial giants are taking matters into their own hands to make greener products with cleaner energy.

Zero Carbon Manufacturing at Zero Cost

A study of "Net-Zero Carbon Manufacturing at Net-Zero Cost" out of the University of Dayton Industrial Assessment Center (UD-IAC) recommends the following strategies for industries looking to reduce their manufacturing energy:

Improve facility energy efficiency
Energy efficiency improvements in buildings can reduce energy consumption by an average of 43 percent, according to the National Renewable Energy Laboratory. Improvements like reducing hot water temperature, turning off lights, and turning down thermostats during off hours can be achieved at no cost. Switching to compact fluorescent or LED lighting, replacing appliances with energy-conserving ones, and adding insulation can generate significant savings with minimal investment.

Invest in onsite renewable energy systems

Once the initial investment in energy efficiency upgrades has been paid off, the UD-IAC recommends that the cash flow from energy efficiency (in the form of savings on utility bills) should be invested in an onsite renewable energy system. This system should be sized so that the combined cash flow from the system and energy efficiency savings completely repay the short-term loan for the system. The net result is that the system is installed at no additional cost to the manufacturer.

Invest in offsite renewable energy

Since it's often not possible for manufacturers to produce all their own energy onsite, cash flow from energy efficiency should be used to purchase Renewable Energy Credits (RECs) once the onsite renewable system has been fully paid off. RECs are tradable commodities representing electricity produced from renewable resources like wind, sun, small hydro, and biomass. Purchasing them has the same effect as purchasing the electricity directly from a producer of renewable electricity. Based on its experience with clients, the UD-IAC concludes that "The savings from energy efficiency in combination with the savings from the on-site renewable system are frequently enough to pay for the RECs required to take a manufacturer to net-zero carbon emissions."

This incremental strategy for reducing manufacturing energy can save not only fossil fuels, but money too. Studies by the U.S. General Services Administration show that LEED-certified buildings use 25 percent less energy than non-certified ones, reducing operating costs by an average of 19 percent. And DuPont reports saving five billion dollars thanks to energy efficiency improvements since 1990.[8]

Distribution

UNLESS you own your own fleet of trucks, there's almost no choice but to ship by fossil fuel-burning modes of transportation. A few companies that do own their own fleets, however, are starting to change that. Coca-Cola, for example, now runs a fleet of 16 refrigerated electric trucks, delivering Odwalla beverages around San Francisco. "When people see Coca-Cola committing to this, it will move the industry forward," said Bryan Hansen, CEO of Smith Electric, the truck's manufacturer. Not to be outdone, Coke competitor Pepsi employs 35 electric trucks in New York to deliver snacks by its subsidiary, Frito-Lay.[9]

For post-petroleum designers not quite ready to deploy their own fleets, FedEx offers delivery by electric truck. Currently, the company has 43 all-electric commercial vehicles deployed in Chicago, London, Los Angeles, Memphis, New York City, Paris, and Hong Kong, as well as 330 hybrids and 58 trucks powered by compressed natural gas. As David L. Cunningham Jr., President of FedEx Asia Pacific, points out, "These electric trucks are not only aimed at improving FedEx fleet efficiency in Asia Pacific, but also promoting the development of all-electric trucks among all vehicle users for a more sustainable future."[10]

Figure 16.4 Electric FedEx Truck
FedEx offers delivery by electric trucks in Chicago, London,
Los Angeles, Memphis, New York City, Paris, and Hong Kong.
Shutterstock.com image; photo by Daryl Lang.

Across the Pacific in Portland, Oregon, another form of petroleum-free product shipment
is catching on: bike delivery. As Chad Walsh writes in Portland's *Neighborhood Notes*, "These very
young bicycle delivery companies all seem to stem from environmentalism, an entrepreneurial
spirit and a sense of play. And they're serious about getting what people and businesses need and
want delivered to them quickly, and often, more affordably than conventional transportation."
Franklin Racine-Jones, owner and CEO of the city's B-Line bike delivery firm, says his cyclists
have logged over 3,000 miles. Delivering organic foods and other products to fellow Portlanders
on two wheels instead of four is saving an estimated 18 tons of carbon dioxide per year.[11]

Portland's bike delivery culture is so developed that firms are starting to specialize:
SoupCycle is a perfect example. The company has made over 50,000 deliveries of fresh soup,
according to founder Jed Lazar. And they not only deliver the soup by bike, they make it
themselves, in flavors like Barack-a-li Cheddar and Miso Happy. "We don't worry about fluctuating gas prices, which makes our expenses much more predictable," Lazar said. "Plus, the
eco-friendly focus of our company has attracted a lot of new customers." And SoupCycle isn't the
only Portland business running on two wheels. More than a dozen others, including plumbers,
landscape contractors, and housecleaners, have followed suit.[12]

Figure 16.5 SoupCycle
Portland's SoupCycle has made over 50,000 deliveries of fresh
soup by bike, logging more than 20,000 miles and keeping over
20,000 pounds of carbon dioxide emissions out of the atmosphere.
Image courtesy of SoupCycle.

Waste Management

WHILE it's possible to reduce or eliminate petroleum from manufacturing without confronting waste management, most of the post-petroleum companies featured in this book take care to manage their waste thoughtfully. The list of 20 natural materials that they employ, shown earlier in this chapter, reveals that they all are biodegradable and non-toxic. Matters become more complicated, however, when toxic additives are introduced, as they often are in petrochemical plastic products. Dyes, stabilizers, modifiers, and other additives can make benign materials harmful if they leach out into the environment from the landfill. Pesticides used in textiles like cotton can do the same. But while exact numbers aren't available, it appears that the companies featured in this book avoid toxic additives and use certified organic raw materials to a high degree.

How Gone Studio Became a Zero-Waste Company

When I started Gone Studio in 2010, I made the commitment to make all our products plastic-free. As I developed the design for our first product—the Greensleeve case for the iPad—my commitment grew even deeper. I developed a plastic-free packaging and shipping scheme, and made my studio a plastic-free zone. But I hadn't thought about waste management. Then one day, as I was cleaning up in the studio, I noticed I didn't have a trashcan. I didn't need one—I'd been working for months with zero waste. And to this day, Gone Studio is a zero-waste company. I reuse or recycle everything.

Since most of the products featured in this book are made from biodegrable materials, they don't require elaborate strategies for recycling at the end of their service. The shoes made by Ethletic, for example, shown in Chapter 15, are made with organic cotton and natural rubber, so they will do no harm other than, at worst, one day taking up space in a landfill. But according to the EPA, landfilling biodegradable natural materials can actually delay their degradation due to the lack of sunlight, oxygen, and microbes. And as we'll see in a following chapter, landfilled bioplastics will also be around a very long time. Bioplastic manufacturer, NatureWorks, for instance, determined that containers made from its compostable corn-based PLA will last as long in landfills as containers made from traditional plastics. Nonetheless, stockpiling biodegradable natural materials and plant-based bioplastics in landfills is better than stockpiling petrochemical plastics that may contain toxins.[13]

Landfilling isn't the only option for the disposal of post-petroleum products, however. Some, like the iPad case from Gone Studio, are compostable. Others are made from recyclable materials like non-biodegradable bioplastic, metal, paper, or glass. The best solution of all, practiced by many post-petroleum designers, is to make products that last a very long time, keeping them out of the waste stream as long as possible.

Notes

1   "Octave P." www.octaveperrault.com/

2   European Bioplastics, "Frequently Asked Questions on Bioplastics," July 15, 2013, http://en.european-bioplastics.org/multimedia/faq-2/

3   Block, Ben, "Can 'Sustainable' Palm Oil Slow Deforestation?" Worldwatch Institute, www.worldwatch.org/node/6082

4   Grover, Sami, "Lotus Wind-Powered Car Factory Approved," July 30, 2008, www.treehugger.com/cars/lotus-wind-powered-car-factory-approved.html; "BMW Factory to Use 100% On-Site Wind," *Environmental Leader*, August 22, 2011, www.environmentalleader.com/2011/08/22/bmw-factory-to-use-100-on-site-wind/

5   Karhof, Merel, "Windworks", www.merelkarhof.nl/merel_karhof_-_product_design/Windworks.html; Karhof, Merel, "Wind Knitting Factory," www.merelkarhof.nl/merel_karhof_-_product_design/wind_knitting_factory.html

6   Kirk, Bill, "'Largest Solar Powered Ballet Shoe Factory' Now in Lawrence," *Eagle-Tribune* (Massachusetts), June 25, 2012, www.eagletribune.com/news/local_news/largest-solar-powered-ballet-shoe-factory-now-in-lawrence/article_57bb4604-092b-5653-bd2b-298ab3c0c956.html?mode=jqm

7   "Environmental Responsibility," Apple, www.apple.com/environment/renewable-energy/

8   Pohlman, Dustin, Smith, Jeremy, and Kissock, Kelly, "Net-Zero Carbon Manufacturing at Net-Zero Cost," Proceedings of the American Solar Energy Society, 2012, Sea Island, Georgia, http://academic.udayton.edu/kissock/http/Publications/2012_ASES_NetZeroCarbonManufacturing.pdf; "Green Building Performance: A Post Occupancy Evaluation of 22 GSA Buildings," White Paper, GSA Public Buildings Service, August 2011, www.gsa.gov/graphics/pbs/Green_Building_Performance.pdf

9   O'Connor, Mary Catherine, "Coca-Cola Launches First Electric Refrigerated Truck Fleet," GreenBiz, September 19, 2013, www.greenbiz.com/blog/2013/09/19/coca-cola-launch-first-electric-refrigerated-truck-fleet

10   "FedEx Express Launches Zero-Emission All-Electric Vehicle Fleet in Hong Kong," FedEx Newsroom, March 16, 2013, http://news.van.fedex.com/fedex-express-launches-zero-emission-all-electric-vehicle-fleet-hong-kong

11   Walsh, Chad, "Pedal Power: Portland's Bike Delivery Services," *Neighborhood Notes*, January 14, 2010, Portland, Oregon, www.neighborhoodnotes.com/news/2010/01/pedal_power_portlands_bike_delivery_services/

12   "Think Bicycles Are Just for Fun? Think Again, Says SoupCycle," Press Release, January 19, 2012, www.prweb.com/releases/2012/1/prweb9116488.htm

13   U.S. Environmental Protection Agency, "The Degradables Debate," www.epa.gov/osw/wycd/catbook/debate.htm; Lilienfeld, Robert, ed., "Review of Life Cycle Data Relating to Disposable, Compostable, Biodegradable, and Reusable Grocery Bags," The ULS Report, March 28, 2008, www.use-less-stuff.com/Paper-and-Plastic-Grocery-Bag-LCA-Summary-3-28-08.pdf

17

New Life for Old Plastic

Industrial Recycling

WHILE only a tiny percentage of today's plastics are recycled into new goods, the industry is moving toward a future where plastic lives on, given new life in a wide variety of products. New products made from recycled plastic are introduced every day, and since they are made of plastic it's not my intention to cover them in detail here. But plastic, as we know, doesn't go away, so it's important to consider what to do with the five billion tons of it we've already produced. Can it all be recycled into new products? Should we let what's already in the landfills rest in peace, or mine it to make new materials and products? New technologies for recycling include landfill mining, waste-to-energy programs that convert plastic to fuel through high-temperature incineration, industrial recycling, and bioremediation—a waste reduction method that uses biological processes to break down pollutants.

Industrial plastics recycling takes the scrap plastic created when factories turn "raw" plastic into products, and grinds it up and reprocesses it to make more "raw" plastic. "As with any manufactured product, there is always going to be discarded material, plastics that are part of the manufacturing process but not part of the finished product," said recycler Blackrock Plastics on its company website. "Companies can choose to simply throw away this post industrial plastic, where it will languish in the landfills, or sell it to a recycling company."

"With a big push for green products and for companies to be environmentally friendly, plastic recycling is becoming big business," the company explained. "Recycling not only reduces the amount of waste material that enters landfills, but it also reduces carbon dioxide emissions and reduces oil usage." Recycled plastic also takes less energy to make than virgin plastic. Recycling one ton of HDPE, for example, saves seven tons of petroleum.[1]

Building Bridges with 100 Percent Recycled Plastic

Increasingly, plastic bound for the recycler is being intercepted by innovators and entrepreneurs and put to work to create new products. New Jersey-based Axion International, for example, buys plastic waste bound for municipal recycling and reprocesses it into heavy-duty structural members for buildings. Their Struxure composite building products are much stronger than the recycled plastic and wood-plastic composite "plastic lumber" common in decks and other light applications. In fact they're so strong that Axion built a bridge with them at Fort Bragg in North Carolina that's capable of supporting vehicles weighing up to 88 tons like the M1 tank. Not only is this new breed of plastic made from dedicated recyclables super-strong, it's also built to last: rot-proof, rust-proof, and corrosion-free.

It's fast too. The company installed a 90-foot bridge spanning the River Tweed in Scotland in just four days. "By taking advantage of our material's strong, yet light-weight nature," said Steve Silverman, Axion's president and CEO, "we were able to cost-effectively ship the entire span to Scotland, and then complete construction on-site in just two weeks. The remarkably fast erection time of only four days for a 90-foot bridge is a major benefit of our unique composite material, as it substantially reduces the complexity and cost of construction, and is good for the environment as well." The Easter Dawyck Bridge supports 45 tons and is the first European roadway bridge constructed out of 100 percent recycled plastic.[2]

Figure 17.1 Axion Struxure Fort Bragg Bridge
New Jersey-based Axion International reprocesses plastic waste from municipal recycling centers into heavy-duty structures like this bridge at Fort Bragg in North Carolina, strong enough to support an 88-ton M1 tank. Image courtesy of Axion International Inc.

Fighting Oil with Plastic

On December 11, 1999, French authorities received an alert from the Maltese tanker, *Erika*. The ship, carrying over 30,000 tons of oil, was experiencing structural problems amid high seas and strong winds. The captain then reported that the situation was under control and he was heading the ship for the nearby port of Donges. But at 6:11 a.m., amid 20-foot seas and winds over 50 mph, the *Erika* suddenly broke in two. As French and British helicopters scrambled to rescue the crew, others reported a growing oil slick nearly ten miles long

Figure 17.2 Erika Installation
RAUM: this French architecture firm used hundreds of plastic oyster
nets to make their seaside installation, *Erika*. Oyster fishing was
one of the industries hardest hit by the oil spill from the project's
namesake, an oil tanker that spilled nearly 20,000 tons of oil nearby.
Image courtesy of RAUM.

spreading across the Bay of Biscay. Over the next several days, the sinking *Erika* would release roughly 20,000 tons of oil, creating the worst spill in French history.

Walking along the beaches of Biscay in 2007, you would still have been likely to see the effects of the spill. You would also have seen an unlikely memorial, not to lost human life (thankfully the entire crew was rescued), but to lost wildlife and the other ill effects of oil. The structure, aptly named *Erika*, was actually a temporary installation designed and built by RAUM Architects as part of the Contemporary Art Biennale of Estuaire. Made from hundreds of plastic oyster nets, Erika takes an ordinary object used by one of the industries hit hardest by the spill and makes it extraordinary. Perhaps ironically, perhaps fittingly, the biennale was sponsored by Total, the French oil company responsible for the spill. I asked RAUM principal Benjamin Boré what inspired the firm to use plastic oyster nets to make a building.

> We wanted to try to use plastic oyster bags because we know it's problematic for the oyster farmers to recycle this material. Most of the time plastic oyster bags are burned in place. We know too that oyster farmers are very affected by different oil slicks, and especially the one resulting from *Erika*. That's why we decided to erect a sort of monument to concentrate all these problematics and to find a way to have a concentration of plastic oyster bags to recycle without any cost to the oyster farmers. After the exhibition, recycling was paid for by the Art Contemporary Biennale and de facto by Total. [3]

Post-Consumer Plastic Recycling

WHILE industrial or pre-consumer plastic recycling continues to grow, some companies are looking beyond the recycling bin to create large-scale programs to make new products from post-consumer plastic as well. Waste Management, Inc., which moves more trash than any other company, has teamed up with Renmatix, a leading manufacturer of bio-based sugar intermediates, to explore turning trash into a variety of bio-based products, including perfume. Renmatix currently uses rural biomass such as agricultural waste to make sugars for manufacturing bio-based materials. But under the new agreement, Waste Management will provide them with urban waste including food scraps, construction debris, paper, and recyclables. Urban trash delivered by Waste Management could be used alone or in combination with other feedstocks to create perfumes, paints, textiles, packaging, plastics, and other products. "This initiative has the potential to harness post-consumer biomass from urban communities as a source for cellulosic sugars," said Mike Hamilton, CEO of Renmatix. "Together we are exploring a new pathway to renewing waste."[4]

Making Tracks with Nike Grind

Nike Grind isn't a new line of athletic shoes, but it is made from them. Through the company's Reuse-A-Shoe program, worn-out sneakers (of any brand) are accepted at Nike stores worldwide. The company's sophisticated repurposing facilities separate out rubber from the outsoles, foam from the midsoles, and fabric from the uppers, grinding each into pellet-sized fragments. The fragments are then formed into surfacing materials for every-thing from running tracks to gym flooring tiles and playground surfacing. Their StepAhead partnership with Home Depot even creates carpet cushion. Making a full-sized soccer field out of Nike Grind can repurpose up to 75,000 pairs of shoes, keeping them out of the landfills. In all, Nike has shredded over 28 million pairs of shoes since 1990, giving them new life in nearly half a million locations around the world.[5]

Renewing plastic waste has developed into an international enterprise. The U.S., for example, ships half of its plastic waste to China. But now, a growing list of countries, including China and Mexico, won't allow the importation of waste of any kind unless it meets significant cleanliness standards. Meeting these standards can make the recycling process cost-prohibitive. But while stricter regulation of plastic waste imports by other countries may be causing some difficulties today, in the long run it will mean less dumping of toxic waste on developing nations and more clean recycling at home.

Can Plastic Recycling Hurdle China's Green Fence?

America's number one export to China isn't autos or electronics; it's trash. In fact, half of the plastic discarded in the U.S. ends up there. But that doesn't mean incoming barges brimming with trash have been an unwelcome sight in Chinese harbors: the country earned over half a billion dollars by accepting U.S. trash in 2011 alone. In 2013, however, over 50 shipments were stopped as China rejected more than 7,600 tons of recyclables. The sudden change in policy was the result of Operation Green Fence, which enforces strict rules for cleanliness on imported waste. Enforcement was no slap on the wrist either, with some sources reporting that violating the Green Fence laws could even result in a death sentence.

According to *PlasticsNews*, Green Fence "has led to a significant drop in imports of plastic waste and put some recyclers out of business, at least temporarily. The policy is bad news for some [U.S.] municipalities, which are having a tougher time with some low-grade plastics that they collect, since they can no longer ship it to China." One recycler that used to send two-thirds of its plastic waste to China said it expects to export less than one-third as a result of the Green Fence operation. "That's a very agreeable thing," said Saureen

Naik, Export Sales Manager of overseas operations with the Naik Group of Industries. "We see the Green Fence as an opportunity to grow domestically, to create new markets for our export material, to create new jobs. Overall, we see this as an opportunity and not a threat." The company plans to invest around $30 million in recycling technology in the U.S. over the next three years. "We've been dumping a lot of our low-end materials into China," Naik added. "And I think that this policy is really an opportunity to examine our actions, impacts and carbon footprints. It provides a chance to take more actions and come up with new technologies that we can really establish here in the U.S. as alternate means and alternate recycling methods for our own scrap."[6]

Waste-to-Energy Conversion

A **POUND** of plastic contains twice as much energy as a pound of coal. And because plastics contain so much potential energy, waste-to-energy conversion is an important part of our future. Already, nearly 100,000 tons of plastic are burned every day in U.S. energy recovery facilities. Waste-to-energy programs that convert plastic to fuel through high-temperature incineration could create a market for certain plastics—films, for example—that are difficult to recycle. They may even provide an alternative fuel for power plants currently burning coal or natural gas. But waste-to-energy conversion has its own environmental issues (discussed in an earlier chapter) and some experts worry they could even undermine recycling programs. "Waste-to-energy needs to be thought through so it doesn't become a reason not to recycle," Steve Miller, CEO of plastic recycler Bulk Handling Systems, told *Waste & Recycling News*. "People might say, 'Oh we don't need to do that. We'll just burn it.' There are ways they can co-exist nicely and have a high functionality but it needs to be carefully designed and implemented."[7]

Plastic waste can also be converted into oil, as it is in the new plants developed by Petrogas in the Netherlands. "We have not only found a solution to the growing plastic waste issue, on top of this we produce oil in a very environmentally friendly fashion," said Petrogas Sales Director Edwin Hoogwerf. He also speculates that the plants will be moneymakers for the local community. "For the local communities this is rather lucrative as production costs are about 27 cents per liter whereas selling it at 70 cents per liter provides a healthy margin. From one kilogram of plastic waste we obtain one liter of diesel oil with only 3% waste, which is sold to the cement industry as an ingredient for asphalt. It is the intention that each plant converts some 22,500 tons of plastic per annum." However, while plastic-to-oil conversion efficiencies may be improving and millions of tons of plastic in landfills need to be dealt with, is using oil to make plastic and then making that plastic into oil really the most efficient use of our irreplaceable fossil fuels?[8]

Biodegradation—using bacteria or other biological means to break down plastic—is another method of transforming waste plastic. Bacteria don't just chew up plastic and spit it out in smaller pieces—they can transform it into less harmful bioplastic. That's what researchers at University College Dublin, Ireland, found when they fed PET plastic to *Pseudomonas* bacteria. By eating the plastic, the bacteria were able to break it down into terephthalic acid, oil, and gas.

When the *Pseudomonas* ate the terephthalic acid, they excreted PHA, a natural polymer produced by many bacteria during fermentation. The PHA could then be used just like any polymer to make plastic.

Plastic-Eating Fungus

Hacking their way through the Amazon rainforest, a team of student researchers from Yale University discovered a fungus with the unique ability to digest plastic. *Pestalotiopsis Microspora* thrives on polyurethane, the polymer used to make foam rubber. Yale students have been collecting rainforest fungi on field trips to Central America for more than seven years, and one student decided to explore the plastic-eating potential of what they'd

Figure 17.3 Yale University Student Expedition
Yale students including Jon Russell (above) discovered a fungus
capable of biodegrading polyurethane on a university expedition to
the Amazon rainforest. Image courtesy of Yale University.

brought back. Pria Anand found that when certain fungi were introduced to plastic, a chemical reaction occurred. Other students developed the experiments to determine which type of fungus was best at devouring plastic, and which type of plastic made the best meal. "While other agents can degrade polyurethane," the university said in a press release, "the enzyme identified by Yale students holds particular promise because it also degrades plastic in the absence of oxygen—a prerequisite for bioremediation of buried trash." This makes *Pestalotiopsis Microspora* a prime candidate for large-scale bioremediation. And with over 12 million tons of polyurethane produced worldwide every year, these voracious fungi won't lack for food.

Canadian high school student Daniel Burd, meanwhile, didn't have to go to the Amazon—he found plastic-eating microorganisms right in his kitchen cupboard. Burd started with common baker's yeast, testing it on plastic bags, and selecting out the most productive strains. By the time he took his experiment to the National Science Fair in Ottawa, his strains of *Pseudomonas* and *Sphingomonas* could break down most of a bag into water and carbon dioxide in just six weeks. Not too surprisingly, Daniel Burd won that science fair.[9]

Landfill Mining

RECYCLING plastic into fuel or new products helps keep it out of our landfills; but what about the 5 billion tons of plastic that are already there? Could we harvest that bounty rather than using up billions of barrels of crude oil every year to make new fuels and plastics? In fact, it's already happening. Packaging company RockTenn has been generating thousands of tons of plastic waste every day for years and storing them in its plastic-only landfill. The company recently penned an agreement with the domestic alternative oil and gas company JBI, whose Plastic2Oil technology creates new fuel from old plastic. Under the agreement, JBI will deploy modular "plug and play" processors at RockTenn's mills to convert mined plastic into fuel. JBI's founder and CEO John Bordynuik called the venture "a viable commercial process to handle not only the critical issue of waste byproduct but also rising energy costs."[10]

But RockTenn's landfills are plastic-only. Harvesting plastic from conventional landfills where it's mixed with other materials presents a more complex problem. And while we know our landfilled plastic isn't going anywhere anytime soon, landfill mining may be here sooner than we think. "By 2020," said waste management expert Peter Jones, "we might have nine billion people on the planet, we could have a very big middle class driving millions more cars, and we could be in a really resource-hungry world with the oil price climbing and a supply situation in Libya, Russia and Saudi [Arabia] where natural gas is limited. It is those drivers, those conditions, which will encourage the possibility of landfill mining."[11]

Rising demand, declining production, and the high prices that result will undoubtedly accelerate the advent of large-scale landfill mining. Other new technologies like waste-to-energy conversion, industrial recycling, and bioremediation will also offer a positive alternative to the current plastic life cycle. But what will be the environmental impacts and unanticipated consequences of the alternatives? They will present both new challenges and new possibilities of their own in the post-petroleum era.

Upcycling

W E don't have to wait for plastic products to reach the landfill before we find creative new uses for them. There are billions of plastic products rolling out of factories every year, and post-petroleum designers are already finding imaginative applications for many of them after their typically brief life of service. Upcycling gives new life to disused products, converting them into everything from jewelry to light fixtures.

Bottle Lights are plastic waste recycled into solar bulbs. Amy Smith at MIT's D-Lab is credited with creating the bulbs, made by simply filling an ordinary used plastic bottle with a mix of water and a few drops of chlorine bleach. The neck of the bottle is then inserted through a small hole cut into the roof of a dwelling. Each Bottle Light emits the same amount of light as a 55-watt bulb, providing light for families who cannot afford electricity. Even families with electric service can save about $6 per month by using Bottle Lights, said Illac Diaz. His MyShelter Foundation, based in the Philippines, sells the bulbs for $1 apiece, including installation. In its first year, the foundation lit over 15,000 homes, with the aim to light one million homes by 2015.[12]

And if you use cans more than bottles, don't despair; those plastic six-pack rings that usually end up clogging our landfills and waterways are also finding creative uses thanks to post-petroleum designers. Bao-Khang Luu, the designer behind Relevé Design, makes his livelihood by upcycling such ordinary objects into unique furnishings like the Allium pendant lamp. This lamp's shade, like a series of others made by Relevé with different shapes, is made entirely from upcycled six-pack rings. "Using a technique developed over a year and a half, the six-pack rings are hand-woven into strands and onto metal lamp rings," Luu explained. "This eliminates the use of new materials or adhesives to connect the six-pack rings together," he added, "and at the end of its lifecycle, each light can be deconstructed easily for upcycling or recycling."[13]

Even the lowly plastic phone card can become high fashion in the hands of an innovative designer. Brazilian designer Mana Bernardes creates products and artworks from plastic cards and bottles, toothpicks, bobby pins, and other everyday items that would otherwise be discarded. Her Colar Espacial Telefônico reveals the potential for the billions of "waste" plastic materials to be creatively reimagined. And Bernardes is helping others learn to do the same, working with the Museum of Rio de Janeiro, the European Design Institute, and other organizations to promote creative and environmentally sensitive upcycling.[14]

Figure 17.4 Allium Pendant Lamp
Bao-Khang Luu's firm, Relevé Design, "transforms commonly discarded
materials into new useful lighting, home accessories, and furniture by
injecting a hefty dose of art and design into upcycling." Image courtesy
of Bao-Khang Luu.

Figure 17.5 Mana Bernardes Colar Espacial Telefônico
Brazilian designer Mana Bernardes uses plastic cards and bottles,
toothpicks, and other everyday items that would otherwise be discarded
to create products and artworks such as her Colar Espacial Telefônico.
Image courtesy of Mana Bernardes; photo by Mauro Kury.

Notes

1 "The Importance of Post Industrial Plastic Recycling," Blackrock Plastics LLC, March 19, 2013, www.black-rockplastics.com/the-importance-of-post-industrial-plastic-recycling/

2 "First Recycled Plastic Bridge," Axion International, www.axionintl.com/PDFs/PRODUCT/BRIDGES/Peeblesshire_BRIDGE_FOR%20DISTRIBUTION_2012.pdf; Bragonier, Emily, "Recycled Plastics Enter Structural Applications," *Environmental Building News*, Volume 19, Number 3, March 2010, www.building-green.com/auth/article.cfm/2010/3/1/Recycled-Plastics-Enter-Structural-Applications/

3 Author interview; Centre of Documentation, Research and Experimentation on Accidental Water Pollution, "*Erika*", www.cedre.fr/en/spill/erika/erika.php

4 "Companies Embark on Program to Explore Viability of MSW as Inputs for Plantrose Process," Press Release, August 23, 2012, http://renmatix.com/waste-management-and-renmatix-announce-agreement-to-explore-conversion-of-urban-waste-to-low-cost-cellulosic-sugar/

5 "Nike Reuse-A-Shoe," Nike, www.nike.com/us/en_us/c/better-world/reuse-a-shoe

6 "US-based Recyclers May Gain from China's 'Green Fence'," *PlasticsNews*, July 12, 2013, www.plasticsnews.com/article/20130712/NEWS/130719975/us-based-recyclers-may-gain-from-chinas-green-fence#

7 Kavanaugh, Catherine, "Weighing the Next 40 Years of Recycling," *PlasticsNews*, September 4, 2013, www.plasticsnews.com/article/20130904/NEWS/130909985/weighing-the-next-40-years-of-recycling

8 "Big Order for Petrogas in Renewable Energy Market," Press Release, September 12, 2013, www.petrogas.nl/Press_Release_-_English-Final.pdf

9 "Yale Students' Trip to Rainforest Yields New Way to Degrade Plastic," *YaleNews*, August 1, 2011, http://news.yale.edu/2011/08/01/yale-students-trip-rainforest-yields-new-way-degrade-plastic; Russell, Jonathan, Huang, Jeffrey, Anand, Pria, Kucera, Kaury, Sandoval, Amanda G., Dantzler, Kathleen W., et al., "Biodegradation of Polyester Polyurethane by Endophytic Fungi," *Applied and Environmental Biology*, Volume 77, Number 17, September 2011, 6076–6084, http://aem.asm.org/content/77/17/6076.full; Burkhart, Karl, "Boy Discovers Microbe that Eats Plastic," Mother Nature Network, July 12, 2009, www.mnn.com/green-tech/research-innovations/blogs/boy-discovers-microbe-that-eats-plastic#

10 Loveday, Eric, "JBI Will 'Mine Plastic' from RockTenn Landfills to Convert to Oil," AutoBlogGreen, August 14, 2011, http://green.autoblog.com/2011/08/14/jbi-mine-plastic-rocktenn-landfill-convert-oil/

11 Kelland, Kate, "Could $100 Oil Turn Dumps into Plastic Mines?" August 26, 2008, www.reuters.com/article/2008/08/26/us-waste-landfill-idUSLJ40413520080826

12 http://aliteroflight.org/

13 "Relevé Design," www.relevedesign.com/press-resources/

14 http://english.manabernardes.com/

18

Bioplastics

Adoption and Resistance

IN the post-petroleum era, plastic products will be made primarily from plants instead of fossil fuels. These bioplastics use plants as their raw materials rather than the fossil fuels ordinary plastic is derived from. The most common bioplastic today is PLA (polylactic acid,) a biobased polymer made from plant sugars used to produce clear plastic water bottles, cups, and clamshell containers. Bioplastics offer several advantages over petroleum-based plastics: they biodegrade much faster, may contain fewer toxins, and have a smaller carbon footprint. PLA production, for example, uses 30 to 50 percent less fossil fuel and generates 50 to 70 percent less carbon dioxide than petroleum-based plastic.[1]

Bioplastics are nothing new. "Biobased polymers have been used for food, furniture and clothing for thousands of years," explained the authors of a report out of Utrecht University in the Netherlands. "The first artificial thermoplastic polymer 'celluloid' was invented in the 1860s. Since then, numerous new compounds derived from renewable resources have been developed. However, many of the inventions related to biobased polymers made in the 1930s and 1940s remained at the laboratory stage and were never used for commercial production. The main reason was the discovery of crude oil and its large-scale industrial use for synthetic polymers since the 1950s."

Synthetic polymers derived from oil pushed biobased polymers almost to extinction, and today bioplastics make up less than one-third of 1 percent of the global plastics market. Still, thanks to their many advantages, bioplastics have a bright future. They are one of the world's fastest-growing markets, increasing at nearly 40 percent per year. According to the Utrecht report, "Up to 90 percent of the current global consumption of polymers can technically be converted from oil and gas to renewable raw materials." But they cautioned, "It will not be possible to exploit this technical substitution potential in the short to medium term. The main reasons are economic barriers (especially production costs and capital availability,) technical challenges in scale-up, the short-term availability of biobased feedstocks and the need for the plastics conversion sector to adapt to the new plastics."[2]

Another study, by scientists at the University of Massachusetts-Lowell researching the sustainability of current bioplastics, found similar challenges. Those authors concluded that

Figure 18.1 Ingeo Biopolymer Pellets
Ingeo plant-based biopolymer pellets from NatureWorks are
used to make textiles, food packaging, clothing, and more.
Image courtesy of NatureWorks.

"None of the biobased plastics currently in commercial use or under development are fully sustainable. Each of the biobased plastics reviewed utilizes: genetically modified organisms for feedstock manufacture and/or toxic chemicals in the production process or generates these as byproducts, and/or co-polymers from non-renewable resources."[3]

Their last concern, that some bioplastics utilize "co-polymers from non-renewable resources," refers to the petroleum- or natural gas-based polymers often combined with biobased polymers and additives in many products. In fact, most products using the term bioplastic in their marketing are made from just such a mix of plant-based and petroleum-based materials. The current PlantBottle by Coca-Cola, for example, is only 30 percent plant-based material—the rest is petrochemical. The company is, however, careful not to refer to the PlantBottle as bioplastic, but "made partially from plants." In Denmark, where the current version of the PlantBottle is only 15 percent plant material, the Danish consumer ombudsman, Henrik Saugmandsgaard Øe, asked the company to revise its marketing materials, saying the 15 percent plant content hardly justifies the designation PlantBottle.[4]

Øe's concerns highlight a dilemma facing today's bioplastics industry: just how much plant material does a plastic have to contain to earn the title bioplastic? Rules vary worldwide. In Japan, for example, industries have committed to a minimum 25 percent renewable content for products and packaging sold as bioplastic. The U.S. Department of Agriculture's BioPreferred product program, on the other hand, includes products with as little as 7 percent renewable material. Yet some BioPreferred products are made from 95 percent renewables. This disparity makes it hard for consumers to know just how much petroleum may be in their bioplastic.

But regardless of exact percentages, as oil supplies run down more of our plastics will be made from plants. And while making plastics from 100 percent biomaterials is still rare, the industry is moving in that direction. One step is to add some biobased additives, modifiers, or "drop-ins" to petroleum-based plastics. "Drop-in bioplastics," according to European Bioplastics, "are biobased or partly biobased non-biodegradable materials such as (partly) biobased Polyethylene (PE), Polypropylene (PP) or polyethylene terephthalate (PET)." Coke's PlantBottles are made with biobased PET, and Toyota uses it in their auto interiors. Ford has combined both in an experimental collaboration with Coke to make interior fabrics from recycled PlantBottles. The multinational food processing and packaging solutions company Tetra Pak is already offering cartons with coatings and caps made from sugarcane, and Dow is experimenting with biobased polypropylene. Drop-ins are expected to play a major role in the short to medium term because their non-biodegradable nature makes them more compatible with the petroleum-based plastics they're mixed with.[5]

Figure 18.2 Tetra Pak Bio-based PE Carton
Packaging manufacturer Tetra Pak now uses plastic made from sugarcane, and currently all 13 billion Tetra Pak packages made in Brazil have up to 82 percent packaging material from renewable sources. Image courtesy of Tetra Pak.

Not All Bioplastics Are Biodegradable?

THAT not all bioplastics are biodegradable may seem counterintuitive: isn't the ability to biodegrade quickly one of bioplastic's main benefits? But biodegradable and non-biodegradable materials don't always mix well. In the worst case, the result is a product that can't be recycled due to its biodegradable content, and can't be composted because of its petrochemicals. Adding non-biodegradable drop-ins to conventional plastics may not be ideal compared to 100 percent bioplastics, but it is preferable to plastics that can't be recycled or composted.

The plastics industry appears eager to adopt bio-based PET drop-ins and additives. Experts predict that "non-biodegradable biopolymers will show the largest growth in the coming years," with bio-based PET expected to account for four-fifths of total bioplastic production capacity by 2017. These non-biodegradable biopolymers may be the short-term future of bioplastics, but as oil supplies diminish, the number of products made from 100 percent bioplastic will increase. And yet, while some 100 percent bioplastics can be composted or landfilled where they break down into harmless particles, it doesn't always work out that way.

Recycling Bioplastic Is No Picnic

Suppose you live in New York, your family or company is planning a picnic, and you want to be extremely green and use only 100 percent biodegradable plastic plates and utensils. According to the New York City Department of Sanitation, "If you want to purchase bioplastic trays, cups, utensils, or other products for an event or for your school or institutional cafeteria, be aware that the NYC Department of Sanitation will NOT be able to collect them for recycling or composting."

"Bioplastics," the Department explains, "look nearly identical to conventional PET plastics, and it's nearly impossible to tell the difference between them in order to separate them out. If they remain mixed together, bioplastics contaminate existing recycling streams because they are made of substances that are incompatible with regular plastics in the recycling process."

The Department doesn't give much hope for composting either. "Most compostable plastics," they explain, "require high-temperature conditions achievable only in a commercial or industrial composting facility to successfully decompose. There are as few as 113 to 200 industrial-grade composting facilities across the U.S. today. Transporting compostable plastics to these facilities, which might be far away, poses logistical and financial challenges. If you want to compost bioplastic items yourself in your own compost bin, you must make sure that the bioplastics you choose will decompose under home composting conditions. The vast majority do not."

With both recycling and composting out of the picture, there's only one option for bioplastics in the Big Apple. "Unless you make arrangements with a private company to collect and transport them to a facility where they can be composted using industrial, high-temperature conditions, they must be discarded as trash." And, the Department reminds you, your bioplastic won't behave much differently from conventional plastic once it reaches the landfill, thanks to the lack of microbes, light, and oxygen needed to break it down.[6]

As it turns out, neither backyard composting nor landfilling allow bioplastics to fully biodegrade. When Woods End Laboratories tested five types of bioplastic bags to see how well they would break down in home compost, they found that none of them degraded completely. Only one, the Mater-bi bag made of corn starch, vegetable oil derivatives, and biodegradable synthetic polyesters, was deemed compostable after 25 weeks. A backyard compost heap simply doesn't have the right combination of naturally occurring microorganisms, oxygen, and sunlight to break down bioplastics. Neither does a typical landfill. According to the EPA, landfilling biodegradable natural materials like food and lawn trimmings actually delays their degradation due to the lack of sunlight, oxygen, and microbes. And bioplastic manufacturer, NatureWorks, determined that containers made from its compostable corn-based PLA will last as long in landfills as containers made from traditional plastics.[7]

University of Plymouth marine biologist Richard Thompson found that plastic grocery bags marketed as biodegradable didn't fare much better in an ocean environment either. His team conducted a simple experiment, tying a selection of bags to the moorings in Plymouth Harbor in southwestern England. "A year later you could still carry groceries in them," said Thompson. When he examined their chemical composition, he found most were a mixture of cellulose starch and petrochemical polymers. As the starch degraded, what remained was even worse than bulk plastic: thousands of clear, nearly invisible plastic microparticles.[8]

Because of these challenges to composting and landfilling 100 percent plant-based plastics, many bioplastics, like the Mater-bi bag, contain biodegradable synthetic polyesters. It may come as a surprise that bioplastics can contain petrochemicals, but as long as they are proven to break down completely in a short time, petrochemical plastics can wear the title bioplastic. The U.S. Code of Federal Regulations sets the standard for which products are allowed to carry the name biodegradable. It states that marketers must provide "competent and reliable scientific evidence that the entire item will completely break down and return to nature (i.e., decompose into elements found in nature) within a reasonably short period of time after customary disposal." According to their definition, products can be labeled "biodegradable" even if they break down into "natural" toxins like the lead and cadmium found in many plastics.[9]

This muddies the bioplastic picture already confused by the lack of recycling and composting options even further. Aren't the tiny plastic particles resulting from degrading petro-chemical plastics even worse for the environment than whole plastics idling in our landfills? The answer is yes. "A new kind of plastic that is biodegradable may in fact represent a step backward," cautioned garbologist William Rathje. "The fact that [petrochemical] plastic does not biodegrade, which is often cited as one of its great defects," he adds, "may actually be one of its great virtues." A virtue because when it does degrade, it can release toxins into the environment.

What Is "Biodegradable"?

When Danny Clark quit his job as a communications engineer in 2008 to start Enso Bottles, he hoped to leave "a legacy that we've done something positive in the environment." By combining biodegradable plant-based PET additives with conventional plastic, Clark created a bottle he claimed was both biodegradable and recyclable.

But Dennis Sabourin of the National Association for PET Container Resources (NAPCOR) disagreed. In 2011, NAPCOR asked PET manufacturers to stop using biode-gradable additives. Claiming that containers made with biodegradable additives can reduce recycling, waste energy, and pose "potentially serious health and safety concerns," the industry organization went so far as to say, "degradable additives provide no real environmental or societal benefit."

The California attorney general's office also disagreed with Clark. Later that same year, it filed suit against Enso and two other water bottle companies, saying Enso's claim that their bottles would biodegrade in less than five years with no harmful residues was false. "Californians are committed to recycling and protecting the environment," said Attorney General Kamala Harris, "but these efforts are undermined by the false and misleading claims these companies make when they wrongly advertise their products as 'biodegradable.'"

According to the attorney general, Enso's claim that the bottles were recyclable was also untrue. As NAPCOR had warned PET manufacturers, recyclers may consider plastic bottles with biodegradable additives a contaminant and separate them from recyclable plastics. "So far, we haven't seen that it does degrade or is not hostile to recycling," said David Cornell of the Association of Postconsumer Plastic Recyclers (APPR). "If it doesn't degrade, then who wants it? If it does degrade, what does it do to recycling?"

For his part, Clark continues to claim that materials enhanced with his company's Enso Restore additive biodegrade 90 percent faster than those without it. "Our products perform as we claim, and we have the data to prove it," he said.

"They're working on it. I will give them credit," added APPR's Cornell.[10]

Bioplastic Feedstocks

RENEWABLE feedstocks aren't perfect either. The use of genetically modified organisms in feedstock manufacture is a concern for some, as is the use of feedstocks that could be used to feed people. The most common feedstocks for today's bioplastics are corn, potato, sugarcane, and beetroot—all food sources. But given bioplastic's tiny percentage of the current market, its feedstocks take up less than 0.001 percent of the world's agricultural land. As the industry organization European Bioplastics points out with true European flair, "This ratio correlates to the size of an average cherry tomato next to the Eiffel Tower." If the bioplastics market grows at 20 percent per year as predicted, however, the arable land and food resources needed to produce feedstocks could become a greater concern.[11]

But already some bio-based plastics are made from non-food sources like switchgrass and agricultural waste. These cellulosic feedstocks, however, require more sophisticated biorefineries that are still scarce because of their complex technologies and the high cost to build and run them. DuPont, for example, recently opened a cellulosic biorefinery in Iowa at a cost of $200 million. The plant will produce cellulosic ethanol and consume over 375,000 tons of corn stover, the inedible stalks left after harvest, every year.[12]

Despite the hurdles of feedstocks and biodegradability, bioplastics are the material of the future, and they are already well established in many of today's products. The ECO mouse, for example, is, according to manufacturer Fujitsu, the world's first biodegradable, plastic-free computer mouse. It joins other computer accessories in the ECO line that the company says is "helping to eliminate the use of oil-based resources, such as plastic and PVC from the manufacturing process."

"We're continuing to prove that it's possible to eliminate the use of non-renewable sources from the IT lifecycle," said Chandan Mehta, product manager at Fujitsu Technology Solutions. "By choosing this mouse, environmentally-conscious businesses can feel good that they are helping reduce CO_2 emissions without sacrificing durability or comfort, and without having to pay any extra."

The shell is made from plastic substitutes called Arboform and Biograde. Sometimes called "liquid wood," Arboform is a moldable bioplastic made from lignin, cellulose fibers, and natural additives. Stronger than polyethylene plastic yet 100 percent biodegradable, it earned its inventors, Helmut Nägele and Jürgen Pfitzer of the Fraunhofer Institute for Chemical Technology in Germany, the 2010 European Inventor Award. Arboform's pliability gives the ECO mouse shell more elasticity than other renewable materials, making it more comfortable to use than a traditional plastic mouse, according to Fujitsu. Biograde is a cellulose-based bioplastic with similar properties.

Beetle Bioplastic

Not all bioplastics come from plants. Dutch designer Aagje Hoekstra makes hers from the shells of dead Darkling Beetles. The shells are made of chitin, a natural polymer also found in crab and lobster shells. After heat-pressing, the shells are still visible in the plastic, which is waterproof and heat-resistant up to 200 degrees centigrade. "I wanted to keep

Figure 18.3 Darkling Beetle Bioplastic Lanterns
The shells of dead Darkling Beetles, which are made of the natural
polymer chitin are the material of choice for lanterns by Dutch
designer Aagje Hoekstra. Image courtesy of Aagje Hoekstra.

the structure of the beetle in the plastic so you know where it has come from," Hoekstra told Dezeen magazine. She has already made jewelry and decorative pieces from her Darkling Beetle plastic, and has plans to make plastic spoons and cups. It's not clear how many consumers are eager to eat and drink from plastic made from beetle shells, but it does appear that Hoekstra's bioplastic utensils don't contain the toxins found in many petrochemical plastic utensils.[13]

Bioplastics offer many of the benefits of petrochemical plastics, and their production results in lower carbon dioxide emissions, less toxic waste, and reduced fossil fuel consumption. Ingeo, for instance, is a PLA biopolymer made by NatureWorks that produces less than one-third the greenhouse gases of common plastics like PVC and PET over its life cycle.[14] As a result of such benefits, nearly one out of three consumers said they were willing to pay 10 percent more for them, according to McKinsey & Co. partner Jorge Fergie. He predicted bioplastic sales will only increase as crude oil prices continue to rise. And thanks to rising oil prices and consumer demand, petroleum-based plastics are likely to see a higher bio-based content in the future. Procter & Gamble, for instance, recently patented a new food packaging material made with 85 percent bio-based content. The Plant PET Technology Collaborative, which includes Procter & Gamble, Heinz, Nike, and Coca-Cola, is working to make packaging, clothing, and other products from 100 percent bio-PET (polyethylene terephthalate made from Brazilian sugarcane). Commitments by Coke to offer 100 percent plant-based bottles by 2020 suggest how fast the industry is moving toward bioplastics. Coke subsidiary Odwalla already sells drinks in bottles made from 100 percent plant-based material. These 100 percent plant-based products represent the leading edge of a bioplastics revolution that will replace petroleum-based plastics in the post-petroleum era.[15,16]

Bioplastics for Carbon Capture

One advantage of plastics is that they capture and sequester CO_2. When oil is used to make plastic, the carbon that would be released if that oil were burned is captured. All the plastic ever created, unless burned, is holding millions of tons of CO_2 in products, landfills, soils, and oceans. Bruce Mulliken of Green Energy News points out that bioplastics made from plants have the same potential for carbon capture:

> Mother Nature does a pretty good job of capturing and storing carbon dioxide. Plants pull CO2 out of the air … [and] if that plant happens to be a tree, the carbon that was pulled from the air remains sequestered in the wood of the tree as long as it is alive, or in the case of trees used for lumber, the carbon can be sequestered in the frame of a house, a piece of furniture or other wood-built object. In wood used as a building product, carbon can remain sequestered for at least a decade or as much as centuries.

Using non-degradable bioplastics to build super durable goods, which can sequester carbon for decades is simply improving on the work of Mother Nature. Instead of wood being a primary, natural way to sequester carbon dioxide, the man-made process could use all kinds of plant life including grasses, waste wood, waste food and waste agricultural products, even algae, to make bioplastics which are then used in the manufacture of products and components used to build super durable goods, like buildings and infrastructure.[17]

Notes

1   Álvarez-Chávez, C.R., Edwards, S., Moure-Eraso, R., and Geiser, K., "Sustainability of Bio-based Plastics: General Comparative Analysis," 3rd International Workshop on Advances in Cleaner Production, São Paulo, Brazil, May 18–20, 2011, www.advancesincleanerproduction.net/third/files/sessoes/5B/7/Alvarez-Chavez_CR%20-%20Paper%20-%205B7.pdf

2   Shen, Li, Haufe, Juliane, and Patel, Martin K., "Product Overview and Market Projection of Emerging Bio-Based Plastics," Technical Report, University of Utrecht, Utrecht, Netherlands, 2009, http://en.european-bioplastics.org/wp-content/uploads/2011/03/publications/PROBIP2009_Final_June_2009.pdf

3   Álvarez-Chávez et al., "Sustainability of Bio-based Plastics."

4   Zara, Christopher, "Coca-Cola Company (KO) Busted for 'Greenwashing': PlantBottle Marketing Exaggerated Environmental Benefits, Says Consumer Report," *International Business Times* online, September 3, 2013, www.ibtimes.com/coca-cola-company-ko-busted-greenwashing-plantbottle-marketing-exaggerated-environ-mental-benefits

5   "'Dropping in': Bioplastics—Same Performance but Renewable," *European Bioplastics Bulletin*, Issue 3, 2012, http://en.european-bioplastics.org/blog/2012/07/13/dropping-in-bioplastics-same-performance-but-renewable/

6   "Bioplastics", NYC Recycles, www.nyc.gov/html/nycwasteless/html/resources/plastics_bio.shtml

7   Long, Cheryl, "The Truth about Biodegradable Plastics," *Mother Earth News*, June/July 2012, www.mothere-arthnews.com/nature-and-environment/biodegradable-plastics-zmaz10jjzraw.aspx#ixzz2ggDAWFM0;   U.S. Environmental Protection Agency, "The Degradables Debate," www.epa.gov/osw/wycd/catbook/debate.htm; Lilienfeld, Robert, ed., "Review of Life Cycle Data Relating to Disposable, Compostable, Biodegradable, and Reusable Grocery Bags," The ULS Report, March 28, 2008, www.use-less-stuff.com/Paper-and-Plastic-Grocery-Bag-LCA-Summary-3-28-08.pdf

8   Weisman, Alan, "Polymers Are Forever," *Orion*, May/June 2007, www.orionmagazine.org/index.php/articles/article/270/

9   U.S. Government Printing Office, "Electronic Code of Federal Regulations," October 31, 2014, www.ecfr.gov/cgi-bin/text-idx?c=ecfr&SID=bce841cb851c93a436cc50e2996cc9d4&tpl=/ecfrbrowse/Title16/16cfr260_main_02.tpl

10 National Association for PET Container Resources, "Degradable Additives to Plastic Packaging: A Threat to Plastic Recycling," www.napcor.com/pdf/Degradable%20Additives%20to%20Plastic%20Packaging%20 2-15-2013.pdf; Soenarie, Angelique, "Eco-friendly Plastic Bottles Stoke Recycling Fight," *USA Today*, February 4, 2011,   http://usatoday30.usatoday.com/money/industries/environment/2011-01-29-water-bottles_N.htm;

Schwartz, Naoki, "Water Bottle Lawsuit: California Attorney General Sues Companies Over False Biodegradable Claims," *Huffington Post*, October 26, 2011, www.huffingtonpost.com/2011/10/26/water-bottle-lawsuit_n_1033795.html; U.S. Government Printing Office, "Electronic Code of Federal Regulations, §260.8 Degradable Claims," www.ecfr.gov/cgi-bin/text-idx?c=ecfr&SID=6beb087d6582cad0e42557e8ef1f12aa&rgn=div8&view=text&node=16:1.0.1.2.24.0.5.8&idno=16

11 European Bioplastics, "Bioplastics", 2014, http://en.european-bioplastics.org/bioplastics/; Bredenberg, Al, "Bio-Plastics Are Getting a Toehold in the Packaging Market," December 10, 2010, http://news.thomasnet.com/imt/2012/12/10/bio-plastics-are-getting-a-toehold-in-the-packaging-market

12 "DuPont Breaks Ground on Commercial-scale Cellulosic Biorefinery in Iowa," Green Car Congress, November 30, 2012, www.greencarcongress.com/2012/11/dupont-20121130.html

13 http://www.aagjehoekstra.nl/coleoptera.php

14 "Ingeo Eco-Profile," NatureWorks, www.natureworksllc.com/The-Ingeo-Journey/Eco-Profile-and-LCA/Eco-Profile

15 "Dow Chemical Explores Methods for Producing Its Key Feedstocks from Renewable Resources," February 28, 2011, www.icis.com/Articles/2011/02/28/9438198/dow-studies-bio-based-propylene-routes.html; Whitworth, Joe, "P&G Files Patent for Eco-Friendly Package Invention," *Food Production Daily*, November 19, 2012, www.foodproductiondaily.com/Packaging/P-G-files-patent-for-eco-friendly-package-invention

16 Moye, Jay, "15 Billion and Counting," June 5, 2013, www.coca-colacompany.com/15-billion-and-counting; Cernansky, Rachel, "Odwalla 'Plastic' PlantBottle Now Made With 100% Plant Materials," treehugger.com, April 5, 2011, www.treehugger.com/corporate-responsibility/odwalla-plastic-plantbottle-now-made-with-100-plant-materials.html

17 Mulliken, Bruce, "Building with Bioplastics: Atmospheric Carbon Storage in Construction Materials—Part 4," *Green Energy News*, Volume 17, Number 18, July 17, 2012, www.green-energy-news.com/arch/nrgs2012/20120072.html

19

Nanoplastics

Possibilities and Perils Big and Small

> Nanotechnology is likely to change the way almost everything—from vaccines to computers to automobile tires to objects not yet imagined—is designed and made.
> (Interagency Working Group on Nanoscience, Engineering and Technology)[1]

Along with the biotechnology that makes plant-based plastic and other innovations a reality, one other "supertechnology" is shaping our post-petroleum future: nanotechnology.

"In the wake of climate change and increasing oil prices, the demand for sustainable and light weight materials that can replace oil-based products has increased," said the founders of SustainComp, a new European project to develop advanced sustainable wood-based composite materials using nanotechnology. "At the same time, bioplastic production capacities are increasing. The combination of bioplastics and nanotechnology is an approach that meets the technical demands of replacing the oil-based materials with sustainable and renewable ones."[2]

Nanotechnology has the potential to change how we make things by enabling us to design and manipulate matter at the molecular scale. At that scale, the laws of quantum physics enable materials to behave in strange and interesting ways. New products made with these nanomaterials offer unparalleled performance—and raise a host of new environmental and health concerns. Many nanotech innovations and concerns stem simply from the small size of the particles themselves, as small as one-billionth of a meter. Concrete, for example, can be made four times stronger simply by grinding its Portland cement into nano-size particles. But particles just a few billionths of a meter wide can enter our lungs and tissues, even pass through cell membranes, in ways that larger materials can't.

While concerns about the effects of nanoparticles on human health and the environment are causing some to question it, nanotechnology has been adopted by almost all industries. Consumer products from automobiles and electronics to cosmetics and medical implants incorporate nanomaterials for greater strength, reduced weight, and many other advantages. Most of these use nanocomposites, materials made from a combination of nanoparticles such as carbon nanotubes and a matrix or binder that is often petroleum-based. Carbon nanotubes have led the nanotech revolution since their introduction in 1991 because of their remarkable properties. They can be much stronger yet many times lighter than steel, they can be made transparent, and they can conduct electricity. They are already common in many consumer products—your car, for example. Autos incorporate carbon nanotube nanoclays in their bumpers to reduce weight without sacrificing strength. These bumpers are, in fact, stronger than the heavy steel ones on the car your grandfather drove. And

Figure 19.1 How Small Is a Nanoparticle?
The size of a nanoparticle is to the size of a soccer ball as the soccer ball is to the Earth. iStock.com image.

they can be molded to integrate with the form of the car. Another example is the carbon nanotube bike frame, now the standard in high-end cycling events like the Tour de France. These frames are made by mixing carbon nanotubes—the strongest material on Earth—with a polymer matrix to hold them together. Carbon nanotube frames are even stronger and lighter than carbon fiber frames, which embed a carbon fiber cloth in a polymer matrix.

Research centers and corporate labs worldwide are producing a steady stream of carbon nanotube-based innovations. Australia's national science agency, the Commonwealth Scientific and Industrial Research Organization (CSIRO), is currently partnering with the NanoTech Institute at the University of Texas at Dallas to boost research into carbon nanotube yarns and textiles, including the development of "bulletproof yarn."

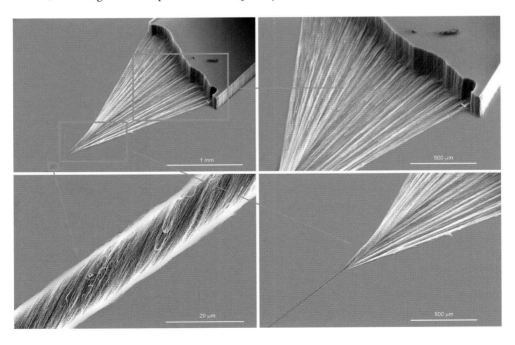

"Carbon fibers about one-third of a millimeter long can be spun into yarns with extraordinary properties," explained a CSIRO press release; "they conduct heat and electricity, and have the potential to produce a new generation of intelligent textiles."[3]

Conductive Plastic

Plastic does many things very well, but conducting electricity isn't one of them. But now nanoscientists at the University of Virginia have used carbon nanotubes to unite the virtues of plastics and metals in an award-winning, ultra-lightweight, conductive material. Their nanocomposite material is a mixture of plastic, carbon nanotubes, and a foaming agent, making it extremely lightweight, corrosion-proof, and cheaper to produce than metal. Their experiments revealed that while carbon nanotubes make up less than 2 percent of the nanocomposite, they increase its electrical conductivity by ten orders of magnitude. They also increase the material's thermal conductivity, improving its capacity to dissipate heat. "Metal is not only heavy; it corrodes easily," said team leader Mool C. Gupta. "And plastic insulators are lightweight, stable and cheaper to produce, but cannot conduct electricity. So the goal, originally, was to take plastic and make it electrically conductive." James H. Aylor, Dean of the university's School of Engineering and Applied Science, foresees that, "The applications for this new material range from thermal insulation, electromagnetic interference shields for commercial and aerospace applications, advanced sensors, lightning protection and more."[4]

Most nanocomposites still require plastic. One reason is that making nanoparticles such as carbon nanotubes is still a very expensive process. Plastic provides a less expensive filler as well as an effective binder to hold the nanoparticles together. Nanotechnology is also expanding the capabilities of conventional plastics. "Most properties of polymers are based on nanostructures," said Franz Brandstetter, a polymer researcher at BASF. "We are creating new polymerization methods to create micro- and nano-structures." BASF predicts that insulation made using this method will be twice as effective as the company's current Basotect foam. In their nanostructuring process, chemical molecules self-assemble, allowing engineers to design molecules with more specific properties. Brandstetter recognizes this as a paradigm shift in design. "Now," he said, "instead of asking 'What will this material do?' we can ask 'What properties do we want?'"

Figure 19.2 "Bulletproof Yarn"
Carbon nanotubes can be hundreds of times stronger than steel yet one-sixth the weight. Researchers at Australia's Commonwealth Scientific and Industrial Research Organization and the University of Texas at Dallas are spinning them into yarn to create "a new generation of intelligent textiles." Image courtesy of CSIRO Manufacturing Flagship Waurn Ponds Microscopy Laboratory.

Plastic that Won't Burn

What could be better than a plastic that releases water vapor instead of hazardous gases when it burns? The plastics common in buildings are often so flammable that they require the addition of flame-retardant chemicals, many of which come with health and environmental concerns. The state of Washington has even banned one class of flame-retardants from use in household items. But nanoscientists from the University of Massachusetts Amherst have created a synthetic polymer that requires no flame-retardants because it simply will not burn. Their polymer uses bishydroxydeoxybenzoin, which releases water vapor when it burns instead of hazardous gases. The researchers said their synthetic polymer is clear, flexible, durable, and much cheaper to make than the high-temperature, heat-resistant plastics in current use. Their work exemplifies how nanotechnology is not only creating new alternatives to petroleum-based plastic, but expanding the capabilities of all plastics.[5]

Nanomaterials for Food Packaging

ONE area where nanotechnology has great potential and raises great concerns is food packaging. As Will Soutter, Editor in Chief of the nanotech information hub AZoNano writes, "Whilst there are still concerns about the degree to which nanomaterials can leach into food from the packaging, and the effect they may have on the health of consumers, most research so far looks promising, and the benefits are highly tangible—several nano-enhancements for packaging are already on the market, helping to prolong the shelf life of food and making it easier to manufacture, process, and manage."

Because the plastics used in food packaging are slightly permeable, the food inside eventually spoils. A nanocoating less than one-millionth of a meter thick, however, can prevent spoilage. In addition, many nanoparticles, like silver and zinc oxide, are naturally antibacterial. The conductive nature of many nanoparticles even has researchers developing smart packaging that will alert consumers—by changing color, for example—when foods start to go bad. But adding heavy metals like silver and zinc to the packaging that contacts our food raises some concerns. "It is not yet completely clear to what extent nanoparticles embedded in packaging films can leach into food products," writes Soutter, "and what the effects of exposure to various nanomaterials on consumer health might be."[6]

Researchers at University College Dublin and University College Cork found that silver nanoparticles in plasticized PVC nanocomposite packaging film can migrate to the food they contain. But they found that migration "likely to be below current migration limits for conventional migrants and a provisional toxicity limit."

"However," they cautioned, "it is acknowledged there is still considerable uncertainty about the potential harmful effects of particles at the nanoscale." The head of the Fraunhofer Institute, Europe's largest consumer research organization, reached a different conclusion. The Institute's research, he told a meeting of the European Parliament, showed that particles three to four nanometers in size "cannot migrate at all from LDPE [low density polyethylene] and therefore from any plastics food contact material." While each of these conclusions reflect research on specific conditions, they reveal that the jury is still out on nanomaterials for food packaging.[7]

Meanwhile, the U.S. National Organic Program says that foods contacting engineered nanomaterials in their production, processing, or packaging will not be allowed to carry the organic label. This includes foods contacting nanoengineered surfaces as well as those with nanoengineered primary packaging. Their ban is a serious blow not only to the producers of countertops and packaging incorporating antimicrobial nanoparticles (which are becoming more commonplace), but also to nanotechnology in general, as the public may be more likely to perceive it as unhealthy now that it is banned from carrying the organic label.[8]

Keeping Food Fresh ... with Nanoclay

Paper and cardboard are still the world's most common packaging materials, but when it comes to food packaging, plastic rules. That's because paper can't match it in reducing moisture penetration. But now researchers at Sheffield Hallam University in the U.K. and Karlstad University in Sweden have invented an alternative made from clay, starch, and a non-toxic plasticizer. The plastic-free product, which they call CaiLar, is ten times more

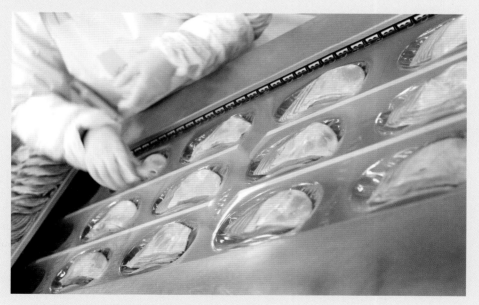

Figure 19.3 O2Block Food Packaging Additive
When oxygen enters food packages, their contents can spoil quickly. But Valencia-based NanoBioMatters has developed new additives combining oxygen-scavenging iron particles with phyllosillicate clay to delay spoilage. iStock.com image; photo by Kaupo Kikkas.

effective than paper at resisting water vapor transmission. "Consumption is increasing in society and it is increasingly important to find replacement materials for the plastic films that dominate today's packages," said Sheffield Professor Chris Breen. CaiLar recently medalled in the Innovators Contest at Globe Forum in Stockholm, and the team is now exploring commercialization.

The European Commission, meanwhile, has invested over 6 million Euros in SustainComp, which aims to develop sustainable nanostructured wood-based biocomposite materials for packaging to replace oil-based products. And the Valencia-based company, NanoBioMatters, has already developed a new series of additives for "oxygen scavenging" in food packaging. Food spoilage typically results when oxygen enters the package through gaps or direct penetration of the packaging membrane. But NanoBioMatters' O2Block technology combines phyllosillicate clay with oxygen-scavenging iron particles to create what the company calls "a simpler, less costly, and more convenient alternative to conventional scavenging techniques." The result could be longer shelf life for foods.[9]

Health and Environmental Concerns

WHILE nanomaterials outperform conventional ones in many ways, they also raise concerns. What happens to these tiny particles when they enter our bodies or the environment? Many studies have shown that some nanoparticles can indeed cause problems when they accumulate in our tissues and in plants and animals. Nanoparticles can behave differently in the body and the environment than bulk materials, and their size alone can be a concern. Nanoparticles can enter the lungs more easily than larger particles, and they can even pass through certain cell membranes. They can also bioaccumulate or build up in plant and animal tissues. This is another area of concern where these particles simply haven't been around long enough to accumulate in natural environments where we can study their long-term effects. Researchers try to simulate bioaccumulation, but it can't be mimicked exactly.[10]

Transient Electronics

Emerging nano-biotechnologies like transient electronics highlight both the promise and the concerns inherent in these rapidly advancing fields. Transient electronics are cell phones, cameras, and medical devices made from "ecoresorbable" and "bioresorbable" materials—materials that break down into tiny particles when composted (ecoresorbable) or even in our bodies (bioresorbable). "These devices are the polar opposite of conventional electronics whose integrated circuits are designed for long-term physical and electronic stability," said Fiorenzo Omenetto, professor of Biomedical Engineering at Tufts School of Engineering. "Transient electronics offer robust performance comparable to current devices but they will fully resorb into their environment at a prescribed time—ranging from minutes to years, depending on the application," Omenetto explained.

"Imagine the environmental benefits if cell phones, for example, could just dissolve instead of languishing in landfills for years."

Omenetto co-authored a paper in *Science* describing the research conducted in collaboration with co-author John Rogers of the University of Illinois at Urbana-Champaign. Rogers's team combined electronics with silk proteins extracted from silkworm cocoons to create an ingestible and fully biodegradable 64 pixel digital camera. Scientists from the University of Arizona and Northwestern University also took part in the research.[11]

Figure 19.4 Transient Electronics
Biodegradable electronic devices like this dissolvable circuit board could introduce new design paradigms for medical implants, environmental monitors, and consumer devices. Image courtesy of Professor John Rogers, University of Illinois at Urbana-Champaign.

But what becomes of the tiny particles as they biodegrade? One study, "Sustainability of Bio-based Plastics," ranked nano-biocomposites as the least desirable type of bioplastics, saying, "The health effects of nano-particles are of concern because their impacts are not well understood. Toxicologists hypothesize that nano-particles may not be detected by the normal defense system of organisms. Their small size can modify protein structures, and they can travel from the respiratory system to the brain and other organs."[12]

The EPA sums up the current state of our knowledge about nanotechnology, saying, "Nanotechnology is a relatively new science and, as a result, the health implications associated with engineered nanomaterials have not been determined." Some advocate for the precautionary principle—keeping engineered nanomaterials out of the marketplace, and therefore the environment and our bodies, until we know for certain how they will behave. But that is far from the approach taken by governmental agencies like the Food and Drug Administration, which has shied away from regulating nanotechnology. At the very least, nanotechnology regulation in the U.S. will remain in flux for years to come.[13]

Titanium Dioxide and Your Health

Titanium dioxide (TiO_2) is the world's most widely used nanoparticle, with worldwide production in the millions of tons per year. It's used as a whitener in paint, sunscreen, toothpaste, even foods like powdered sugar donuts. A study entitled "Titanium Dioxide Nanoparticles in Food and Personal Care Products" found that children potentially consume 2–4 times as much TiO_2 per kilogram by weight as an adult. The study also found that some toothpastes and sunscreens contain over 10 percent titanium. TiO_2 is classified by the International Agency for Research on Cancer as "possibly carcinogenic to humans." With those concerns in mind, I asked Professor Maria Vittoria Diamanti for her thoughts on the current state of TiO_2 toxicology. While not a toxicologist herself, Professor Diamanti is a faculty member at the Politecnico di Milano and author of numerous studies on TiO_2, particularly in building applications.

Should we be concerned about the seemingly large quantities of TiO_2 that children are ingesting, as this study reports?

Titanium dioxide, by itself, is considered to be a biologically inert material, as it is a naturally occurring compound. Yet, concern is growing about its nanosized forms. Animal and human studies show that inhaled nanoparticles (NPs) are less efficiently removed than larger particles by the macrophage clearance mechanisms in the lungs, causing lung damage, and that NPs can translocate through the circulatory, lymphatic, and nervous systems to many tissues and organs, including the brain.

The study cites other studies reporting risks from nanoparticular TiO_2 due to inhalation, including inflammation and a possible link to asthma. Is inhalation a greater concern than ingestion?

Although inhalation is the most vulnerable entrance point, it probably exerts the lowest risk, given the low exposure time for common people; conversely, it can be a hazard for people working in the manufacturing of TiO_2 NPs, or TiO_2-containing materials. However, the human studies conducted so far do not suggest an association between occupational exposure to TiO_2 and an increased risk for cancer.

How about absorption through the skin, as in the case of sunscreens?

Current experiments performed on TiO_2-containing creams show that NPs do not penetrate through healthy skin, thus do not reach viable skin cells and distribute to other organs and tissues.

Finally, the study points out that nearly 70 percent of all TiO_2 produced is used as a pigment in paints, and that while several studies have indicated that TiO_2 tends to be less hazardous to organisms than other nanomaterials such as multiwall carbon nanotubes, others have shown it can bioaccumulate in plankton and inhibit algae growth.

The possible release of titanium dioxide NPs from the built environment (chalking effects of photocatalytic paints, plasters, raw concrete) may be a source of contamination of urban waters, leading to ecotoxicological issues on aquatic life. In this case, short-term exposures revealed no toxic effects on aquatic life, but long-term exposure should also be evaluated due to the persistence and poor solubility of TiO_2. Scarce information is available in the scientific literature; yet, the potential exposure dosages are extremely low.[14]

Notes

1   Interagency Working Group on Nanoscience, Engineering and Technology, "National Nanotechnology Initiative: Leading to the Next Industrial Revolution," Report, Washington, DC, 2000, www.whitehouse.gov/files/documents/ostp/NSTC%20Reports/NNI2000.pdf

2   Institute of Nanotechnology, "EU to Invest Millions in Nanotech for Sustainable Packaging," August 21, 2009, www.nano.org.uk/forum/viewtopic.php?t=3711&sid=4c9ae91ffe38d8d2f82130a89b3937e2

3   Commonwealth Scientific and Industrial Research Organization, "Spinning a Bullet-proof Yarn," March 15, 2010, www.csiro.au/Organisation-Structure/Divisions/CMSE/Fibre-Science/Carbon-Nanotubes-3.aspx

4   Elvin, George, "Nanotechnology for Green Building," Webcast, April 22, 2009, www.brighttalk.com/webcast/691/2060

5   UMass Amherst News & Media Relations, "UMass Amherst Scientists Create Fire-Safe Plastic," May 30, 2007, www.umass.edu/newsoffice/article/umass-amherst-scientists-create-fire-safe-plastic

6   Soutter, William, "Nanotechnology in Food Packaging," AZoNano.com, July 6, 2012, www.azonano.com/article.aspx?ArticleID=3035

7   Cushen, M., Kerry, J., Morris, M., Cruz-Romero, M., and Cummins, E., "Migration and Exposure Assessment of Silver from a PVC Nanocomposite," *Food Chemistry*, Volume 139, Issues 1–4, August 15, 2013, 389–397, www.sciencedirect.com/science/article/pii/S0308814613000691; Addy, Rod, "Fraunhofer Expert: Nanoparticles

Don't Migrate from Food Plastics," *Food Production Daily*, April 2, 2013, www.foodproductiondaily.com/Packaging/Fraunhofer-expert-nanoparticles-don-t-migrate-from-food-plastics; Witworth, Joe, "Migration Factors of Nanosilver in PVC Packaging Studied," *Food Production Daily*, April 11, 2013, www.foodproduc-tiondaily.com/Packaging/Migration-factors-of-nanosilver-in-PVC-packaging-studied

8   Elvin, George, "USDA Bans Foods Containing or Contacting Nanoparticles from Carrying 'Organic' Label," Green Technology Forum, March 24, 2011, http://gelvin.squarespace.com/green-technology-forum/2011/3/24/usda-bans-foods-containing-or-contacting-nanoparticles-from.html

9   "Spain's NanoBioMatters Develops New Series of Oxygen Scavengers for Plastics Packaging," Press Release, October 27, 2010, www.nanobiomatters.com/wordpress/wp-content/uploads/2010/10/NanoBioMatters-launches-O2-scavenger-release.pdf

10   U.S. Environmental Protection Agency, "Research Investigates Human Health Effects of Nanomaterials," www.epa.gov/nanoscience/quickfinder/hh_effects.htm

11   Thurler, Kim, "Smooth as Silk 'Transient Electronics' Dissolve in Body or Environment," TuftsNow, September 27, 2012, http://now.tufts.edu/news-releases/smooth-silk-transient-electronics#sthash.UOTeF3gI.dpuf

12   Álvarez-Chávez, C.R., Edwards, S., Moure-Eraso, R., and Geiser, K., "Sustainability of Bio-based Plastics: General Comparative Analysis," 3rd International Workshop on Advances in Cleaner Production, São Paulo, Brazil, May 18–20, 2011, www.advancesincleanerproduction.net/third/files/sessoes/5B/7/Alvarez-Chavez_CR%20-%20Paper%20-%205B7.pdf

13   U.S. Environmental Protection Agency, "Research Investigates Human Health Effects of Nanomaterials."

14   Elvin, George, "Professor Maria Vittoria Diamanti on Titanium Dioxide Toxicity," Green Technology Forum, February 21, 2012, www.greentechforum.net/green-technology-forum/2012/2/21/professor-maria-vittoria-diamanti-on-titanium-dioxide-toxici.html

PART FIVE

Principles of Post-Petroleum Design

– 20 –

Cycles and Flows

Living Systems

O UR post-petroleum world may be built not only with different materials and technologies than our current one, but different design principles as well. The principles of design described in this chapter are drawn from the work of the dozens of post-petroleum designers interviewed and studied for this book. The products they make use less petroleum, and they are typically made with:

Renewable materials
Recyclable materials
Non-toxic materials
Low energy processes
Low carbon emissions
Local artisanry

These are basic principles of sustainable design and manufacturing. They are admirable, but not very surprising, coming from designers striving to reduce their use of petroleum. But there are other, less obvious commonalities, grounded in a deep understanding of the flows and interconnectedness found in nature. While they do not necessarily articulate them in these terms, these principles occur again and again in post-petroleum design:

Energy flows
Cycles
Resource balancing
Resilience
Interdependence

These principles are also principles of something else: living systems. The dozens of post-petroleum designers interviewed had not necessarily spoken about emulating living systems, but their work speaks for them. In the preceding part of this book we looked at some of the practicalities of post-petroleum design—material sourcing, manufacturing, distribution and waste management. Now let's explore some principles that may guide these pragmatic decisions and the people who make them.

Energy Flows

PETROLEUM may be the first thing we think of when someone says "energy," but there is much more to the concept than just oil. Perhaps we would be wise to see energy in everything and begin to recognize how it moves and flows, concentrates and disperses. Then we can design in synergy with it rather than just using it up in its crudest forms like oil, gas, and coal. Look, for example, at how nature sustains and grows the most fundamental life form, the tree. Sunlight falls on the leaves, which are designed as perfect solar collectors, dispersed around the tree's perimeter, reaching for the sun like living solar panels. Through photosynthesis, the tree then converts sunlight into food for the tree. The byproduct of this process? The oxygen we breathe. In fact, all the byproducts and outputs of nature's energy transformations become food or input for other processes. There is no "waste." And while a tree absorbs energy from the sun, it also draws energy in the form of nutrients from the soil. When the tree dies, it becomes food for microbes and insects in the soil, ultimately becoming soil that nourishes new tree growth.

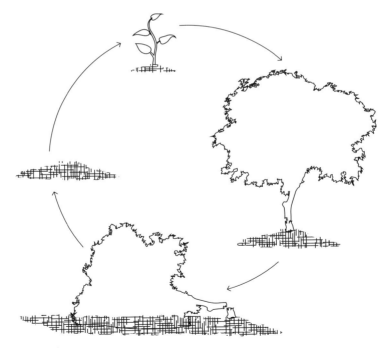

Figure 20.1 Cyclical Energy Flows in Nature

In nature, waste from one process becomes food in
another. Illustration by Maria Meza.

When we begin to see ourselves as part of an infinite web of energy, we quickly realize how foolish we have been in our use of the primitive forms of it we draw from the Earth. Too often, we harm the Earth to get at it, we pollute the Earth to refine it, and we harm the Earth again when we burn it. Much of the potential energy in fossil fuels is lost in processing and transmission.

Nature's renewable sources of energy like the sun and wind, in contrast, enable us to use energy right at its point of production, as a tree does, as all of nature does. Energy in nature is circular—byproducts and outputs becoming food and inputs for other processes; and it is local—it isn't wasted in distribution, but used on the spot. It is also in continuous motion; even when it is stored like heat in a rock or food consumed by an animal, it is always flowing. We could learn to use small amounts of energy locally and quickly, moving the place and time of consumption ever closer to the place and time of production so we don't waste so much in transmission and storage. Energy flows in nature are also self-regulating, "able to maintain their essential variables within limits acceptable to their own structures in the face of unexpected disturbances." An animal that receives too much solar energy seeks the shade. A cloud that builds up too much electrostatic energy releases it as lightning.[1]

Could we apply a deeper understanding of nature's energy flows to the way that we design, make, distribute, and use things? We are beginning to practice a crude form of this through life cycle assessment, which tells us about the energy consumed in the manufacturing, distribution, use, and disposal of our consumer products. It points to a world where we recognize ourselves as a part of this flow, not separate from it. Isolating ourselves from life and land in the past has too often misled us into seeing our planet as a sort of enormous shopping mall, full of resources for us to consume, and as a giant garbage heap for the waste and pollution we create. But there is no standing outside the flow of energy; we are an inextricable part of it, and we greatly affect its flow. We can do harm, as we have too often done with fossil fuels, or we can do good, as we are beginning to do with renewable fuels and materials.

Energy without Electricity

When I committed to making Gone Studio's manufacturing process zero energy, I thought I might be creating considerable hardship for myself. I thought that making all our products by hand might be drudgery. But forgoing electricity has proven to be one of the best business decisions—and life decisions—I've ever made. Once I got the hang of working with zero-energy tools like a hand-powered die press and a foot-powered sewing machine, I found them to be much more satisfying than electric equipment. Because their power comes from their operator, it's much easier to feel the material, like cutting a log with a handsaw instead of a chainsaw. And of course it's better for the environment than relying on grid-connected tools, which, in Gone Studio's case, would mean relying on coal-powered utilities.

But the most unexpected side effect of working without power tools is the quiet. Whereas electrically powered equipment would be chugging or banging away, hand-powered tools are nearly silent. This allows me to connect more deeply with the material and focus more attentively on the work at hand. Instead of a distraction or drudgery, work becomes a pathway to meditation and mindfulness. And the most surprising side effect of working without electricity? It doesn't take any longer. Working without electricity can, of course, take longer than using power tools, but I optimize the design of our products to be assembled without electricity. We could set up solar panels and use electric equipment without fossil fuels or carbon emissions, but I've found the electricity-free environment and work so satisfying that I plan to stick with them.

Figure 20.2 Working with Zero-Energy Machinery
The author's inventory of zero energy tools include a
foot-powered sewing machine. Photo by Jayne Rohlfing.

Energy flows in conventional manufacturing are often "one-way." We too often extract energy from the Earth and give back waste and toxins. A more holistic view of energy flows recognizes this imbalance and seeks to minimize non-renewable energy inputs and energy waste. In many ways, the cleanest industrial process is the one we don't use, the greenest building the one we don't build. Eliminating energy-consuming processes altogether, of course, minimizes their waste and resource use to zero. This is what Amazon aimed to achieve in its Frustration-Free Certified Packaging program. Seeking to reduce "wrap rage," the program simply eliminated packaging altogether. The rage went down, and so did the energy and resources required to make the packaging. What opportunities lie hidden in other design and manufacturing problems—opportunities to save vast amounts of energy when we recognize its flow?

The flow of energy in manufacturing doesn't have to stop at zero either. Can we use waste instead of non-renewable fossil fuels as energy? With current technologies, it's not as easy as it sounds. Waste-to-energy conversion of plastic, for example, is currently a very high-energy process involving incineration at high temperatures. Innovations like biodegradation, which uses bacteria or other biological means to break down plastic, and cogeneration, which uses waste energy from one process as the source for another, could help us ensure that the energy used to reuse waste doesn't exceed the energy gained from it.

Cycles

In nature, energy flows not in a continuous, linear stream, but in a complex network of entwined and interacting substreams. These substreams affect each other in innumerable ways, cresting and ebbing as they converge and disperse. Just like waves on the sea, these interacting energies can form peaks and valleys in response to internal or external forces. These peaks and valleys can recur rhythmically in cycles of pulsed energy. Even the cycling of day and night is a manifestation of complex interacting energies within our solar system. The result of these interactions is a cycling not only of energy in its many forms (light, heat, food, and fuel) but other resources like water and minerals.

Some of nature's cycles can appear random, probably because we do not entirely understand the complex web of forces influencing them. Others, like the cycling of day and night, appear quite uniform. Understanding nature's cycles can help us design more sustainably. Walk through any city at night, for example, and you can spot the buildings that ignore the day/night cycle. Their lights burn brightly even though they're unoccupied, and their heating or air conditioning and other systems are probably running just the same as when they're fully occupied during the day. Smarter buildings pay attention to this simplest of nature's cycles, reducing lighting, heating or air conditioning and other system outputs at night, and saving large amounts of energy and money in the process.

One of nature's most important cycles is the closed loop of inputs and outputs. In nature, waste becomes food. Even the end of life for a plant or animal brings new life as food for others. Our consumption of oil is perhaps the epitome of disregard for this simple rule. We take this resource, which took millennia to form from organic materials, use it briefly, and give back pollutants and carbon emissions. It is a fundamental violation of nature's rule of making food from waste, of sustainable, regenerative cycles where output from one becomes input for another.

Too often in petroleum-era manufacturing, waste has been harmful rather than nutritional. We let it contaminate our air and oceans or buried it for future generations to deal with. We also frequently denied the true value or cost of the energy and resource inputs that feed our production. Water, fossil fuels, minerals, and other natural resources have been virtually given away to corporations that profit from them. Oil has been a prime example of this unsustainable practice which fails to properly value the industrial inputs or resources that nature has created. A report by the International Monetary Fund showed that post-tax subsidies to petroleum

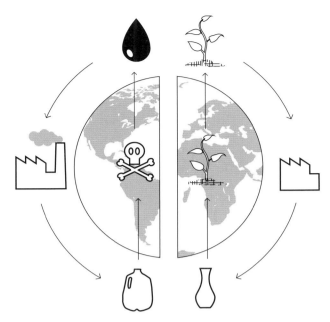

Figure 20.3 Cyclical Nature and Linear Manufacturing
Renewable materials can be grown, processed, used, and recycled
with minimal impact. Petrochemicals often incorporate toxic
additives which can harm the environment when products made
from them are disposed. Illustration by Maria Meza.

companies from world governments reached nearly $1 trillion in 2011. Researchers found that post-tax subsidies in some countries exceeded spending on education and healthcare by as much as 700 percent. And these numbers do not even include the low or zero cost these companies pay for oil in the first place.[2]

In nature's web of regenerative cycles, there is no such thing as a free lunch. When government (i.e., taxpayer) subsidies to fossil fuel companies reach $1 trillion per year, are we giving some energy companies a free lunch? What will be the fate of renewable energy sources like solar, wind, and ethanol when federal subsidies supporting them run out? Conversely, can we take advantage of energy we've already produced and recycle it to power our post-petroleum future? According to a report from Columbia University, if all the plastic sent to U.S. landfills were instead sent to waste-to-energy facilities, it would generate enough electricity to power over five million homes per year. And since the plastic now in our landfills isn't going anywhere for a very long time, the possibility of mining it to fuel our future is very real.[3]

Perhaps the only upside of producing waste by the trillions of tons per year is that we may be creating the next "fossil fuel." If we can learn from nature and complete the cycle, if we can recognize that nothing goes away, perhaps we can one day "close the loop" and turn the trillions of tons of trash in our landfills into fuel. "The opportunities to reduce waste, and in fact live from waste," said David Holmgren, co-originator of permaculture, "are historically unprecedented. In the past only the most destitute made a living from waste. Today we should acknowledge those who creatively reuse waste as the very essence of living lightly on the earth."[4]

Captains of Industry, Learning from Nature

In 1923, my grandfather emigrated from Scotland to North America to set up some of our largest petrochemical-based textile factories for the Celanese Corporation. His patents for textile machinery hang on the wall of my office. He was a good man, smart and skilled, but I suspect he wasn't any more worried about where his petrochemicals came from or where they went than anyone else was in those days.

Today, we know better. The linear thinking of my grandfather's era—that resources can be taken and not replaced, and that waste can be discarded and not recycled—has largely given way to a more holistic way of thinking. We now recognize the need to draw our energy from replenishable sources and recycle our waste into new materials. Growing up in the hills of rural Scotland, my grandfather no doubt witnessed the cycles of nature. But it may not have occurred to him or his peers that cycles like the rotting of a tree that feeds insects, microbes, and ultimately new plant and animal life would make a logical or successful business model. But they can.

Resource Balancing

NEW technologies like waste energy recovery may help us better model our industrial processes on nature's cycles. But nature doesn't rely on future technological advances to solve problems that are being created today. Instead, natural systems adjust to balance production with available inputs. In other words, while we have output trillions of tons of trash to the Earth every year and hoped that future generations may use it as input, the Earth turns outputs like the "waste" from a rotting tree into inputs supporting new life. Photosynthesis is a good example. The Earth receives energy from the sun and transforms it into oxygen and other inputs that support life. Within a single tree, production is limited according to the inputs available—light, water, and soil nutrients. Through this systemic balancing act, nature minimizes waste and maximizes the efficient use of energy and other resources. Comparing the life energy balance of the tree with that of a plastic water bottle reveals how far we have to go in terms of energy efficiency. To make the water bottle, we excavate non-renewable energy from the Earth, process it in energy-intensive ways, distribute it in ways that use more energy, use it once, and throw it "away."

As economist E.F. Schumacher observed many years ago, we fail to recognize the value of nature's "capital"—the rich resources including oil that we are using up at an alarming rate. Fossil fuels were Schumacher's prime example of what he called natural capital. "No one, I am sure, will deny that we are treating them as income items although they are undeniably capital items," he wrote in *Small Is Beautiful*. If we treated them as capital, "we should be concerned with conservation; we should do everything in our power to try and minimize their current rate of use." If we did recognize fossil fuels as capital, he added, we would dedicate the money acquired from their depletion to finding "alternative methods of production and patterns of living so as to get off the collision course on which we are moving with ever-increasing speed."[5]

Like Schumacher, David Holmgren, the co-originator of permaculture, believes we should treat fossil fuels and other natural resources as capital to be conserved rather than income to be squandered. "In the language of business," he writes in *Essence of Permaculture*, "renewable resources should be seen as our sources of income, while non-renewable resources can be

Figure 20.4 Greensleeve Case for iPad

The design of the Greensleeve Case for iPad by Gone Studio was optimized to reduce waste, plastic content, and manufacturing energy to zero. Image courtesy of Gone Studio; photo by Chuck Gentile and Jim Baron.

thought of as capital assets. Spending our capital assets for day-to-day living is unsustainable in anyone's language." By looking at resources from an energy balancing perspective, he notes, we could not only conserve the natural capital we've inherited from the Earth, but rebuild it. "Inappropriate concepts of wealth," he stated, "have led us to ignore opportunities to capture local flows of both renewable and non-renewable forms of energy. Identifying and acting on these opportunities can provide the energy with which we can rebuild capital, as well as provide us with an 'income' for our immediate needs." The result of living like nature and balancing energy and resource consumption to available, renewable inputs is an economy and a world that thrive on renewal and resilience.[6]

Emulating natural systems that balance production with available inputs affects not only manufacturing but also design. That was the case with my own company, Gone Studio, in the design of our first product. My first design for our iPad case was based on the assumption that it would be made from plastic like the vast majority of other cases out there. Then the BP Gulf oil spill occurred, and I committed to make all our products plastic-free. Wool was my new material of choice, and its texture, workability, and other characteristics all led to changes in the design. When I committed to make the manufacturing process electricity-free, that again changed the design. Working with a foot-powered treadle sewing machine certainly motivated me to minimize the amount of sewing required, and minimizing the seams actually strengthened the case as a whole. Finally, I also decided to make Gone Studio waste-free and reuse any material (wool, in this case) left over from manufacturing. Again the design changed, and I worked with innovative nesting software to minimize the amount of wool left over from the large rolls after the individual case forms were cut from them. At each step, a conscious decision to minimize energy and resource inputs led me to adjust the design and manufacturing accordingly.

Notes

1   Schieber, Jürgen, "Chapter 7: Self Regulating Systems—Atmospheric Gases—Greenhouse Effect," www. indiana.edu/~geol105b/1425chap7.htm

2   Clements, Benedict, et al., "Energy Subsidy Reform—Lessons and Implications," International Monetary Fund, January 28, 2013, www.imf.org/external/np/pp/eng/2013/012813.pdf; Croady, David, et al., "Petroleum Product Subsidies: Costly, Inequitable, and Rising," International Monetary Fund, February 10, 2010, www.imf. org/external/pubs/ft/spn/2010/spn1005.pdf

3   "Landfill Plastic Could Power 5m Homes, Says Report," *Environmental Leader*, October 13, 2011, www. environmentalleader.com/2011/10/13/landfill-plastic-could-power-homes-says-report/

4   Holmgren, David, *Essence of Permaculture*, www.holmgren.com.au/DLFiles/PDFs/Essence_of_PC_eBook.pdf

5   Schumacher, E.F., *Small Is Beautiful: Economics as if People Mattered*, New York: HarperPerennial, 1989.

6   Holmgren David, *Essence of Permaculture*.

21

Resilience and Interdependence

Resilience

BECAUSE nature is made up of dynamic flows, all things are in a perpetual state of change. Some changes appear abrupt, some slow. The glass on your computer screen, for example, is actually a liquid—a very slow-moving liquid. Continents appear rock-solid, yet drift across a planet that is, itself, moving through space. Natural systems, plants, and animals either adapt or die, so they evolve to adapt. Like nature, the world of human enterprise is in continuous flux, and the same rule—adapt or die—also applies.

A currently popular term for adaptability is resilience. "Resilience," according to Alex Wilson, President of the Resilient Design Institute, "is the capacity to adapt to changing conditions, and to maintain or regain functionality and vitality in the face of stress or disturbance." While sharing virtually the same meaning as adaptability, resilience has gained favor lately as a design response to climate change. Not only are resilient buildings designed to reduce energy use and carbon emissions, they are designed to adapt to a changing climate. For example, seaside buildings may sit higher above the shore to accommodate rising sea levels while others incorporate beefed-up cooling systems to handle rising temperatures. Resilient systems are designed to provide for basic human needs through their durability, simplicity, use of locally available, renewable, or reclaimed resources, and the diversity and redundancy of their systems.[1]

Resilient design is gaining traction not only because it accepts climate change as the new reality, but because it takes a global, systemic approach to design. The University of Southern Mississippi's Gulf Coast Research Laboratory, designed by Lake|Flato Architects, is a good example. Because the original laboratory was lost to Hurricane Katrina in 2005, the architects looked to nature to ensure resilience in a future likely to see more major storms. They were quick to notice that many of the trees on site had survived the storm, which damaged the building beyond repair. They not only preserved the trees to shelter the new lab from future storms, they also emulated their root structure in the new lab's foundations. They also avoided plastics like PVC and recycled plastic decking in above-ground applications to avoid having it swept out to contaminate the Gulf of Mexico in a future storm.[2]

Designs like Lake|Flato's Gulf Coast Research Laboratory are examples of biomimicry, using the study of nature to create designs and processes that solve human problems. Through

Figure 21.1 Gulf Coast Research Laboratory
The design of the University of Southern Mississippi's Gulf
Coast Research Laboratory by Lake|Flato Architects incorporates
principles of resiliency from trees on site which survived
Hurricane Katrina. Image courtesy Lake|Flato Architects.

biomimicry we can learn to model our own systems with the efficiency, beauty, and economy of natural systems. HOK architects, for instance, have teamed with Biomimicry 3.8 to create a design strategy that takes nature's lessons in resilience and compiles them into a comprehensive database of resilient design. Their Genius of Biome process profiles how native species have adapted over time and asks what lessons their adaptations offer for building on site. In a pilot project to replace an orphanage and children's center devastated in Haiti's 2010 earthquake, the team turned to the native kapok tree. The design of the new orphanage emulates the tree's branching pattern in its earthquake-resistant structure, and the tree's bark in its energy-conserving envelope. But that doesn't mean the new structure looks like a kapok tree. As Frank Lloyd Wright argued long ago, the goal of architecture is not to imitate nature's forms, but to study the principles behind them—principles like resilience—and apply them to the discipline of design.[3]

Optimized Adhesives from Shells and Spiders

By studying nature, today's scientists and designers are developing new, petroleum-free materials with remarkable properties. For example, almost every product requires some kind of adhesive, and alternatives to petroleum-based adhesives can be hard to come by. Using petrochemical adhesives, however, can raise concerns: urea formaldehyde, for example, is classified as a probable human carcinogen by the EPA. By looking at the nanoscale formation of bone, abalone shells, and spider silk, researchers from Northwestern University and the University of California, Santa Barbara, have unlocked the secrets of some of nature's strongest materials. Their study showed that these optimized adhesives hold elements of materials together and yield just prior to the elements' breaking points so as to prevent the entire structure from breaking. "Abalone shell and bone can heal themselves due to the weak bonds, such as hydrogen bonds or ionic bonds, that can reform," researcher Paul Hansma told PhysOrg.com.

In a paper published in the journal *Nanotechnology*, the researchers drew several conclusions that might seem contrary to our typical ideas about adhesives:

- Nature is frugal with resources: it uses just a few percent glue, by weight, to glue together composite materials.
- Nature does not avoid voids.
- Nature makes optimized glues with sacrificial bonds and hidden length.

Their observations of nature open the door to new insights into artificial glues, self-healing materials, and the promise of stronger, lighter, and more efficient and economical adhesives without petroleum.[4]

Interdependence

ALL of these principles—energy flows, cycles, energy and resource balancing, and resilience—suggest a deep interdependence, a connectivity within and between systems wherein components and processes are nested. Energy flows within and between these systems and their components result in mutual influence; components and processes in one system respond to cycles in another, and outputs from one system become inputs to another. Indeed, even the notion of "one system" is a mental construct to model the behavior of a world made not of neatly packaged "systems" but of overlapping, interacting energies. When we do model the systems, components, and processes of nature, though, we see how deeply interdependent they are in both space and time. Glaciers melting in Greenland today, for example, may endanger homes in Florida later this century.

A Ray of Sun, a Lump of Coal

One summer morning I had the luxury of sitting on the beach on the Atlantic coast, watching the sun rise. "What a magnificent source of energy," I thought. We can capture its energy right at the point where we need to use it, as on a home's rooftop solar panel, convert it to electricity, and use it without fear of carbon emissions or pollution. Its beauty and simplicity made a sharp contrast with the fossil fuels I grew up with. I thought back to a winter walk past the coal-fired power plant that used to heat the buildings at the university where I teach. Two huge trucks were dumping black coal that stood out against the snow-covered landscape. I stooped down and picked up a lump of it, staining my hand just as it had stained the snow. What struck me most was thinking about where that piece of coal came from and how it got there. It was dug out of the ground, leaving who knows what scars on the landscape. And while the land may heal in a few hundred years, that natural resource is gone forever. It's gone up in smoke, wafting from the smokestacks that tower above the power plant in the air, some of it falling on the garden in my backyard, returning to the soil as toxic particles that may find their way into the vegetables I feed my children.

Harnessing the power of the sun, in contrast, need leave no trace. We can use it up without harmful side effects that can impact people far away in space and time. Coal and oil, however, are often harvested far from their point of use, and their processing and use can have negative impacts on faraway places and future generations. If only we could take our leaders and show them where the energy that heats their offices comes from. Let them stand among the gray rocks of a strip mine that used to be a forest; let them follow the smoke from the stacks and see how it falls on our gardens, lawns, fields, and streams; let them hold a dirty lump of coal in their hand, then throw open the windows and stand in the warmth of the sun, and decide.[5]

Post-petroleum designers minimize harmful impacts over space and time, asking questions such as, "Where does this material come from?" and "How will it affect future generations?" This means considering each step in their products' life cycles—raw material extraction, processing and manufacturing, transportation, use, and reuse, recycling or disposal. They are proving it is possible to design products with the beauty, power, and permanence of the sun, if we thoughtfully consider their impacts on all life on Earth now and in the future.

Could, for example, buying a pair of sneakers in Boston affect people in Pakistan—positively? Ulrika Mensch of Ethletic shoes, featured in Chapter 15, says "Yes!" Her company's footwear is not only 100 percent plastic-free, it's made with organic, Fairtrade-certified cotton canvas tops and 100 percent natural rubber soles. The rubber is sourced from responsibly managed forests certified by the Forest Stewardship Council, and Ethletic pays a Fair Trade premium that provides education and healthcare programs to its rubber tappers and manufacturers in Pakistan and Sri Lanka. "The whole idea behind the sneakers is to take great responsibility regarding the environmental and social aspects," said Mensch. And clearly, that responsibility extends around the planet and into the future.[6]

That sense of responsibility stems directly from understanding how nature works. The nature-based principles often found at work in post-petroleum design are:

Energy Flows
Nature's energy flows include much more than just fuels. Nature's energies in all their forms tend toward cyclical, self-regulating, decentralized, and regenerative patterns. Understanding our place in this complex web of energies, we can optimize our designs and our products to work with, rather than against, them.

Cycles
Energy often flows in cyclical patterns where the outputs from one process become inputs to another, thereby eliminating waste. Designing with awareness of nature's cycles—even the simplest ones like night and day—can make the resulting products more sustainable.

Resource Balancing

Natural systems adjust to balance production with available inputs. This is true for energy as well as other resources like food and water. Nature minimizes waste and is the ultimate recycler. By distinguishing between energy income and energy capital, products and processes can be optimized to balance energy use with available energy income. Products can, for example, be designed to serve as inputs to new processes or products at the end of their service.

Resilience

Because nature is made up of dynamic flows, all things are in a perpetual state of change. "Adapt or die" is as true in design and commerce as it is in nature. Resilience is the ability of our designs and products to adapt to changing conditions. Many post-petroleum designers practice biomimicry, taking lessons from nature and emulating the resilience they see in the bending of a tree, the slow shifting of a streambed, or other aspects of natural systems.

Interdependence

Energy flows within and between natural systems, resulting in mutual influence, with components and processes in one system responding to cycles in another. Recognizing these deep connections, post-petroleum designers minimize harmful impacts over space and time, asking questions such as, "Where does this material come from?" and "How will it affect future generations?"

Notes

1   Logan, Katherine, "Resilient Design: 7 Lessons from Early Adopters," November 1, 2013, *Environmental Building News*, www.buildinggreen.com.

2   Ibid.

3   Ibid.; Biomimicry Group Inc. and HOK Group Inc., "Genius of Biome Report," 2013, www.hok.com/thought-leadership/genius-of-biome/

4   National Cancer Institute, "Formaldehyde and Cancer Risk," www.cancer.gov/cancertopics/factsheet/Risk/formaldehyde; Hansma, P.K., Turner, P.J., and Ruoff, R.S., "Optimized Adhesives for Strong, Lightweight, Damage-resistant, Nanocomposite Materials: New Insights from Natural Materials," *Nanotechnology*, Volume 18, 2007, 1–3, http://bucky-central.me.utexas.edu/RuoffsPDFs/Optimizedadhesives155.pdf; Zyga, Lisa, "Nature's Frugal Glues Provide Insight for Optimized Adhesives," PhysOrg.com, January 11, 2007, http://phys.org/news87722200.html

5   Elvin, George, "A Lump of Coal, a Ray of Sun," Green Technology Forum, January 30, 2011, www.greentech-forum.net/green-technology-forum/2011/1/30/a-lump-of-coal-a-ray-of-sun.html

6   Author correspondence.

PART SIX

Life in the Post-Petroleum Era

22

Post-Petroleum Consumers

Whether it's municipalities implementing bans on plastic bags or schools creating litterless lunch programs, awareness is growing and people and organizations are taking action to challenge the status quo.

(Jay Sinha, Co-founder, Life Without Plastic)[1]

Individual Choices

THE push for a positive, post-petroleum future based on nature's principles isn't coming from designers and manufacturers alone. Every year, more consumers are demanding it, and more governments and institutions are requiring it. This breadth of demand, spanning designers, manufacturers, consumers, and regulators is creating a critical mass, an energy from all sides that can sustain, and has already begun, a powerful movement. And like many movements, it all begins with individuals.

Every year, the average American family discards enough plastic to cover their entire backyard. In 40 years they would find themselves hip deep in plastic. Maybe if it went into our backyards, where we could see it, we'd use less. Instead, it fills our landfills and oceans. But some consumers are saying, "Enough," and saying no to plastic.[2]

New Year's Day 2010 found Vancouverite Taina Uitto hauling all the plastic out of her kitchen and bathroom. She was following through on her new year's resolution to live the year plastic-free. "People always say they don't use that much plastic," she told the *Vancouver Sun*, "but until you collect it even for a week and pull all the plastic from your kitchen, you don't know. It's a shocking exercise." Uitto is still living plastic-free, doing without the few things she can't find a plastic-free alternative to, making some products (like soap) herself, and doing a lot more cooking from scratch because, as she explains, "nearly everything in the center aisles of the grocery store is off limits." She's even doing without a boyfriend who told her that living plastic-free was "the worst thing ever."

But she's the first to say she's gained a lot more than she's lost. Uitto said she feels much better without all the plastic waste and "all the toxins that plastic leaches into our water and our food." She's now tackling the even bigger challenge of building a plastic-free cabin on Denman Island north of the city.[3]

Breaking the Plastic Burden

Taina Uitto was getting fed up. She'd been arguing for five minutes with the Ikea clerk, who insisted that her purchase wasn't leaving the store without a plastic shopping bag. "Store policy," he parroted in response to her every argument. With glares from the people in line behind her growing more lethal by the minute, she met the store manager, who escorted her and her purchase out the door plastic-free.

Why was this normally mild-mannered Vancouverite so adamant about refusing plastic?

"I was one of those people who would always forget my reusable bag in the car and take the plastic bag," said Uitto. "I had this growing unease about that—feeling like I wasn't doing the right thing—and I always carried a big burden about it."

The turning point, she said, was a presentation about ocean plastic pollution by the leaders of 5 Gyres, a California-based marine research organization. Co-founders Anna Cummins and Marcus Eriksen spoke about what they'd seen as they sailed all five gyres, or ocean systems.

"What we've seen across 25,000 miles of ocean over the last few years," said Cummins, "is that this is a global problem. Plastic trash saturates our societies, pollutes our streams and rivers, and washes out to sea. It can be found on virtually every shoreline in every ocean in the world."

"That really hit me pretty hard," said Uitto. "But it wasn't until about half a year later that I decided to give up plastics."

One of the first exercises in her plastic-free regimen was to face up to how much plastic she had already accumulated. "I did it in my bathroom and in my kitchen," she confided, describing how she pulled every bit of plastic out of the two rooms that typically contain the most. "Now I always recommend it as a way for people to gain awareness of where the plastic is coming from, what items would be easy to give up, and the sheer quantity of it."

Banishing plastic from her household was only half the battle though. Every day had its plastic-induced skirmishes like the one at Ikea, and at times it seemed like resistance was futile. "You have to stay vigilant at all times," she said. "Plastic is constantly coming at you—people putting a straw in your drink, things like that. You really have to stay true to your rules because otherwise you'll just go for that convenience item."

But along with fending off plastic-wielding baristas and furniture store clerks came the opportunity to educate. "It doesn't take long for people to get it," she said. "I've had a number of instances where people will come back to me two weeks after learning I'm plastic-free and say, 'I haven't been able to stop thinking about what you said.' They want to help, and that's a really positive thing."

"Since I quit plastic," Uitto continued, "I'm spending less money because I'm buying less stuff, and that allows me to buy higher quality products. Just re-finding the value in natural materials like wood and glass is such a lovely thing. They feel better, they look better, and my house feels more sophisticated."

Uitto shares her experiences through her blog, Plastic Manners, from her home on Denman Island, just off Vancouver. Not surprisingly, it's plastic-free, built on 38 acres that she calls a "little bit of Heaven." She's also working with 19 Vancouver families in their quest to go plastic-free for a year, and a documentary is in the works.

Taina Uitto walks the walk, refusing to let plastic into her life as she spreads the word about its dangers and the liberation of living without it. That may seem like too much of a challenge for us plastic-bound mortals, but she would be quick to remind each of us that every plastic bottle, bag, or straw we refuse is one less that may end up leaching toxins in a landfill or mistaken for food by a marine bird or fish. Each time we say no to plastic, we move the world one step closer to healthier oceans and marine life, healthier soil, and ultimately, a healthier you and me.[4]

Figure 22.1 Taina Uitto
Plastic-free living pioneer Taina Uitto collects plastic
debris from a Vancouver Island beach. Image
courtesy of Taina Uitto; photo by Megan Baker.

These are extremes—pioneers devoted to showing the world what life can be like without plastic. They are not advocating that we all live plastic-free, but they are demonstrating that we can all cut back dramatically on our plastic use without sacrificing much. Alternatives abound, and these plastic-free pioneers have become expert at finding them and sharing them with others. It's clear from their stories that they do sacrifice in order to live plastic-free; they make products that the rest of us buy at the store and they do without many things the rest of us enjoy. But they also share some more important things that they've gained. Taina Uitto told the *Vancouver Sun* her life feels a lot less cluttered without plastic, and the things she's bought to replace them look and feel a lot nicer. Her bathroom is a good example, where she reports she now has "five things instead of 500 things." Matthew Stewart and his girlfriend, Sarah Milton, took Uitto's challenge to quit plastic for one year. They found themselves making things like almond milk that they used to buy in the store. "We spent a lot of time in the kitchen together," Stewart observed, "it was really kind of romantic."[5]

Plastic-free pioneer Beth Terry kicked the plastic habit in 2007. In 2012 she chronicled her post-plastic adventures in her book *Plastic-Free: How I Kicked the Plastic Habit and How You Can Too*. Terry said she began eating better when she chose to turn down the plastic-packaged junk foods crowding the supermarket aisles. She also shared something deeper: "Living plastic-free is inextricably entangled with awareness, consciousness, mindfulness. In a world of plastic, we don't have to think about where the products we use come from or where they're going. Our lives are unexamined." Apparently when we give up plastic, we free ourselves of a lot more than just petroleum.[6]

Collective Action

INDIVIDUAL action can be a strong driver of social change. Working together, we can make change stronger, faster, and longer lasting. Around the world, groups of students, families, and investors have gotten together to take their individual actions to the community level. Over 50 university campuses worldwide have joined the Global Plastic Free Campuses Program, established by the Plastic Pollution Coalition, and many more have independent programs. Students at St. Louis University in the Philippines, for example, have started a Plastic-Free Wednesdays program in which campus vendors will use no plastic carryout containers. "Every student, faculty member, non-teaching personnel or any canteen customers who wishes to buy packed foods will have to bring his own food container," said Albert Francis Abad, president of the university's Supreme Student Council. Customers can borrow utensils, but they have to leave a valid ID as collateral. Their program is typical of hundreds of plastic reduction campaigns at schools and universities worldwide.[7]

Outside the classroom, communities are also banding together to reduce the impact of plastic on their environment. Plastic Free Hawai'i is typical. The group is "a coalition of community members and business owners that strives to educate the stores, schools restaurants, residents and visitors of Hawai'i on the environmental and health benefits of going plastic free in order to minimize the consumption and pollution of plastics in our islands."[8]

There are global communities too. One of the most innovative is the Transition Town movement, which links community-based groups into a global network. The global Transition Network supports community-led responses to climate change and shrinking supplies of fossil fuels. Their goal is to transition from an oil-dependent economy to an oil-independent one. Their message is that "as the Age of Cheap Energy (1850–2008) passes the point known as Peak Oil and gives way to the Age of Unaffordable Energy (2008–?) we are increasingly at risk, economically and socially. We can't just open the oil spigot and expect more cheap and easily accessible energy to fuel our homes, businesses, leisure, transport, factories and agriculture." Their goal is "resilience and happiness" in the post-petroleum era.

But members of the Transition Network, recognizing that virtual communities have their limits, have banded together to form over 1,000 registered local Transition Towns. Those in cities like New York and London have thousands of members. Shuswap in Transition in Salmon Arm, British Columbia has ten. But this tiny community of mostly Shuswap Nation Native Americans is fiercely committed to a future free of our current dependency on oil. "I used to worry that my kids were going to come along one day and say, 'Why didn't you do anything? You knew about this, why didn't you do anything?'" said Shuswap in Transition leader, Karen Andreassen. "Now I'm doing something—small, but I think a lot of people doing small things can make a difference."[9,10]

Not all groups working to reduce plastic are place-based like these Transition Towns, schools, and community groups. Not surprisingly, online communities are proliferating, bonding people with vastly different backgrounds, locations, and interests around the common cause of minimizing plastic. Facebook communities like Stop Ocean Plastics, Life Plastic Free, Think Beyond Plastic, and Plastic Pollution Coalition bring thousands of like-minded people together, providing resources, events, inspiration, and a forum for sharing ideas and stories. Just as in political movements with strong social media components like the 2012 Arab Spring, the Internet may prove to be the common ground where the post-petroleum era is forged.

Author, educator, and environmentalist, Bill McKibben, has emerged as a leader in post-petroleum politics through a skillful and passionate mix of scholarly writing, inspirational speaking, community organization, and civil disobedience. Decades of work on the front lines of the environmental movement have led him to focus foremost on oil and its impacts in recent years. "We have met the enemy, and they is Shell," wrote McKibben in his *Rolling Stone* magazine article, "Global Warming's Terrifying New Math." In it, he cited a study by the Carbon Tracker Initiative showing that the reserves held by the world's fossil fuel companies contain enough carbon dioxide to, in his words, "wreck the planet" unless we stop them. We need to act quickly, he said, and we need to point the finger: "A rapid, transformative change would require building a movement, and movements require enemies … and enemies are what climate change has lacked."[11]

Oil companies have often obliged in making themselves easy enemies. Rex Tillerson, CEO of Exxon Mobil, for instance, said of his company's foray into shale oil drilling, "We are losing our shirts today. We're making no money." That may sound strange coming from the man who made just shy of $100 million per day as CEO of the world's fifth-richest corporation.[12]

McKibben believes in a wide range of actions to fight big oil and climate change, from civil disobedience to political pressure. His most recent strategy emphasizes divestment, calling on college students to demand that their universities' endowment funds dump their investments in fossil fuel companies. Other institutions, investors, and pension funds, he says, should do the same.

Lifestyle changes, McKibben argues, aren't working. "People perceive, correctly," he said, "that their individual actions will not make a decisive difference in the atmospheric concentration of CO_2." But there is always the danger that the void left by divestment on the part of universities and other institutions will simply be filled by less scrupulous investors. Oil is just too profitable and there are too many investors willing to look past its environmental impacts. After all, three of the world's 11 richest companies are oil companies, with a combined market value of over one trillion dollars.[13]

Whether or not divestment will succeed in altering the behavior of the fossil fuel companies remains to be seen. But it already provides a strategy for investors to stop what permaculture co-founder Bill Mollison calls "investing in our own destruction." McKibben advocates looking at our own investment portfolios and our own oil, coal, and gas consumption, and divesting ourselves from fossil fuel profiteering as much as possible. When we do, we "invest in our own resurrection," as Mollison says, redirecting our funds toward environmentally responsible investments. In concert with other individual actions divestment can help us reduce our dependence on fossil fuels. When we act together as a community, something McKibben works hard to foster, we can accomplish even more.

Art

MONEY talks when it comes to voicing our concerns about the environment, but art can sometimes speak even louder. Around the globe, artists are increasingly calling attention to the plastic pollution problem through their work. Many use the plastic waste filling our waterways and landfills as their medium. Devebere, for example, was an urban "bottle cave" installed by Maciej Siuda and Rodrigo García González at the Muzeum Wspólczesne in Wrocław, Poland in 2012. By filling large plastic bags with thousands of used plastic water bottles and then evacuating the air, González and Siuda were able to make large architectural forms that occupied the city's waterfront. Their structure engaged locals and tourists alike and even traveled to other European cities, making those who experienced it think more deeply about the scale of our global plastic waste problem.[14]

Even businesses can use art to call attention to issues they care about. With their Vac from the Sea project, appliance manufacturer Electrolux aimed to raise awareness about the global shortage of recycled plastics. The project not only raised awareness; thanks to the work of some inspiring artists, it helped move Electrolux closer toward its long-term sustainability goals. "Electrolux vision is to produce vacs from 100% recycled material," said Cecilia Nord, VP of Environmental and Sustainability Affairs in Electrolux; "yet this isn't possible due to a shortage of high quality post consumer recycled plastic. The project gives us a platform for raising awareness about this planet's poor management of plastics, and how plastic waste destroys our oceans."

Figure 22.2 Devebere by Maciej Siuda and Rodrigo García González
Sometimes the best medium for calling attention to plastic pollution
is plastic itself. Rodrigo García González and Maciej Siuda gathered
thousands of used plastic water bottles for their traveling exhibition,
Devebere. Image courtesy of Rodrigo García González.

To make people more aware of the problem, Electrolux turned some of their vacuum
cleaners into art incorporating ocean plastic waste. The company worked with organizations
and volunteers worldwide to collect plastic from the seas around Hawaii, Thailand, France, and
Sweden. They then created a special series of vacs from the collected plastic, each representing a
specific ocean. The Vac from the Sea program also helped Electrolux launch a new line of vacuum
cleaners, the Green Range, made from 70 percent recycled plastic. Vac from the Sea won many
awards too, including a 2011 IPRA Golden Award from the United Nations in collaboration with
the International Public Relations Association.[15]

Figure 22.3 Vac from the Sea
Electrolux collected plastic from the world's oceans and commissioned artists to create a special series of vacs from the collected plastic, each representing a specific ocean. Image courtesy of Electrolux.

Retail Leaders

BETWEEN the consumers calling for more plastic-free products and the designers and manufacturers providing them is a growing culture of post-petroleum retailers. Some offer plastic-free goods as part of a wider selection of green products. A few dedicate their entire inventory to plastic-free merchandise. The latter ones share a deep commitment to the principles that guide post-petroleum designers and "less plastic" consumers. But they also recognize that good intentions aren't enough to sustain a business, and their success is living proof of the growing demand for plastic-free and less plastic products.

Dedicated plastic-free stores can be found online and, increasingly, around the corner. The Soap Dispensary is a refill store frequented by Vancouver plastic-free lifestyle pioneer Taina Uitto. While some of the store's bulk soaps, household cleaners, and personal care products are kept in plastic jugs, offering them in bulk allows their customers to reuse containers again and again, keeping thousands of one-time-use bottles out of the landfill. Not surprisingly, their products are also biodegradable and animal cruelty-free. But, as they explain on their website, "The inspiration for The Soap Dispensary was born from a desire to reduce our plastic footprint." Austin, Texas grocery store, In.gredients, doesn't attempt to sell everything plastic-free, but they have committed to a zero-waste program that includes selling all their goods packaging-free and pushing their vendors to provide them that way as well. Even their eggs come in reusable containers from Vital Farms, where organically fed, free-range chickens roam fields featuring mobile fences and lay their eggs in "MCUs", Mobile Chicken Units.[16]

Plastic-free retailers aren't all about selling goods, either. The Soap Dispensary, for example, offers workshops on topics as diverse as managing allergies, composting, and making your own cosmetics. In.gredients sponsors community events, performances, and volunteer programs. Both author blogs sharing insights on what The Soap Dispensary calls "living a less disposable lifestyle." People, they realize, are the key to global change. As In.gredients explains on their website, "Our business model isn't the silver bullet that will spawn colossal change in the food packaging industry. Rather, we hope to teach our community how just a few simple changes to the way we live can reduce waste and promote healthy living."

Other retailers focus on the online community. Plastic Antidote, the online store of the Plastic Pollution Coalition, offers hundreds of plastic-free products such as bowls made from bottlecaps, handbags made from recycled newsprint, and even a "Go Plastic-Free Starter Kit" complete with stainless steel water bottle, stainless steel drinking straw, and recycled PET plastic utensils. Life Without Plastic has been offering online customers "products that are completely devoid of plastic" since 2006.

Saying No to Plastic

Taina Uitto, who lives plastic-free, shares her tips for buying less:

- Buy bulk whenever possible and use paper bags for produce.
- Bring natural wax paper to buy meats and cheese. Ask for a portion that is not already packaged, wrapped in your paper.
- In place of cling wrap, try wraps made from reusable hemp and cotton infused with bee's wax.
- Carry cloth shopping bags or ask for paper or compostable plastic bags.
- Avoid convenience foods—cook from fresh ingredients. If you must buy prepared foods, buy in jars and reuse them around the house.
- Buy wine and beer in bulk, in refillable bottles and growlers. Or make your own beer and wine and control the packaging that way.
- Buy metal, stackable tiffin boxes (widely used in Asia and Africa) and frequent restaurants that will fill them.
- Carry your own ceramic coffee cup and refuse plastic stir sticks.
- Some soaps, shampoos, and cleansers can be purchased in bulk. Look for paper-wrapped tampons or use Luna Pads. Make your own cosmetics.
- Recycle metal, glass, and paper and compost food waste—you won't have as much garbage and little need for garbage bags.[17]

Life Without Plastic

Chantal Plamondon and her husband, Jay Sinha, founded online retail company, Life Without Plastic, in 2006, "to help all living beings, including the Earth, by working toward decreased reliance on plastic."

Not many people start stores based on what their products don't have in them. What inspired you to start Life Without Plastic?

Our inspiration for Life Without Plastic has come from many sources. We have both always been interested in helping and appreciating the environment and living in healthy ways. Our son was an enormous influence. He's ten now, and was the primary catalyst for starting this business. Before he was born, we started researching toxins in the environment, and that led us to the endocrine-disrupting chemicals leaching from plastics, especially when searching for a non-plastic water bottle and glass baby bottles. We looked around a lot for a stainless steel bottle and the only one we could find on the market was by Klean Kanteen, which at that time was a small California cooperative. We ordered one, tried it out, and loved it.

When our son was born, Chantal was breast-feeding but we needed bottles to store breast milk. The more we researched and learned about endocrine disruptors coming out of plastics, the more the thought of a wee babe drinking out of a plastic container made us cringe. The most common ones found in consumer products mimic the hormone estrogen, can affect development, and have been linked to certain cancers, for example, bisphenol A and phthalates. We couldn't find glass bottles anywhere—this was 2003. We finally came across Evenflo of Ohio, which was still making them. Glass bottles were, of course, the norm just over a generation ago. We contacted Evenflo, and they were happy to sell us glass bottles, but they only did wholesale, so the minimum order was 1,000! That got us thinking. You could call it a lightbulb moment. We knew there were others out there increasingly looking for safe alternatives to plastics. With the glass baby bottles and the stainless steel water bottles and our first stainless steel food containers we launched Life Without Plastic back in 2006.

I'm curious about Chantal's native Wendat heritage and how it has influenced your work.

Chantal's Huron Wendat ancestry has influenced her whole outlook on life, and definitely influences her work with Life Without Plastic through its emphasis on helping the environment and a holistic approach to everything. It has instilled in her a deep reverence for nature and natural materials. Everything we need can be found in nature. There is no need to create artificial versions that pollute and toxify rather than biodegrade naturally. Indigenous peoples lived close to the Earth, and many still do. They find all they need directly from nature. That is a powerful, life-giving example to live by.

Jay has a background in biochemistry and ecotoxicology. How has that influenced your work?

Because we test many of our own products, understanding the science behind the tests helps us feel confident that our products really are safe. Everything we sell we have made use of in our everyday lives at some point, so our testing also includes using our own products to ensure their functionality, quality and durability. We would not use them ourselves—and we certainly would not sell them—if we were not confident of their safety.

Figure 22.4 Chantal Plamondon and Jay Sinha, Life Without Plastic
Chantal Plamondon and her husband, Jay Sinha, founded Life Without Plastic in 2006 to offer an online retail alternative to petrochemical-containing products. Image courtesy of Life Without Plastic; photo by Mike Beedell.

Are you able to achieve plastic-free shipping?

Absolutely. From the start this has been a key priority. Products are packed tightly with minimal packaging and using recycled materials, such as newspaper, as much as possible. We reuse all boxes we receive, or recycle unusable ones. All the packing materials are either paper, cellulose wadding, or cornstarch peanuts. The tape is paper tape, or where a clear tape is required, cellulose tape. Packaging is one of the worst culprits when it comes to plastic pollution and non-recyclable plastic waste. Furthermore, how strange it would be for us to be offering wonderful plastic-free products and then swaddling them in plastic as we ship them out.

How can you tell if you're succeeding in your mission?

We know we are succeeding because awareness about the health and environmental problems associated with plastics is building everywhere. But we are a small part of what is now a dynamic movement with numerous participants all over the world. Plastic pollution is increasingly becoming an issue covered by the mainstream media. We are extremely inspired and invigorated by the rise of organized activism to deal with the plastics issue from various angles. Whether it is municipalities implementing bans on plastic bags or schools creating litterless lunch programs, awareness is growing and people and organizations are taking action to challenge the status quo. This is increasingly leading to exciting partnerships between businesses, NGOs, governments and communities.[18]

The plastic-free movement does indeed seem to be building momentum. Headlines containing the term "plastic-free," are up 33 percent since Google began tracking them in 2007. That suggests a growing interest in all things plastic-free, including merchandise. As demand increases, how will plastic-free retailers change and grow in the future? Pioneers with an established following like Life Less Plastic will hopefully continue to prosper, but don't expect to see a boom in dedicated plastic-free retailers. The reason is that plastic-free products will in all likelihood be a growing part of all retailers' inventory. In this respect they will follow the same pattern as green building products. Ten years ago, green building supply stores were springing up around the country. Now, green building supplies are abundant at your local hardware store. It's likely that plastic-free products will be similarly assimilated into every retailer's inventory.

Notes

1   Author interview.

2   U.S. Environmental Protection Agency, "Municipal Solid Waste Generation, Recycling, and Disposal in the United States: Facts and Figures for 2011," Report, www.epa.gov/osw/nonhaz/municipal/pubs/ MSWcharacterization_508_053113_fs.pdf; Cornell Lab of Ornithology, "The Average American Yard,"

2011, http://content.yardmap.org/explore/the-average-american-yard/; Executive Office of Energy and Environmental Affairs, State of Massachusetts, "Volume-to-Weight Conversions for Recyclable Materials," www.mass.gov/dep/recycle/approvals/dsconv.pdf

3   Shore, Randy, "Her Life without Plastic Is Harder than You'd Think," *Vancouver Sun*, October 7, 2013, http://blogs.vancouversun.com/2013/10/07/her-life-without-plastic-is-harder-than-youd-think/

4   Author interview.

5   Ibid.

6   Terry, Beth, *Plastic-Free: How I Kicked the Plastic Habit and How You Can Too*, New York: Skyhorse Publishing, 2012.

7   "Plastic Free Campuses," Plastic Pollution Coalition, 2010, http://plasticpollutioncoalition.org/projects/plastic-free-campuses/; Elvin, George, "Students start Plastic-Free Wednesdays campaign," Green Technology Forum, http://gelvin.squarespace.com/green-technology-forum/2012/4/26/students-start-plastic-free-wednesdays-campaign.html

8   "About Plastic Free Hawai'I," http://kokuahawaiifoundation.org/pfh

9   Transition Network, www.transitionnetwork.org

10 Wickett, Martha, "Trying to Beat the Oil Addiction," *Salmon Arm Observer*, January 4, 2012, www.saobserver.net/news/136668433.html

11 McKibben, Bill, "Global Warming's Terrifying New Math," *Rolling Stone* online, July 19, 2012, www.rollingstone.com/politics/news/global-warmings-terrifying-new-math-20120719#ixzz2A1oGcePd

12 Dicolo, Jerry, "Exxon: 'Losing Our Shirts' on Natural Gas," *Wall Street Journal* online, June 27, 2012, http://online.wsj.com/article/SB10001424052702303561504577492501026260464.html

13 "The World's Biggest Public Companies," Forbes, 2014, www.forbes.com/global2000/list/

14 Devebere, 2014, http://cargocollective.com/devebere

15 "Electrolux and Vac from the Sea awarded by United Nations," Electrolux, October 27, 2011, http://group.electrolux.com/en/electrolux-and-vac-from-the-sea-awarded-by-united-nations-12115/

16 Plastic Pollution Coalition, "Plastic Antidote," http://plasticantidote.com/; In.gredients, http://in.gredients.com; The Soap Dispensary, http://thesoapdispensary.com/

17 Shore, "Her Life without Plastic Is Harder than You'd Think."

18 Author interview.

23

Regulations and Incentives

Regulation

The only way the transition to clean energy will ultimately succeed is if new rules are established … that require the private sector to invest in a low-carbon future.
(Deborah Gordon, Senior Associate, Carnegie Endowment Energy and Climate Program)[1]

Individual and collective action creates a strong "bottom-up" demand from consumers for products using less plastic and petroleum. But sometimes bottom-up demand isn't enough. We all want to use less gas, for instance, but without top-down enforcement of speed limits, many people would continue to drive fast and use more gas. When bottom-up individual and collective action fails to achieve the common good, governments often intervene to force a change in behavior. Even as far back as 1300, the King of England banned the use of coal in London because "the fumes of coal had a peculiarly corrupting effect upon the air, and were most injurious to health." When the ban failed, "a commission was issued for the purpose of ascertaining who burned sea-coal within the city and its neighborhoods, and to punish them by fine for the first offence, and by the demolition of their furnaces if they persisted." Even that failed, though, resulting in a law making coal burning a capital offense. It only took one execution to bring an end to coal burning in London.[2]

While we're not likely to see anyone executed for using plastic or petroleum, some European governments are developing surprisingly strong regulations to limit or even end their use. Germany, for example, is taking a proactive approach that uses taxation and private investment incentives to free itself from coal and oil. The country's Energiewende (Energy Turn) program incentivizes private sector investment in renewable energy and imposes a surcharge on every citizen's electric bill to subsidize it. By 2040, when the U.S. plans to get only 16 percent of its energy from renewable sources, Germany expects to receive 66 percent of its own from renewables thanks to the program. And while the surcharge raises energy bills now, most Germans see it as an investment in the future.

Rainer Baake, Director of Agora Energiewende, explained: "Germany is not organizing this Energiewende to harm its economy—quite the opposite—we see the advantages. We have a lot of people in industry who realize this is a fantastic opportunity to be the first mover and sell technologies not only here in Germany, but also in other countries." PBS correspondent Rick Karr asked Baake what advice he would give his U.S. counterparts. "Sooner or later," he replied, "this transition to renewable energy has to come, so the question is do you want to be one of the first movers—do you want to belong to that group of countries that is producing with the energy sources of the future—or do you want to prevail with the old fossil system for a few more decades?" Many other countries around the world have similarly ambitious plans to wean themselves from petroleum and other fossil fuels sooner rather than later.[3]

As for plastic, many countries are moving to reduce its use as well. The entire European Union is considering a ban on the microplastic particles used in many cosmetics. In the Netherlands, the industry has already volunteered to replace 80 percent of its microplastics with other materials by 2015. These tiny, non-biodegradable plastic particles, found in skin scrub, bath products, and even toothpaste, are a particular concern because they often end up in waterways. There, they can absorb toxins and be eaten by fish and marine wildlife, working their way up the food chain.[4]

In the U.S., California is considering legislation it believes can reduce marine plastic pollution by 95 percent by 2025. Assembly members Mark Stone and Ben Hueso have introduced a bill that would require producers of plastic pollution to meet strict plastic reduction targets within clearly defined timeframes. How producers meet the targets would be up to them, but this could include everything from improved product design to support for increased recycling. The bill is expected to save taxpayers and local governments money by reducing waste management, litter cleanup, and recycling costs.[5]

Plastic Bag Bans

> Why would you make something that you're going to use for a few minutes out of a material that's basically going to last forever, and you're just going to throw it away?
>
> (Jeb Berrier, *Bag It*)[6]

If legislation to reduce plastic pollution had a Most Wanted List, its number one outlaw would be the single-use plastic shopping bag. Worldwide, most legislation to ban plastic focuses on these bags. California is banning them statewide, and their motivation is not only environmental, but economic. The state spends over $30 million each year removing littered bags from streets and sending them to the landfill. The city of San Jose alone spends about $1 million per year to repair recycling equipment jammed with plastic bags.[7]

Despite these costs, we tend to think of plastic grocery bags as "free" because most stores don't charge separately for them. But they do charge. Grocery stores add between two and five cents per bag to the cost of food for every plastic bag they hand out. That adds up to between $17 and $30 per year for each of us.[8]

Plastic bag bans are spreading rapidly in the U.S., where Los Angeles, San Francisco, Austin, Seattle, Portland, Long Beach, and many other cities have already banned the bag. California's plastic shopping bag ban takes effect in 2015. Plastic bag manufacturers, however, aren't taking the ban lying down. As soon as Governor Jerry Brown signed the ban into law, a referendum committee was formed in hopes of repealing it. That committee has just one California-based member, from plastic bag company Durabag. The other four are from Superbag Corporation in Texas, Hilex Poly Corporation from South Carolina, Heritage Plastics out of Mississippi, and New Jersey Formosa Plastics Corporation USA. According to the *Sacramento Bee*, "Out-of-state plastic companies hoping to block California's freshly signed ban on single-use plastic bags have poured over $1 million into [the] referendum campaign."[9]

"Hawaii was the first state to ban plastic in all of its counties," noted Surfrider Foundation Hawaii Coordinator, Stuart Coleman. Honolulu Mayor Kirk Caldwell added that, "Now the entire Island is going to be plastic free and I think that's really important because we're surrounded by water and these bags are blowing everywhere." An exemption to his city's ban that allowed the continued sale of biodegradable plastic bags was taken out in 2014. Legislators were concerned that bags containing only small amounts of biodegradable material, or biodegradable material that does not break down quickly enough under some circumstances, were still being allowed to pollute the state's shores. Compostable bags, which are more clearly defined and regulated, are still allowed.[10]

Internationally, Delhi banned plastic bags in 2009, but after repeated enforcement efforts failed to stop residents from using them, violators now face up to seven years in prison. Many countries have bans in place too, including Italy and China which estimates it saved $40 billion in the first year of its ban. The European Union is currently weighing legislation that would cut plastic bag use by 80 percent, and France has placed them under its General Tax on Polluting Activities beginning in 2014. Early adopter Ireland, which imposed a plastic bag use tax in 2002, has reduced consumption by 90 percent.[11]

With global plastic bag production exceeding one million bags per minute, the spread of bans and taxes could put a serious dent in oil consumption, carbon emissions, and plastic pollution. An Australian study, for example, found that the country could reduce carbon dioxide emissions by over 42,000 tons per year by switching from single-use plastic grocery bags to reusable ones.[12]

Product Transparency

LEGISLATION in the form of bans and taxes isn't the only way to reduce plastic consumption. One of the most promising is the move toward "product transparency." The term refers to means of making product ingredients and impacts more transparent to consumers—a kind of nutrition labeling for products. As this new trend in consumer information unfolds, a number of variations are emerging, including environmental product declarations, product ingredient reporting, and health product declarations. All of these are reporting measures intended to disclose the ingredients of products and their environmental impacts over their life cycles. Unlike nutrition labeling for food, they are currently voluntary. But that doesn't mean they won't have a big impact on future product choices made by consumers and material choices made by designers.

The green building rating system Leadership in Energy and Environmental Design (LEED), developed in the U.S., for example, is adopting environmental product declarations as a way for users to earn credit toward green building certification of their projects. And while LEED certification may not carry the force of law, more municipalities are turning to it every day as a requirement for construction in their jurisdictions.

The growing trend toward product transparency will require manufacturers to disclose the ingredients of their products because consumers have a right to know what's in the products they're buying. Future product transparency reports may even include chemical inventories or chemical hazard assessments. This could be of particular concern to some plastic product manufacturers, since consumers may become wary of plastics revealed to contain toxic ingredients.

But product transparency reports will benefit those products that can show non-toxic, sustainably harvested ingredients, reduced greenhouse gas emissions, renewable energy sources, and minimal waste. Some manufacturers are already using positive product transparency reports as a marketing tool. The Association of the Nonwoven Fabrics Industry (INDA), for example, is using environmental performance reporting to showcase the sustainability of some of its products, which include clothing, packaging, and a variety of consumer products, both plastic and plastic-free. According to INDA President Dave Rousse, "Designing greener products is becoming increasingly important in all industries. It is critical for raw material suppliers, roll goods suppliers, end product and process equipment manufacturers within the nonwoven industry to keep up with this trend to develop and showcase their products' environmental performance." The association is using life cycle assessment software from Sustainable Minds to measure the environmental performance of its products. The results are important not only in helping customers understand the impact of their products, but in the design of those products too.[13]

Sustainable Minds co-founder and CEO, Terry Swack, sees life cycle assessment (LCA) as a critical input to the design of green products, not just a beneficial output for their marketing. "Designing greener products," she said, "starts with bringing life cycle thinking and a whole product systems approach to the beginning of the design process. It's no longer about just designing the artifact. There's so much more to design when we have responsibility for the whole product system throughout its life cycle."[14]

As designers increasingly use product life cycle impacts as input to the design process and consumers see those impacts spelled out in more stringent product labeling, will it mean less plastic in our products? This question is receiving more attention in green building than ever before, thanks to the increasingly close examination of building product ingredients called for in green rating systems like LEED and the 2030 Challenge For Products. In all likelihood, the pressure for product transparency will spread from building products to consumer products. As it does, some plastic products may fare better than others, but consumers will have a better understanding of what's in their products and what their life cycle impacts are.

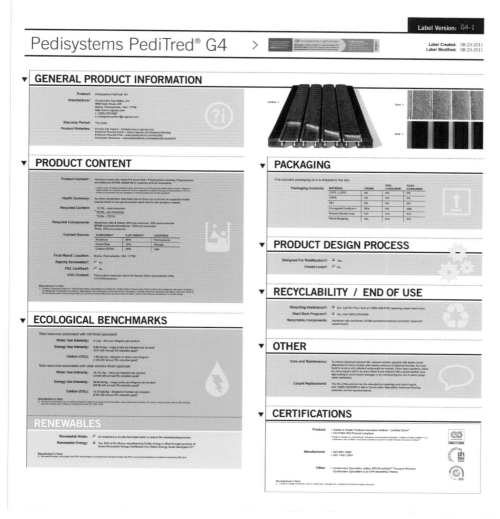

BUILDING PRODUCT TRANSPARENCY LABEL

This online label is a declaration of the make-up of the product, highlighting critical lifecycle information and potential human health impacts. It strives to be comprehensive, relevant, verifiable, and able to evolve as the products and processes change.

Figure 23.1 Product Transparency Label

Product transparency labels, "nutrition labels for products," give consumers critical information on their products' ingredients and life cycle environmental impacts. Image courtesy of Construction Specialties, Inc.

Reclassifying Plastic Waste as Hazardous

Writing in the journal *Nature*, ten scientists from North America, Europe, and Asia have called on world governments to reclassify the most harmful plastic waste as hazardous material. Currently, most nations classify plastic as solid waste, a view that, according to the authors, ignores scientific evidence that plastic debris is laden with highly toxic pollutants. "We believe that if countries classified the most harmful plastics as hazardous," they wrote, "their environmental agencies would have the power to restore affected habitats and prevent more dangerous debris from accumulating. Ultimately, such a move could boost research on new polymers and replace the most problematic materials with safer ones." Taking a page out of history, the authors modeled their proposal on what's been called the most successful international environmental agreement in history: the classification of chlorofluorocarbons, or CFCs, as hazardous under the 1989 Montreal Protocol. That global agreement brought a halt to CFC production within seven years.

The four most hazardous types of plastic the authors would like to see reclassified immediately include polyvinylchloride (PVC), polystyrene, polyurethane and polycarbonate. "We feel," they conclude, "that the physical dangers of plastic debris are well enough established, and the suggestions of chemical dangers sufficiently worrying, that the biggest producers of plastic waste—the United States, Europe and China—must act now."[15]

Increased product transparency and consumer awareness are already having an impact on manufacturing. One sign of this is the growing demand for "extended producer responsibility." Extended producer responsibility (EPR) suggests that manufacturers take more responsibility for the "end" of the product life cycle—reuse, disposal, or recycling. Increasingly, this means recognizing that nothing goes away, and that all products and their component materials affect the environment and our health after we are through with them. There are currently over 75 EPR laws in effect throughout the U.S., laws like California's 2010 Carpet Stewardship Bill which requires carpet retailers to help divert used carpet from landfills.

Outside the U.S., stricter EPR laws are common. The European Union's Packaging Directive, for example, makes product producers responsible for their post-consumer packaging waste, which must be recycled. Such a law in the U.S., where nearly one-third of all municipal solid waste is packaging, would have a profound effect, potentially diverting over ten million tons of plastic from our landfills every year.[16]

Notes

1   Gordon, Deborah, "Understanding Unconventional Oil," Report, Carnegie Endowment, Washington, DC, 2012, http://carnegieendowment.org/files/unconventional_oil.pdf

2   Tomlinson, Charles, *A Rudimentary Treatise on Warming and Ventilation*, London: John Weale Architectural Library, 1850, http://books.google.com/books?id=v0o1AAAAMAAJ&pg=PA63&lpg=PA63&dq=1306+l ondon+executed+coal&source=bl&ots=c5KcilQpnj&sig=9y607EnUSoFpx5FKN-8TbRr7sQc&hl=en&s a=X&ei=fPGcUqzXLum6yAH1soDIDg&ved=0CD4Q6AEwAg#v=snippet&q=executed%2C%20for%20 burning%20sea-coal%20in%20London&f=false

3   Ponsott, Elisabeth, "Will Germany Banish Fossil Fuels before the U.S.?" Grist, January 23, 2013, http:// grist.org/climate-energy/will-germany-banish-fossil-fuels-before-the-u-s/?utm_campaign=daily&utm_ medium=email&utm_source=newsletter&utm_content=headline

4   "Lower House Finds Micro Plastics in Cosmetics Unacceptable!" Plastic Soup Foundation, http://plasticsoup-foundation.org/geen-categorie/tweede-kamer-vindt-microplastics-in-cosmetica-onaanvaardbaar/

5   Monroe, Leila, "Can We Keep Plastic Pollution Out of Our Oceans?" Natural Resources Defense Council Staff Blog, April 15, 2013, http://switchboard.nrdc.org/blogs/lmonroe/can_we_keep_plastic_pollution. html?utm_source=fb&utm_medium=post&utm_campaign=blog

6   Beraza, Suzan, "Bag It: Is Your Life Too Plastic?" Film, 2011, www.bagitmovie.com/

7   Monroe, Leila, "Can We Keep Plastic Pollution Out of Our Oceans?"; "Should Cities Ban Plastic Bags?" *Wall Street Journal* online, October 8, 2012, http://online.wsj.com/article/SB10000872396390444165804578006832 478712400.html

8   Ibid.

9   White, Jeremy, "Plastic Industry Gives $1.2 Million to Repeal Bag Ban," Sacramento Bee, October 22, 2014, www.sacbee.com/news/politics-government/capitol-alert/article3228336.html#storylink=cpy

10 Joaquin, Tannya, "Mayor Caldwell Signs Amended Plastic Bag Ban Bill," Hawaii News Now, September 26, 2014, www.hawaiinewsnow.com/story/26628087/mayor-caldwell-signs-amended-plastic-ban-bill

11 "Plastic Bags Taxed from 2014," Service-Public.fr, November 21, 2013, www.service-public.fr/professionnels-entreprises/actualites/00768.html; "Delhi's New Plastic Bag Ban Carries Stiff Penalties," Environmental News Service, September 12, 2012, http://plasticbagbanreport.com/delhis-new-plastic-bag-ban-carries-stiff-penalties/?utm_source=feedburner&utm_medium=email&utm_campaign=Feed%3A+PlasticBagBanReport+ %28Plastic+Bag+Ban+Report%29

12 Dilli, Rae, "Comparison of Existing Life Cycle Analysis of Shopping Bag Alternatives," Sustainability Victoria, April 18, 2007, www.zerowaste.sa.gov.au/upload/resources/publications/plastic-bag-phase-out/LCA_ shopping_bags_full_report[2]_2.pdf

13 "About Nonwovens," Association of the Nonwoven Fabrics Industry, www.inda.org/about-nonwovens/

14 "Transparency", Perkins + Will, 2014, http://transparency.perkinswill.com/default.cshtml?url=/main; "Building Product Transparency Label," Construction Specialties, 2014, http://transparency.c-sgroup.com/; "Sustainable Minds Eco-concept Modeling & LCA Demo," December 17, 2009, www.sustainableminds.com/ watch-the-demo

15 Rochman, Chelsea, Browne, Mark, Halpern, Benjamin, Hentschel, Brian, Hoh, Eunha, Karapanagioti, Hrissi, et al., "Policy: Classify Plastic Waste as Hazardous," *Nature*, Volume 494, February 13, 2013, 169–171, http:// www.nature.com/nature/journal/v494/n7436/full/494169a.html; Weiss, Kenneth R., "Some Plastics Should Be

Classified as Hazardous, Scientists Say," *Los Angeles Times* online, February 13, 2013, http://articles.latimes.com/2013/feb/13/science/la-sci-sn-some-plastics-should-be-classified-as-hazardous-scientists-say-20130212

16 Pearson, Candace, "Waiting for Take-Back Programs for Building Materials," *Environmental Building News*, November 1, 2013, http://buildinggreen.com; Caliendo, Heather, "EPR Laws Continue to Spread," *Plastics Today*, February 10, 2012, www.plasticstoday.com/articles/EPR-laws-continue-to-spread-0210201201; Monier, Véronique, et al., "Development of Guidance on Extended Producer Responsibility (EPR)," Report to the European Commission, Bio Intelligence Service, 2014, http://epr.eu-smr.eu/introduction; U.S. Environmental Protection Agency, "Plastics," www.epa.gov/osw/conserve/materials/plastics.htm

24

Challenges in Post-Petroleum Design

Environmental Challenges

SINCE the challenges we face in any paradigm shift often come in the form of objections, I've adopted a question and answer format for this chapter.

Are natural materials really more environmentally friendly than petrochemical ones?

Not all plastics are harmful, and not all natural materials are benign. The aim of post-petroleum design is both to use the best and healthiest materials, energy sources, and manufacturing processes and to be proactive about the simple fact that, sooner than we think, we will have to make our products without oil. Yet as earlier chapters have shown, many petrochemical plastics do contain toxins that can harm us during their use and contaminate the soil, water, and air during their manufacture and after their disposal. And all are by definition non-renewable since they come from fossil fuels.

As oil runs out and we ramp up our use of renewable raw materials, we will need to pay greater attention to our products' environmental and health effects. If, for example, we were to replace all of today's polyester fabrics with cotton without changing the way it's grown, we could face dire environmental consequences. Cotton can be grown without harmful pesticides and monoculture farming, but that's not often the case today. We will need to find new and creative methods for producing large amounts of natural materials in ways that minimize environmental damage. It can be done, it is being done in many places, and it has to be done to replace our petrochemical raw materials as oil runs out.

Won't switching to bioplastics and natural materials use up all our food supplies and arable land?

Bioplastics feedstocks, as mentioned earlier, take up less than 0.001 percent of the world's agricultural land. And by the time bioplastics become the dominant form of plastic, more of their feedstocks will come from non-food sources—agricultural wastes like corn stover and inedible stocks like algae and switchgrass. As for natural raw materials like cotton, wool, wood and cork, the question is not so much whether we can grow enough to replace petroleum-based plastics, but whether we can grow them sustainably. Sustainable farming and harvesting is a complex topic that can't be fully covered here, but we would be wise to set our goals for it, not according to an abstract ideal of perfect sustainability, but in comparison to the documented environmental effects of the petroleum and plastic processing it replaces. In addition, nanotechnology and biotechnology, if wisely managed, could help us maximize the use of natural raw materials. These technologies are already being employed, for instance, to turn natural switchgrass into bioplastic-producing "factories." But questions both environmental and ethical will have to be resolved.[1]

Social and Economic Challenges

Isn't switching to post-petroleum materials and energy sources an overwhelming task, given our current dependency on oil?

Our current worldwide economic infrastructure depends on oil, but it can't stay that way. Consensus estimates suggest that what oil remains at the end of this century will be too expensive for ordinary uses. We have no choice but to find alternative materials and energy sources regardless of our stance on the environmental and health effects of petroleum. But why wait until the end of the century, when an abrupt and unplanned-for end of oil could ruin our economy? As this book has shown, there are thousands of designers, manufacturers, material suppliers, and retailers already living the post-petroleum vision. And there are millions of consumers eager to forgo the negative environmental and health effects of petroleum.

But a smooth transition will require more than a design movement or a shift in consumer demand. Change at the scale of our petroleum-based infrastructure will require the help of government. And while skeptics might argue that governments are none too quick to initiate change, the global shift to renewable energy, although slower than it needs to be, is nonetheless an example of large-scale government cooperation. And just as governments are working to transform the utility grid to accommodate renewable energy with the creation of a new "smart grid," the changeover of our design, manufacturing, and commercial infrastructure to fit the reality of a post-petroleum world is not only possible, it's inevitable.

Don't we need plastics for some things?

There are some plastic performance characteristics that can't be matched by other materials at a reasonable price. But as oil supplies dry up, that will change. Bioplastics and other alternative materials will expand their market as the petroleum to make plastic becomes scarcer and more expensive. Plastic companies know this, and many are already developing plant-based plastics. For now, we should be saving what oil remains for plastic's highest uses—medical implants, aeronautics, advanced electronics—rather than squandering it by producing a million single-use plastic bags a minute.

Design Challenges

What challenges does post-petroleum design raise for designers?

While the designers featured in this book are quite proficient at working with petroleum-free materials and processes, most designers still lack expertise in this area. The best cure for this is education. Education in post-petroleum design will most likely come in three phases. First, post-petroleum designers are already leading by example. While this book profiles some of the most innovative, there are many more out there, and their numbers are growing every day. As their numbers grow, more resources focusing on their work will become available. As society as a whole becomes more proactive about the end of oil, books, blogs, talks, and organizations will continue to spring up, pointing the way for those seeking more knowledge. Finally, in the near future, formal education will prepare students for leadership in post-petroleum design, manufacturing, and business, just as it will have to prepare all students for life in the post-petroleum era.

What challenges does post-petroleum design raise for manufacturers?

Just as our petroleum-based economy as a whole will face growing pains as we replace oil, individual manufacturers will too. We already see this as many struggle to meet rising fossil fuel-based utility costs and ponder the high first costs of switching to renewable energy. Materials raise a similar dilemma; green materials can cost more than less environmentally healthy ones, and most consumers want products that are both eco-friendly and affordable. Individual manufacturers can't do much about the economic infrastructure imbalances that make some harmful materials and processes appear cheaper than their green counterparts—imbalances like the hidden cost to taxpayers of oil company subsidies and plastic pollution. Even internal manufacturing infrastructure like equipment and supply chains can be hard to change. But opportunities to change will be supported by growing consumer demand for greener products and possibly even stronger environmental regulations from governments like we're starting to see in Europe and elsewhere. Here again, manufacturers will have to change before the end of the century.

Will consumers accept post-petroleum alternatives to petrochemical plastics?

Consumers appear not only willing but eager to buy greener products, as long as they don't cost much more than their less green competitors. As economies shift into post-petroleum mode, governments take more initiative to fight climate change, and consumers look for more alternatives to plastic, the demand for post-petroleum products will only grow.

Bioplastics are already proving that the performance of nearly all petroleum-based plastics can be matched by petroleum-free alternatives. Advances in nanotechnology and biotechnology have dramatically improved the performance of some natural materials for specific uses, but must be applied wisely lest they do more harm than good. And ultimately, consumers don't prefer petrochemical plastic for its own sake, but for its performance characteristics—low cost, strength, light weight. As new and ancient technologies and materials converge to match or exceed those characteristics, consumers will opt for those that are less harmful to human and environmental health.

This convergence will offer designers a new palette of materials in the post-petroleum era. As Dr. Debbie Chachra, Associate Professor of Materials Science at Olin College of Engineering, explains, "In the last century or so, chemists and chemical engineers have … developed thousands of plastics for use in tens of thousands of applications, if not more. That means that we'll need to find replacements for these oil-based plastics for every one of those uses, probably from previously unconsidered renewable sources. It'll be a different world."[2]

Notes

1   European Bioplastics, "Bioplastics," 2014, http://en.european-bioplastics.org/bioplastics/

2   "Guest Informant: Debbie Chachra," WarrenEllis.com, April 25, 2012, www.warrenellis.com/?p=13968

25

Designing Our Post-Petroleum Future

Running Dry

TODAY, the American Petroleum Institute's 1972 adage "A nation that runs on oil can't afford to run short" takes on an ominous tone. What becomes of a nation that runs on oil when all the cheap oil is gone? Already, we see wildly fluctuating gas prices and an eagerness to find more oil without proper regard for the environment. We see landfills brimming with toxic materials, and billions of plastic particles clogging the world's waterways and choking out marine life. Unless we plan now for life beyond oil, this scenario will only worsen as oil runs out.

Nations that run on oil may well go to war to keep running, if they haven't already. The fights that broke out in the lines waiting for rationed gas in 1972 may look mild compared to those over the last drops. And if we continue to ignore the inevitable, whole economies could stumble or fall, the infrastructural machinery that built them grinding to a halt as the oil that fueled them runs out.

In a rapidly industrializing world, prices and supplies will become increasingly volatile. China has become the world's second-leading importer of oil, yet it imports less than half as much as the number one importer, the United States. That's a big concern for the U.S. because, although we've reduced our consumption slightly of late, we're still deeply dependent on foreign oil. And when your lifeline is in the hands of others, you put yourself at risk. "I would say the number one risk to the stability of global oil prices—which can have big economic and security ramifications—is the potential for major conflict in the Middle East and instability in oil-producing countries," says Michael Levi, Director of the Program on Energy Security and Climate Change at the Council on Foreign Relations.[1]

And yet assumptions about continued growth in global oil production can be founded on potentially false assumptions of stability. As the most recent forecast by the U.S. Energy Information Administration cautions, "The Reference case [which EIA sees as the most likely future scenario] assumes that OPEC will maintain a cohesive policy limiting supply growth, rather than maximizing total annual revenues. It also assumes that no geopolitical events will cause prolonged supply shocks in the OPEC countries that could further limit production growth." Recent geopolitical history suggests such assumptions may be optimistic.[2]

Already, we can see rising tensions over the remaining supply intensifying, with the potential for all-out conflict increasing daily. Threats in 2012 by Iran to close the Strait of Hormuz, which carries about 40 percent of the world's seaborne oil, met with a response from the U.S. that suggested the possibilities. "We've invested in capabilities to ensure that the Iranian attempt to close down shipping in the Gulf is something that we are going to be able to defeat," U.S. Defense Secretary Leon Panetta said. Those capabilities included the aircraft carrier *U.S.S. Stennis*, which was making its way to the Persian Gulf as he spoke.[3]

As events that might have once seemed like science fiction play out across the globe, the end of oil is becoming an increasingly popular theme in "eco-pocalyptic" books and films, perhaps because it seems so plausible. Works like James Howard Kunstler's 2008 novel *World Made By Hand* paint a dire image of a future where the conveniences brought about by petroleum and plastic are replaced by global suffering as technology, commerce, and everyday life are suddenly propelled backward into preindustrial hardship. The images of post-petroleum life portrayed in film and literature are too numerous (and for the most part too grim) to enumerate here. Suffice it to revisit the warning of former Secretary of Energy James Schlesinger on the subject: "Unless we take serious steps to prepare for the day that we can no longer increase production of conventional oil, we are faced with the possibility of a major economic shock—and the political unrest that would ensue."[4]

The end of oil is not a question of if, but when. The brief rise in its production we are currently enjoying only leaves that much less for future use. "The oil industry is expected to invest huge sums in petroleum production and oil infrastructure in the years ahead, up to an estimated $1 trillion over the next decade alone," concludes a report by the Carnegie Endowment. "The opportunity costs are massive." Already, it takes more than five times as much energy to extract a barrel of oil in the U.S. than it did in the 1930s. Scarcity and the difficulty of extracting what's left will only send prices higher.[5]

Ironically, a world without oil might prove more livable than one with unlimited oil and the plastic it creates. In 1945, as plastic was just beginning its postwar boom, chemists Victor Yarsley and Edward Couzens envisioned life in the coming Age of Plastic: "Plastic man will come into a world of color and bright shining surfaces where childish hands find nothing to break, no sharp edges, or corners to cut or graze, no crevices to harbor dirt or germs." Their description of plastic man's life continues on "until at last he sinks into his grave in a hygienically enclosed plastic coffin." As for exactly how plastic man's life would end, DuPont chemist and co-inventor of nylon Julian Hill was quite specific: "I think the human race is going to perish by being smothered in plastic."[6]

Today's plastic person can indeed teethe on a plastic pacifier made with toxic bishenol-A and be laid to rest in a plastic casket, but the plastic paradise envisioned by Yarsley and Couzens may elude us thanks to dwindling oil supplies. The question, as the end of oil draws nearer, is whether we will sit idly by as it approaches or take charge of our future while there's still time. If we wait for dwindling supplies to reduce our oil consumption, it will be too late. Post-petroleum designers are already working to reduce the amount of oil we use. Their work is about proactively designing our products, our cities—everything—to avert those hardships and enjoy healthier, more sustainable living for all.

Figure 25.1 Portia Munson's "Pink Project"
The predominance of plastic in modern society is emphasized in New York
artist Portia Munson's "Pink Project." Munson used thousands of discarded
pink objects to call attention to "the marketing of femininity and the
infantilization of the female gender." Image courtesy of Portia Munson.

Experts suggest we would also be wise to leave as much oil in the ground as we can, because just burning what we already have stockpiled could pour an unacceptable amount of carbon dioxide into the atmosphere. Oil company reserves, they suggest, are "five times more than we can ever safely burn." From their perspective, oil reserves are like stockpiled nuclear weapons; if we use them, it will be to destroy ourselves.[7]

Life in the Post-Petroleum Era

Peak oil means peak plastic. And that means that much of the physical world around
us will have to change.

(Debbie Chachra, Associate Professor of Materials Science, Olin College of Engineering)[8]

Throughout the twentieth century, our lives were dominated by oil. It got us where we needed to go, it fueled our economic expansion, and it formed the plastics we shaped into our everyday objects. We used it up at an alarming rate, and gradually we came to see the effects of its extraction, refinement, and consumption. Oil stoked the engines of progress, while we turned a blind eye to its irreplaceability and its negative effects. But these effects weren't the fault of oil, which is, after all, just an inert material. We had intentions, and oil fit them like a glove. Now, no matter how efficient we can make our energy and auto industries, we will still need to reduce the carbon footprint of our plastics industry dramatically, especially considering that our use of plastic is doubling about every 13 years.[9]

Oil gave us power over nature and it gave us a new "wonder material," plastic. "From the early twentieth century onward," wrote plastic historian, Jeffrey L. Meikle, "plastic has signified greater human control over nature." But he continues, "By the late 1960s, the word plastic had emerged as a complex metaphor in American culture, signaling the hazards of materialism and a sterile technological future."[10]

Perhaps from the early twenty-first century onward, post-petroleum design will signify greater human cooperation with nature. And while life in the post-petroleum era will be different than it is now, the performance of our products may not change as much as Professor Chachra seemed to suggest when she said that "much of the physical world around us will have to change." Bioplastics and other alternative materials may in time match the performance of today's petroleum-based plastics. But the effects of their material harvesting, processing, use, and end-of-use may be radically different. Instead of taking non-renewable oil from the earth, where it took millennia to form, mixing in sometimes toxic additives, and landfilling most of the resulting products, our goods could come from renewable, non-toxic materials processed in environmentally friendly ways to create healthy products we can cherish and ultimately reuse, recycle, or compost.

The signs of change are all around us, not only within the pages of this book. The positive post-petroleum era envisioned here will be characterized not only by new materials and technologies of design, but new uses for the millions of tons of plastic we've already accumulated. Because petrochemical plastic is one of the most energy-laden materials on Earth, much of it will be converted to fuel through more efficient and safe incineration than we use today, even more sustainable bioconversion using plastic-eating bacteria, or technologies yet to be discovered. Landfills will be mined for plastics to be converted to energy or new materials; even oceans will be trawled for it, cleaning up the billions of bits that foul them today. What plastics remain in circulation will be recycled, and at a much higher rate than the paltry 8 percent we've achieved so far. Through nanotechnologies and biotechnologies, if they can be sustainably managed, we may develop new materials with properties that plastic could only dream of.[11]

One hundred years from now, the plastic we throw away today will still be around; abundant oil to make new plastic will not. It won't be there to run our cars and industrial machinery, either. How will we live? It's impossible to know, but one thing is certain. We will live without petroleum. The question is, what will the transition be like? Will we continue to ignore the undeniable—that the end of oil is approaching faster than we think? Will we face the catastrophe that our denial could bring—an abrupt end to our oil supply and the accompanying shock to our economy? Or will we be proactive, acknowledging the inevitable end of oil, and designing a world free from its environmental and health effects, a cleaner, healthier world where we renew and restore the Earth's resources? We have all the technology and know-how to begin now. Post-petroleum designers have already begun.

Designing the Post-Petroleum Era

IT is during the design of our products that their environmental performance is determined. With that in mind, post-petroleum design reflects not so much a change in materials or processes as a change in design thinking. Philosopher Roland Barthes captured the wonder of the new "miraculous substance" called plastic and the design thinking it embodied when he visited an exhibition of its wonders in 1957. "More than a substance," he wrote, "plastic is the very idea of its transformation … And it is this, in fact, which makes it a miraculous substance: a miracle is always a sudden transformation of nature. Plastic remains impregnated throughout with this wonder: it is less a thing than the trace of a movement."[12]

Today, Barthes would witness plastic as itself the subject of transformation, a transformation by design. This transformation to post-petroleum design maintains the best attributes of the material he admired in 1957—its adaptability, versatility, low cost, "the stuff of alchemy" as Barthes marveled—but without the harmful effects of its petrochemical inputs as new plastic materials emerge from bioplastics, natural alternatives, and materials yet to be created.

And if plastic has been "less a thing than the trace of a movement," then the same could be said about post-petroleum plastics. The movement they trace, however, promises to be one of cooperation with nature rather than a fight against it. In their respect for nature, many of the products of post-petroleum design are reminiscent of Shaker furniture or the Japanese handcraft objects called Mingei. "Things reflect the society that made them," said Sori Yanagi, the late director of the Japan Folk Crafts Museum. "For beautiful things to be made, not only the makers but the users and the entire distribution network between must be healthy."[13,14]

Because users, makers, materials, and processes form an integral whole, I've emphasized the full life cycle and not just the design phase throughout this book. I've focused on post-petroleum designers and let them tell their own stories, while also describing common principles and attitudes in their work. In this way, post-petroleum designers are carrying on the spirit of craft traditions like the Shakers and Mingei, interpreting them with the latest materials and technologies of production; not looking backward or copying traditional forms, but looking ahead. As Sori Yanagi said, the challenge facing modern designers and manufacturers is to draw out the spirit of folk crafts and give it substance within the context of our modern, changing environment.[15]

Good Tools, Right Use

Tools extend the hand, the human reach. Not just outward in conquest—too often we have used technology to degrade life on earth when that has been our aim. But can technology help us reach inward to better understand ourselves, our role in society, and our place among all living things? I believe it can. For one thing, it can lift us up beyond the subsistence of life without tools. Even Wendell Berry and other critics of high technology accept certain tools for their ability to raise our quality of life. Good tools help us live better, healthier lives.

But they do more than ease the drudgery of manual labor. They help us complete ourselves. A fine wood plane satisfies in its use, connects us more deeply with the source of our work, the material, and augments our inspiration and creativity. Even a scanning electron microscope can be a wonder, opening our eyes to an unseen world and helping us learn and create in ways we could never have dreamed of without it. Employed with imagination and creativity, it can help us solve problems and improve quality of life significantly.

What matters is our aim in applying our tools and technologies. What do we want to accomplish? Why is it important? Who is it helping? Does it do harm? We need to keep asking ourselves these questions as our tools become ever more powerful. Without proper guidance, a fine wood plane can injure a finger. An ill-conceived genetically modified organism, however, holds the potential for far greater harm. Contemplating this, I always think of how my father-in-law, a devout Christian, closes his mealtime blessings: "Lead us in the right use of Your gifts." Amen to that.[16]

Many years ago, I met a Japanese woodworker who defined skill as "the ability to care." His insight struck me deeply as the defining characteristic that makes traditional Japanese crafts like Mingei so beloved. Oil and plastic are not evil; with them we have reached unprecedented heights of prosperity. But we are just now learning to use our resources more skillfully—learning to fully exercise the ability to care we must exercise in order to live sustainably. We now have the technology to produce large numbers of goods in the same spirit as the one-off artifacts of yesterday's craft traditions. Do we have the skill to design products and processes that prove our ability to care? We have the technology to create bioplastic products with all the appeal of the fluid plastic forms that defined the twentieth-century vision of the future. We can produce clothing from biomaterials every bit as comfortable, lightweight, and weatherproof as polyester. We can imitate and exceed the playfulness and performance of the plastic objects we love, but without all their undesirable effects. It all depends on our intentions, on design.

The design strategies, tools, and materials we use to shape our post-petroleum world won't be those we used to shape our pre-petroleum world. Responsibly managed nanotechnology and biotechnology will likely play a role, as will new technologies yet to be discovered. The work of Ecovative, the company making packaging, building materials, and other products from their innovative Mushroom Material is a good example (Chapter 10). I asked co-founder Eben Bayer how the environmentally friendly methods used by his company differ from what we might imagine when we think of nanotechnology. He replied,

Figure 25.2 NASA Astronauts Wearing Armadillo Merino

Astronauts aboard the International Space Station frolic in merino wool
shirts from Armadillo Merino. Image courtesy of Armadillo Merino.

When I think about nanotechnology, it's this field of incredible promise that Drexel
laid out in the 80s. At some point in college I realized that when you look at living
systems in nature you've basically got a lot of molecular nanotechnology already
assembled into some pretty unique devices. Part of what we're doing at Ecovative is
recognizing that there's some pretty complex equipment available, and you can find
ways by building systems around it to utilize it in new ways.

That's what we're doing with the solid state culture of filamentous fungi [the
foundation of their Mushroom Materials.] Rather than trying to break an organism
down to excrete some new property, we're leveraging the fact that it creates this
structural matrix and at the same time excretes the enzymes needed to break down
things like lignin and cellulose to create a growing composite. In a sense we get
lucky that it has those attributes. In another sense I think there are opportunities to
leverage living cells like that, complex cells from nature, to do complex tasks. I very
much view that as molecular nanotechnology.[17]

Leveraging natural materials through innovative processes is also the foundation of the work
of Armadillo Merino, the company putting a new spin on merino wool with its next-to-skin
protective clothing for professionals in high-risk environments (Chapter 15). The company

Figure 25.3 Jon Coen Making Grain Surfboard
Surfer and freelance writer Jon Coen builds a Grain
surfboard from local woods engineered using computer
numerically controlled machines. Image courtesy of Grain
Surfboards; photo by Nick LaVecchia.

selects only the finest merino wool fibers, each less than one-third the thickness of a human hair, thereby ensuring maximum softness and comfort against the skin. By using superfine fibers Armadillo is able to "compact spin" 45 of them into the cross section of every strand of yarn, significantly increasing the fabric's strength and durability. Finally, wool's natural flame resistance adds fire safety to the list of user benefits. This synergy of advanced technologies with natural materials points to the future rather than the past. Maybe that's why NASA has chosen Armadillo Merino for its astronauts to wear onboard the International Space Station.

Grain Surfboards, like Armadillo Merino, Ecovative, and the other designers featured in this book, may be ambassadors of a new, post-petroleum era in design. Grain's use of local, sustainable woods and local workshops where people can make their own boards using Grain parts, artfully combined with computer numerically controlled machining technology, may offer all the benefits of the traditional wooden Alaia board yet improve upon it with lighter weight, better performance, and faster, less expensive manufacturing (Chapter 12).

This is the spirit of post-petroleum design; not to rely on natural materials and handcraft alone—that would be a step backward—but to bring new technologies and materials to the fore, as long as they are consistent with the principles of nature. Around the world, people are designing, making, and living in greater awareness of these principles. This movement is happening at all scales, from major auto manufacturers producing electric vehicles to individuals saying no to plastic bags at the supermarket. Governments, too often the last responders in an environmental crisis, are taking action as well. What these individual, corporate, and governmental actions have in common is a commitment to reduce our dependence on oil through post-petroleum design and manufacturing. Corporations are adopting it to build consumer loyalty by doing the right thing for the environment, and people are demanding it for the health of the planet and future generations. Governments recognize post-petroleum design as the way to energy independence and security; even the U.S. Armed Forces have vowed to go petroleum-free by 2040.[18]

Post-petroleum design, with its reliance on natural, renewable materials, low-energy processing, and waste reduction, offers us an opportunity to do regenerative work. Materials, rather than simply being consumed, will flow in sync with nature's cycles. Outputs from one process will become inputs for another. Resources like oil and coal, formed over millennia, will be used over millennia, not used up in less than two centuries. As much oil and coal as possible will be left in the ground, considering the harm they can do when used. Materials and energy used will not only be renewed but multiplied to increase their abundance and ensure future prosperity. We will replenish and heal our planet, replenishing ourselves by helping all living things to thrive. But the healing can't happen by itself; it can only happen by design. It will happen. How do I know? Buckminster Fuller said it best: "The best way to predict the future is to design it."

Notes

1   Stafford, James, "Falling Oil Prices and the Shale Boom: An Interview with Michael Levi," OilPrice.com, December 5, 2012, http://oilprice.com/Interviews/Falling-Oil-Prices-and-the-Shale-Boom-An-Interview-with-Michael-Levi.html

2   U.S. Energy Information Administration, "International Energy Outlook 2014," www.eia.gov/forecasts/ieo/more_overview.cfm

3   Rayment, Sean, "Armada of International Naval Power Massing in the Gulf as Israel Prepares an Iran Strike," *The Telegraph* online, September 15, 2012, www.telegraph.co.uk/news/worldnews/middleeast/iran/9545597/Armada-of-international-naval-power-massing-in-the-Gulf-as-Israel-prepares-an-Iran-strike.html

4   "James R. Schlesinger's Statement before the United States Senate," November 16, 2005, PlanetForLife.com, http://planetforlife.com/oilcrisis/oilschlesinger.html

5   Gordon, Deborah, "Understanding Unconventional Oil," Report, Carnegie Endowment, Washington, DC, 2012, http://carnegieendowment.org/files/unconventional_oil.pdf; Nelder, Chris, "Watts Up, Vaclav? Putting Peak Oil and the Renewables Transition in Context," GreentechMedia.com, June 5, 2013, www.greentech-media.com/articles/read/watts-up-vaclav

6   Yarsley, V.E. and Couzens, E.G., *Plastics*, Harmondsworth: Penguin Books, 1945; Allen, Henry, "Their Stocking Feat: Nylon at 50 & the Age of Plastic," *Washington Post*, January 13, 1988.

7   McKibben, Bill, "The Great Carbon Bubble: Why the Fossil-fuel Industry Fights so Hard," *Grist*, February 7, 2012, http://grist.org/fossil-fuels/the-great-carbon-bubble-why-the-fossil-fuel-industry-fights-so-hard/

8   "Guest Informant: Debbie Chachra," WarrenEllis.com, April 25, 2012, www.warrenellis.com/?p=13968

9   PlasticsEurope, "Plastics—the Facts 2012: An Analysis of European Plastics Production, Demand and Waste Data for 2011," Report, www.plasticseurope.org/documents/document/20121120170458-final_plasticsthe-facts_nov2012_en_web_resolution.pdf

10 Meikle, Jeffrey L., *American Plastic: A Cultural History*, New Brunswick, NJ: Rutgers University Press, 1997.

11 Wirthman, Lisa, "How a Company Recycles Ocean Plastic Twice the Size of Texas," Forbes.com, March 14, 2013, www.forbes.com/sites/ups/2013/03/14/how-a-company-recycles-ocean-plastic-twice-the-size-of-texas/; White, Ronald D., "Neville Browne Sees Great Future in Plastic Bottle Recycling," *Los Angeles Times* online, September 20, 2013, www.latimes.com/business/la-fi-himi-brown-20130922,0,1400270.story#axzz2nrfXSK8l; "Biobased Materials: Essential for the Next Generation of Products," Sustainable Biomaterials Collaborative, www.sustainablebiomaterials.org/

12 Barthes, Roland, *Mythologies*, New York: Hill and Wang, 1957.

13 Andrews, Edward Deming and Andrews, Faith, *Religion in Wood: A Book of Shaker Furniture*, Bloomington: Indiana University Press, 1966.

14 *Kindred Spirits: The Eloquence of Function in American Shaker and Japanese Arts of Daily Life*, San Diego, CA: Mingei International, 1995.

15 Ibid.

16 Elvin, George, "Good Tools, Right Use," Green Technology Forum, June 12, 2007, www.greentechforum.net/green-technology-forum/2007/6/12/good-tools-right-use.html

17 Author interview.

18 Elvin, George, "U.S. Armed Forces to Go Petroleum-free by 2040," Green Technology Forum, March 29, 2012, http://gelvin.squarespace.com/green-technology-forum/2012/3/29/us-armed-forces-to-go-petroleum-free-by-2040.html